Under the Southern Cross

Isaac Gordon Bradwell (Courtesy, Gordon C. Bradwell).

UNDER THE SOUTHERN CROSS

Soldier Life with
Gordon Bradwell and the
Army of Northern Virginia

Compiled and Edited by:
Pharris Deloach Johnson

MERCER UNIVERSITY PRESS

1979   1999

TWENTY YEARS OF PUBLISHING EXCELLENCE

ISBN 0-86554-667-3
MUP/496

© Mercer University Press
6316 Peake Road
Macon, Georgia 31210-3960
1999 All rights reserved

First Edition.
Second printing October 2000.
∞The paper used in this publication meets the minimum requirements of
American National Standard for Information Sciences — Permanence of
Paper for Printed Library Materials, ANSI Z39.48-1984.

Art on Jacket: The Last Salute, by Don Troiani
Bookjacket design by Jim Burt

Library of Congress Cataloging-in-Publication Data
Bradwell, Isaac Gordon, 1843-1934.
    Under the Southern Cross : soldier life with Gordon Bradwell and the Army of
Northern Virginia / compiled and edited by Pharris Deloach Johnson.
        p. cm.
    Comprises articles written by Bradwell which appeared in Confederate veteran
magazine.
    Includes bibliographical references and index.
    ISBN 0-86554-667-3 (alk. paper)
    1. Bradwell, Isaac Gordon, 1843-1934. 2. Confederate States of America. Army. Georgia
Infantry Regiment, 31st. 3. United States — History — Civil War, 1861-1865 Personal
narratives, Confederate. 4. Georgia — History — Civil War, 1861-1865 Personal narratives.
5. United States — History — Civil War, 1861-1865 — Regimental histories. 6.
Georgia — History — Civil War, 1861-1865 — Regimental histories. 7. Soldiers — Georgia
Biography. 8. Confederate States of America. Army of Northern Virginia Biography. I.
Johnson, Pharris Deloach. II. Confederate veteran (Nashville, Tenn.). III. Title.
E559.5 31st. B73   1999
973.7'458 — dc21   99-28401
                                                                        CIP

To Annie

CONTENTS

FOREWORD

As the twenty-first century approaches, a tumultuous four-year period from nineteenth-century America continues to capture our imagination. Publishing houses, large and small, still produce books on Robert E. Lee, "Stonewall" Jackson, Abraham Lincoln, and a host of other prominent figures from the War for Southern Independence, or Civil War, as it is commonly called. Social Customs, military strategy, and political philosophy of the early 1860's are still subjected to intense scrutiny and debate. The latest resurgence in interest has prompted scholars and amateur historians alike, to search for obscure soldier diaries and letter collections, potentially fresh material to satisfy a growing demand. Reprints of titles published long ago are again available.

I first became aware of Isaac Gordon Bradwell in the mid-1980's. A lifelong interest in my ancestral regiment initiated a ten-year research endeavor that culminated with my book, *A History of the 31st Georgia Volunteer Infantry*. One of the first sources I consulted was the *Confederate Veteran* magazine, the literary arm of the United Confederate Veterans organization, and other related groups whose mission was to preserve the memory of the Confederacy and the Old South. Mr. Bradwell, a veteran of the 31st Georgia, contributed seventy-three articles of war reminiscences during the last twenty-five of the magazine's forty-year existence. Nearly every aspect of a young private's life in the Lawton-Gordon-Evans brigade is vividly described. Bradwell, with the exception of a few brief periods of absence due to illness, could be counted on to be present when the muster roll of the "Arnett Rifles" was called, as his noble service record substantiates.

A volunteer at eighteen, Bradwell was with his company at the time of its inception and was in combat at the time of Lee's surrender at Appomattox Court House. His candor and honest approach answered many of this researcher's questions, while providing many leads in the process. Intimate details of the 31st Georgia and its personalities gave me insight that could not have been found anywhere else. Details of some incidents, later verified from obscure sources, were provided by the proud Confederate veteran. A product of a family that strongly believed in the value of education, Bradwell obviously was a lover of literature, especially if it pertained to the conflict of his youth. I originally assumed that Bradwell kept a diary in the war, but no record of one exists. In brief, the unforgettable events witnessed by an impressionable young Georgian found their way into narrative form many years later, in piecemeal fashion, courtesy of the *Confederate Veteran* magazine.

Colonel Pharris Johnson is to be commended for what he has done with the Bradwell articles. I had never realized that when placed in proper order, chronologically as to when events occurred, the collection encompasses the entire war. Why Bradwell did not write a book of his experiences is not known. Perhaps he did not have the means or resources. Fortunately, the creativity and determination of Colonel Johnson, the compiler of Bradwell's chronicles, have resulted in a work that will be enjoyed and utilized by future generations. *Under the Southern Cross: Soldier Life with Gordon Bradwell and the Army of Northern Virginia*, is a fitting tribute to its author and the tragic times in which he lived. As with most memoirs composed long after the guns were silenced, there are occasional facts and names confused, but these do not materially detract from the writings. Not only was Bradwell an active participant and witness in America's bloodiest war, he was a student of it as well. The perspective of this educated man is a fine addition to the history of Georgia and his brigade's distinguished role in Lee's Army of Northern Virginia.

Gregory C. White

PREFACE

My great-grandfather, Benjamin Berrian Brewton, was a member of the 61st Georgia Volunteer Regiment during the Civil War. This regiment, with the 13th, 26th, 31st, 38th, and 60th regiments along with the 12th battalion, was a part of the Lawton-Gordon-Evans Brigade of the Army of Northern Virginia. While researching information on this brigade in the *Confederate Veteran* magazine, I found numerous articles written by Isaac G. Bradwell. An examination of the magazine's comprehensive master index, prepared by Broadfoot Publishing Company, revealed that Bradwell contributed over seventy articles during a twenty-five-year span. I began reading the articles and realized that Bradwell wrote a very full account of his participation in the war. I pieced together his material in chronological sequence, and this book resulted from the effort.

The source of the articles, the *Confederate Veteran*, is one of the most significant nongovernmental sources of information about Confederate veterans. The forty-volume magazine spanned the period of 1893 to 1932. As explained in *Tracing Your Civil War Ancestor* by Bertram Groene, the monthly publication contains "the largest collection of Confederate memoirs, anecdotes, incidents, and personal stories in existence." Of course, as Douglas Southhall Freeman writes in his book *The South to Posterity*, the information in the *Confederate Veteran* articles ranges from "exceedingly tall tales" to information sometimes providing "the answer to a historical riddle, or an eye-witness' clear account of some incident that never had been explained."

Bradwell's collection of articles is made more complete by virtue of his remarkable record during the war. Other than a few relatively brief absences, he was with his company from November 11, 1861 when it was formed until its members surrendered at Appomattox on April 9, 1865. Captain George Lewis first organized this company as the Arnett Rifles, and it later became Company I of the 31st Georgia Regiment. Bradwell participated in most of the regiment's battles and skirmishes from the company's arrival in Virginia in the spring of 1862 until the close of the war.

Bradwell was a mere private in the ranks, but writes with the great understanding and insight of a seasoned senior officer. His keen ability to grasp the larger context of military operations is evident in his commentary. He also adds to the creditability of the narrative by pointing out the events that "came under my own observation" versus those described to him by his comrades.

In his accounts Bradwell covers with vivid recall the activities in Lee's army, as well as those while his regiment was still in Georgia. He demonstrates his ability to capture small, but important details when he describes rainy weather as a contributing factor to the rout of General Edward Johnson's lines on May 12, 1864 at the battle of Spotsylvania:

> The previous night was dark and rainy, making the leafy covering of the earth as soft and noiseless as a carpet to the feet of the advancing army. Under this favorable condition the enemy moved up their front line during the night as near General Johnson's position as possible without detection, with instructions to make a bold rush at four o'clock in the morning and capture the position.

Bradwell is candid in his writing. Although there is an obvious Confederate bias, he also heaps criticism on the troops in gray, and particularly their officers, where he thinks it is due. For example, he speaks of the leadership of his brigade as "shameful" during the Battle of Fredericksburg. He made this observation because of mismanagement and lack of coordination within his brigade that led to a disastrous, haphazard advance on the enemy.

Bradwell provided further criticism of his regiment in describing a skirmish at Middletown, Virginia, in July of 1864. He tells of his fellow soldiers and regimental commander fleeing from the enemy. According to Bradwell,

> They [the Yankees] ran because they had good reason, and we ran when there was no great cause for us to do so...Looking to the left I saw to my astonishment, our old Colonel going through that piece of woods to the rear in full flight...He was evidently panic stricken and was acting in the most undignified

manner for a field officer, who ought to be a brave man and a model for all his men.

Bradwell was a man of his times. As such, his prejudices show in much of his writing. Comments on the nobility of the Anglo-Saxon race and disparaging observations on the ethnic makeup of the Federal army are plentiful.

Bradwell frequently commented on the courage of soldiers on both sides. On several occasions he alleges that the Federal commanders employed alcohol to hearten their troops. Of course, as we know, the malady of hard drink was not exclusively on the Federal side. As Bell Irvin Wiley put it in his classic book, *The Life of Johnny Reb*, Southern commanding generals also "were appalled at the prevalence of the vice." Bradwell states his observations on this subject when he writes:

> They [drinkers] were the biggest cowards in the army. Perhaps a little liquor just then would have given them some stamina. But I have known this remedy to have a bad effect on some who happened to have it, and caused them to expose themselves unnecessarily and suffer the consequence. We did not have it and did not need it; we had a greater stimulant to our courage—the consciousness that we were fighting for our homes and everything we held sacred; but our enemy, I am sure, employed it as means to hearten their men in the Wilderness campaign. I am certain of this fact from the appearance of their dead, the faces of which were as black as a negro, where those of the dead Confederates were pale and natural.

He often wrote of the chivalry and virtues of the Confederate soldier. For example, during the Gettsysburg Campaign when his brigade entered the town of Gettysburg, Pennsylvania, he describes the event thusly:

> The younger set [townspeople], however, of both sexes, considered it a holiday and turned out in force. They were anxious to know when we were going to burn the town. Crowds of these youngsters hung to us everywhere we went,

asking this same question. Our only answer was that Southern solders didn't burn towns.

Bradwell praises the optimism of the Southern troops. He eloquently describes his feelings during the final dreadful days of the retreat from Petersburg as follows:

> Matters grew worse and worse from day to day; but a few of us held on to our guns and ammunition, determined to cut our way out, free ourselves from the enemy, and continue the fight to the bitter end unless we could secure some fruits of the long contest and the sacrifice of so many of our brave men who had died in defense of the South. Animated by this thought, we resisted the ever-present pangs of hunger, fatigue, and the efforts of the enemy to destroy us, with a faint hope that something would turn up to our advantage, as had often been the case before when fortune seemed to be against us.

Many of Bradwell's articles overlap chronologically, and he wrote several on exactly the same events. His favorite subject seemed to be General Jubal Early's 1864 Valley Campaign. He wrote at least seven articles on various aspects of this topic alone. With this repetition considered, I arranged the articles in approximate chronological order. In the case of duplicated articles, I chose the one providing the most complete account. Readers may consult the bibliography for a listing of Bradwell's articles. The only editing performed was to correct obvious typesetting errors in the original publication, and to eliminate some paragraphs that duplicate information in his other accounts. These articles are footnoted accordingly. Readers will note that despite the editing, there is still some repetition present that was necessary to preserve continuity in the narrative.

Bradwell's spelling and word separation differs from modern usage. For example, he writes "battle field" and "some one" as two words rather than one. He also does not capitalize the word, "negro." This was a stylistic standard from the editors of the magazine.

One of the more interesting parts of his accounts is his description of some of the most famous participants in the war. Bradwell describes generals and privates with equal insight. Below are two of his poignant observations on General Robert E. Lee and Charlie Billet, a fellow private in Bradwell's unit.

> *Gen. Robert E. Lee.* With these conditions confronting him [before his 1862 Maryland Campaign], General Lee did not hesitate to plan a new offensive in which everything seemed to be in favor of the enemy. Trusting to his good fortune and the overcaution of the enemy, he boldly crossed over into Maryland to operate far away from his base, while the enemy had his capital and base at his back. This campaign seems to have been highly inadvisable when we consider the great risks it involved; but these were not greater than many others which he took before and after this. There can be no rules to govern a general in war. He must be his own judge when to strike and how.

> I think I never saw a horse perform his part so beautifully as did old Traveller on this occasion [grand review of the troops in the winter of 1863-1864] or a rider sit more gracefully in the saddle. But to see General Lee at his best he must be seen on horseback, where he appeared to be perfectly at home.

> *Charley Billet* [Bradwell's fellow soldier in the 31st Georgia]. In this engagement [Spotsylvania] many of our best men who had done conspicuous service went down and among them the brave Charley Billet, unknown in history, unwept by his countrymen, and forgotten. Somewhere in Virginia, perhaps in an unmarked grave, the bones of our comrade rest, while his soul has joined the multitude of brave spirits who made the extreme sacrifice for their country. This article is written as a just tribute to the memory of a brave comrade who fell in defense of his country, whose name and deeds otherwise would never be known.

He often concludes his articles by asking other veterans to write to him. Many of them did, and he sometimes cites these letters in correcting errors in his previous articles. Bradwell's letters and notes must have comprised a wonderful archive of Civil War materials. His

Confederate pension application references his personal library as one of his noted assets. Unfortunately, I was unable to find any extensive collections of his papers. We *do* have the many articles he wrote for the *Confederate Veteran*, however, and they provide comprehensive accounts of soldier life and the history of his brigade.

We know that Bradwell did contemplate a book-length treatment of his memoirs. In 1933 and 1934 he corresponded with Douglas G. Carroll of Brooklandville, Maryland, concerning the possible publication of the memoirs. After review of the manuscript, Carroll concluded that publication would not be profitable at that time. The econmics of publishing during the height of the depression era no doubt came into play.

Bradwell's correspondence with Carroll is instructive, however, as it relates to the former Confederate's motivation for writing as he did about the conflict of the 1860s. Bradwell says:

I had no idea from the first of receiving any pecuniary advantage from it [writing], but to correct much false history and many errors in the minds of honest people who have read books written by authors who intentionally misrepresented facts. I want my friends and the world to know the truth of the great struggle of the Southern people and what they suffered for what they thought was right. How they fought without hope four years against the whole world and what kind of men commanded their armies. [Maryland Historical Society, Baltimore; Manuscript 2337.]

Students of Georgia Civil War history will readily recognize Lillian Henderson's *Roster of the Confederate Soldiers of Georgia* as a beginning reference for research. Although there are some errors in these volumes, I have often thumbed through the pages looking at the brief accounts of Georgia's Confederate infantry soldiers. This information includes material from muster rolls and pension records, but does not tell about how the men lived, fought, and sacrificed in support of their country. Nor does it describe what motivated the soldiers to suffer under such terrible conditions. Sometimes, we are fortunate to find a memoir or autobiography that gives us insight to the men whose names make up these rolls. Bradwell's articles give a human touch to the stories behind the rosters, statistics, and service records—and substance to our understanding of these men and events.

Yes, Bradwell wrote many of these articles as an old man. They must be read critically because of the lapse of time. However, his writing indicates that even in his 80's, he possessed a sharp mind and ability to recall vivid detail. Very importantly, some of the information he presents is unavailable elsewhere. His eye-witness accounts form a captivating history that is of value to anyone interested in the activities of the 31st Georgia Regiment, the Lawton-Gordon-Evans Brigade, and the Army of Northern Virginia.

ACKNOWLEDGMENTS

A number of people contributed information and provided encouragement for this book. I gratefully acknowledge the help of these individuals.

During the early stages of my research, Sibyl Swanner Holman Dorsey, Crenshaw County Registrar, at Luverne, Alabama, was very helpful in finding biographical material on Gordon Bradwell. During my research trip to Alabama, she also provided introductions to local residents and acquainted me with Bradwell records available in the Crenshaw County Courthouse. This very personable lady was most gracious with her time.

Sig and Cora Morgan, of Brantley, Alabama, granted me an interview during which they provided information on the Bradwell family and recollections of Bradwell's talks on the Civil War to the local school children.

Another resident of Brantley, Marjorie P. Pinckard, furnished further information on Gordon Bradwell's life in that town. Her kindness in providing this material led to other important sources for my research.

Dupont Strong, a nephew of Gordon Bradwell, recounted to me meetings with his uncle in 1929 and 1932. Dupont indicated that even though Gordon was an aged man at the time, Bradwell was "quite lucid and entertaining." Readers will find further details of Strong's recollections in Bradwell's biographical sketch.

Gordon C. Bradwell, of Athens, Georgia, provided much valuable genealogical data on the Bradwell family. Gordon's grandfather, James Sumter Bradwell, was a brother of Isaac Gordon Bradwell. Gordon and his wife, Eleanor, also provided much encouragement for this project and the photos of Isaac Gordon Bradwell and his second wife, Henrietta.

James Morgan, publisher of the *Luverne Journal* in Luverne, Alabama, identified several sources for information on the Bradwell family. A request for information provided in his newspaper led to additional contacts.

In addition to providing the Foreword to this book, Gregory C. White, of Canton, Georgia, reviewed the manuscript, made excellent suggestions, and pointed out areas for further research. His outstanding book, *A History of the 31st Georgia Volunteer Infantry*, provides a thorough and informative account of this noted regiment's history.

Much thanks is in order for Bob Krick, Chief Historian at the Fredericksburg and Spotsylvania National Military Park, and Civil War historian Keith Bohannon. These gentlemen enthusiastically provided encouragement for this project.

Sincere appreciation goes to Don Troiani for permission to use his classic print, *The Last Salute*, for this book's dust jacket. Mr. Troiani's assistant, Jo-Val Codling, was very accommodating in processing my request. Further assistance with illustrations was expertly provided by Frank Wood of Frank and Marie-Therese Wood Print Collections, Alexandria, Va.

Heartfelt gratitude goes to my sister, Linda Hester, of Thomasville, Georgia, for her encouragement on pursuing my love of history. Her assistance in helping develop my manuscripts for publication is always dependable and gracious.

The personnel of Mercer University Press provided thoughtful and comprehensive support for this project. I express special thanks to Marc A. Jolley, Assistant Publisher, for his interest in Bradwell's Civil War accounts and his recognition of their importance. I greatly appreciate the skill, patience, and vision of this outstanding publisher and gentleman.

Isaac Gordon Bradwell:
A Biographical Sketch

Isaac Gordon Bradwell, known as Gordon to his family and friends, was the son of Daniel and Jane McCutchen Gordon Bradwell, from South Carolina. Daniel's parents, Thomas and Catherine Durr Bradwell, lived in the Charleston District. Born in 1775, Thomas died in September 1857 close to the town of Charleston, and within three miles of his place of birth. Daniel's mother, Catharine, died in the same district in 1859. Jane was the daughter of David and Mary McKnight Gordon of South Carolina.[1]

Born September 5, 1800, Daniel Bradwell's place of birth was ten miles from Pond Bluff, the former plantation of General Frances Marion. The plantation was in St. Mathew's Parish, South Carolina. Daniel finished his classic studies at Bethany Academy in Iredell County, N.C., and graduated with a M.D. degree from Charleston Medical College in 1825.[2]

Daniel and Jane Bradwell married in 1828 and moved from South Carolina to Georgia in the early 1830s. Prior to 1841, Daniel moved his family to Houston County. Born on March 15, 1843 near Ft. Valley, Gordon was the third Bradwell son.[3]

---

[1] *Bible Records of Decatur County*, Bainbridge Chapter of the Daughters of the American Revolution, May 15, 1974, 1:50.; The Bradwell family hailed from Dorchester, S. C. According to an account written by Daniel Bradwell, the first of his American Bradwell line was Thomas Bradwell. Isaac Bradwell, son of Thomas, was Daniel Bradwell's grandfather. Isaac Bradwell had one son, Thomas B., by his first wife, Elinor Laton Bradwell. Two of Isaac's brothers, Thomas B. and Jacob B., emigrated to Liberty County, Georgia about 1754 as part of a small colony of settlers who were members of the Midway Church at Midway in Liberty County, Georgia.; Letter, Daniel Bradwell to Sumter Bradwell, June 4, 1876. A transcript of this letter and other material kindly provided to the editor by Gordon C. Bradwell of Athens, Georgia.

[2] Ibid.

[3] U.S. Census, Georgia, 1830 and 1840.

Gordon Bradwell's parents moved the family to Gadsden County, Florida about 1845. However, the elder Bradwell did not like the new location and moved the family in 1854 to the town of Bainbridge, in Decatur County, Georgia. His motivation was to find better schools for his children, and Bainbridge featured some of the area's finest.[4]

In 1857, Gordon's mother, Jane, died at the age of 51. Daniel buried her on the family plantation, about a mile and one-half from Bainbridge. Daniel and Jane had nine children, all of whom were living at the time of Daniel's death. Daniel's second wife was Mary N. Baker, of Liberty County, whom he married on July 20, 1858.[5]

Dr. Daniel Bradwell was a man of prominence. By 1860, he owned 10,800 acres of land and 79 slaves. Daniel's substantial plantation was southeast of Bainbridge, close to the Flint River. His two-story brick home in Bainbridge was just east of the Quincy Road. He also owned stores and warehouses in the town. Daniel served as justice of the Decatur County inferior court during the war and worked to care for the families of soldiers fighting for the Confederacy. Among other activities, he oversaw the successful elimination of a small pox epidemic in the county during 1863. After the war, Yankee occupation soldiers used Daniel's residence as their headquarters.[6]

Daniel's wife Mary died in 1869. By 1871 he moved to North Carolina, where he bought a farm. His last marriage was to Isabella Watts in Statesville, Iredell County. He and Isabella had one child, Durr, in 1873. Daniel died in 1881 at the age of 80.[7]

---

[4] "I.G. Bradwell," *The Brantley Reporter*, Brantley, Ala., October 24, 1912. Also, see 1870 Crenshaw County census records, microfilm roll T9, 21.; Decatur County Deed Book J, 67.

[5] Daniel Bradwell will, Iredell County, North Carolina, Will Book 4, 425.; *Decatur County, Georgia Early Marriage Records and Wills, Georgia Pioneers*, 1987. See appendix §1 for letter.

[6] Frank S. Jones, *History of Decatur County Georgia*, (Spartanburg: The Reprint Co., 1980 254.; *Confederate Veteran*, March 1921, 29:102-103.; Daniel Bradwell will, Iredell County, North Carolina, Will Book 4, p. 425.; Name card file, Georgia State Archives, Atlanta, Ga.; *Confederate Veteran*, March 1921, 29:102-103.

[7] *Bible Records of Decatur County*, Vol. 1, Bainbridge Chapter of the Daughters of the American Revolution, May 15, 1974, 50. Annotation in this publication: "This bible record from an old bible in possession of Mrs. Annie Campbell

With his younger brothers Louis and Sumter, Gordon Bradwell attended school in Bainbridge from the fall of 1856 until the spring of 1861. He planned to attend the University of North Carolina the following year. In the fall of 1861, however, Bradwell enlisted in the company of Captain George W. Lewis, a local tailor. This company, called the "Arnett Rifles," later became Company I of the 31st Georgia Volunteer Regiment. The men spent almost seven months in and around Savannah before the Confederate government ordered the regiment to Virginia in May 1862 as part of General A. R. Lawton's Brigade. Later, General John B. Gordon and then General Clement A. Evans commanded this unit, known also as the Georgia Brigade.[8]

Bradwell had a remarkable career in the Army of Northern Virginia. By his own account he was in twenty-nine battles and many skirmishes during his three years and five months in Confederate service. After seeing much action from the Seven Days' campaign to Cold Harbor, his brigade then moved with General Early on his 1864 Valley campaign. They entered the Petersburg trenches in February 1865 and were also at the final Appomattox surrender.[9]

Gordon Bradwell had one known furlough of twenty-four days during January of 1864 when his commander allowed him to return home. He was never seriously wounded, but was sick on several occasions that necessitated his absence from the army. These periods are well described in his letters. One time frame was from August to November 1862, when he had typhoid dysentery. As a result, he missed the battle of Sharpsburg. He was sick again in May 1864 after the battle of Spotsylvania and remained out of Lee's ranks for one month.[10]

Bradwell participated in the Gettysburg campaign, but missed the first day of the battle due to fever and fatigue. He and his comrades

---

Bradwell of Bainbridge, Georgia."; Daniel Bradwell will, Iredell County, North Carolina, Will Book 4, 425.; Isaac Gordon Bradwell's siblings were Catharine, Matilda, Emily, Thomas Marion, Alexander Moutrie, Elenor, Louis, and James Sumter.; Letter, Daniel Bradwell to Sumter Bradwell, June 4, 1876.

[8] *Confederate Veteran*, October 1923, 31:382.

[9] Ibid., September 1923, 31:338-339.

[10] Ibid., March 1920, 28:102-103.

were among the last Confederates to leave Pennsylvania soil on their return to Virginia after the battle.[11]

At the battle of Monocacy on July 9, 1864, Bradwell was the only one of twelve men in his company not wounded, although he had numerous bullet holes in the blanket that he wore rolled across his chest. Gordon's Brigade took the majority of the Confederate losses during this battle and Bradwell describes the casualties as "the veterans of many battle fields."[12]

He was in the Petersburg defensive lines from February to April 1865. While there, he took part in the unsuccessful attempt to capture Ft. Steadman. During the battle General Gordon assigned Bradwell to escort captured Union General McLauglin to the rear, an event he describes in several of his articles. Bradwell was one of the very last soldiers to leave the Confederate works on April 2 in the retreat from Petersburg.[13]

A 1912 sketch in the *Brantley Reporter* newspaper sums up Bradwell's military career as follows:

> To enumerate all the battles, marches, suffering endured, would make this article too lengthy. Suffice it to say, however, that he and a few of his comrades survived all these; and when the last gun was fired at Appomattox Court House, the regimental colors furled, and their arms stacked, he and the small remnant, ragged, barefoot, and almost starved, set out on their long journey for their homes in Georgia.[14]

During his trip home after the Confederate surrender at Appomattox, he received a new suit of clothes in Augusta and threw the old ones in the Savannah River. As Bradwell put it, "Divesting myself of my old ragged duds I had worn so long, I cast them with all the living things they contained into the Savannah River to float on and out to the Atlantic Ocean."[15]

---

[11] Ibid., October 1922, 30:370, 428.

[12] Ibid., May 1920, 28:176-177.

[13] Ibid., January 1915, 23:20-23.

[14] "I.G. Bradwell," *The Brantley Reporter*, Brantley, Ala., October 24, 1912.

[15] *Confederate Veteran*, March 1921, 31:102-103.

Bradwell continued his trip home via train to Atlanta, Macon, and then to Albany. He made the last part of the journey by stage and arrived at his father's home in Decatur County on May 4, 1865. After a few days rest, he joined the small number of black workers still present on his father's farm in gathering the crops. He became foreman of his father's business interests and also farmed on his own account.[16]

After working for his father, Bradwell entered the teaching profession, where he spent twenty-four years. He stayed in Decatur County until 1875, and then moved to Florida. He remained there for three years and then moved to Alabama in September of 1878. He first taught school at Honoraville in Crenshaw County and continued as a teacher there for 14 years. Bradwell originally planned to go to Texas as his brother Thomas had, but stayed in Alabama on the advice of a former officer of the 31st, Captain John A. Walker. Bradwell had a chance encounter with the captain in Eufaula in 1878 and Walker advised him against going because of yellow fever epidemics in Texas. In 1923 Bradwell wrote, "I took his advice and am here yet."[17]

In 1894 Bradwell settled in Brantley, a town located on the Conecuh River in southern Crenshaw County. Founders started the town as a railroad depot in 1891 on the line that went from Troy to Searight. Bradwell taught school in Brantley for three years. As reflected in a 1912 newspaper account, he "manifested a keen interest in the religious, moral, and financial progress of the town." He was also an active democrat and attended at least one state convention in Montgomery.[18]

Bradwell bought land in southern Crenshaw County in September 1881, and then sold much of the land to people wanting house lots in the new town of Brantley. His real estate interests were considerable and he sold thirteen lots in the town. Bradwell built a fine home on one

[16] "I.G. Bradwell," *The Brantley Reporter*, Brantley, Ala., October 24, 1912.; *Confederate Veteran*, March 1921, 29:102-103.

[17] *Confederate Veteran*, November 1923, 31:419.

[18] "I.G. Bradwell," *The Brantley Reporter*, Brantley, Ala., October 24, 1912; *History of Brantley*, Mrs. Joe Wyatt, unpublished, 1950.; Alabama Confederate pension application, I.G. Bradwell, April 25, 1922, microfilm roll 22. Alabama Department of Archives and History, Montgomery, Alabama.; Bradwell attended the 1884 convention from Decatur County. Bradwell letter, June 6, 1884, provided to the editor by Gordon Bradwell of Athens, Ga.

of his properties, and the house still stands today at 127 Main Street. By 1922, his assets had an assessed value of $4,355, including 143 acres of land, three dwellings, and two vacant lots.[19]

Although his retirement left him with little income, his land holdings caused Bradwell no small difficulty in obtaining a pension from the state of Alabama in 1922. The state first denied the stipend based on the value of his taxable property. Part of his protest to the Alabama Pension Commission auditor was as follows:

> I am entitled to draw a pension as well as my comrades, some of whom gave little or no service to the country while I was on the firing line until the last shot was fired at Appomattox. Since that time I have been helping the state to pay these pensions by my honest effort and industry. But I am now old and am not able to work as I once could and my health also is failing.[20]

After working through his state representative, the state auditor granted Bradwell the pension in 1923.[21]

Bradwell married twice. His first wife was Henrietta Ophelia Shine Bradwell. She was born September 15, 1849 and died in Montgomery, June 13, 1913. Bradwell married her in 1887, when he was forty-four years of age. They did not have any surviving children. His second wife was also named Henrietta, a native of Virginia. He married her on December 30, 1914. She was forty-eight at the time of their marriage and some twenty-three years younger than Bradwell. He met her in Virginia on a trip to attend a Confederate veterans' convention, and he later went back to the "Old Dominion" and married her. On his return to Alabama, he arranged for a brass band to meet them at the Brantley railroad depot to welcome his bride to her new home. He died in December 1934 at the age of ninety-two, leaving his full estate to his wife.[22]

---

[19] Alabama Confederate pension application, I.G. Bradwell, April 25, 1922, microfilm roll 22. Alabama Department of Archives and History.

[20] Ibid.

[21] Ibid.

[22] *Crenshaw County News*, June 19, 1913. Crenshaw County Will Book B, p. 103.; 1910 Crenshaw County Census, Precinct 9, 25A.; Letter from Marjorie P. Pinckard, Brantley, Ala., January 15, 1998.

Bradwell, known affectionately as "Brother Bradwell," was a faithful member of the Brantley Methodist Church. Local residents remember that in his later years he served as the Sunday School superintendent and also worked as a custodian of the church.[23]

Bradwell's interest in the Civil War continued throughout his lifetime. In addition to writing numerous articles for the *Confederate Veteran*, he regularly visited the local schools to lecture on the Civil War. Sig Morgan, of Brantley, remembers that Bradwell always wore a distinctive gray knit cap and old uniform when he gave these talks and could become quite animated when discussing the war, no doubt his favorite subject. He made these presentations for many years and as his obituary states, "Just a few days before his death he made a very interesting speech at the school house, telling the children and visitors of his Civil War experiences."[24]

He proudly marched in local Confederate veteran parades and was a commander of Camp Gracie, Number 474, of the United Confederate Veterans at Luverne, Alabama. Bradwell was quite active into his ninth decade, and continued to write prolifically about the Confederacy and his recollections of the war of his youth.[25]

[23] Sig Morgan, interview with editor, April 25, 1997, Brantley, Alabama.

[24] Ibid.; Alabama Confederate pension application, I.G. Bradwell, April 25, 1922, microfilm roll 22. Alabama Department of Archives and History; Telephone interview, Dupont Strong, and editor, January 20, 1998. "I remember Gordon Bradwell very well. He was my great-uncle. As a boy of 11 or 12, we visited him at least twice at his Brantley home. His mind was very sharp and his recall most lucid. As I remember on one trip he was clean shaven and the other had a Vandyke beard. After dinner he would tell us stories about the war. He spoke almost as a philosopher as he described those long ago events. He could really tell some war stories. However, he was not bitter about the war. In fact, he said the South had no business winning because we were in the wrong. His wife was from Virginia, and after he died, she went back there."; Obituary, *Luverne Journal*, December 26, 1934.

[25] Sig Morgan, interview with editor, April 25, 1997, Brantley, Alabama.

In prewar Decatur County, Georgia, the courthouse was the site of rallies and pro-secession speeches. This photo is from the mid-1850s.

Colonel Hugh M. King was an attorney in prewar Bainbridge, Georgia and served as the town's mayor. King is third from right, second row. (Courtesy, David Sanders)

The boat landing at the bluff of Camp Beaulieu on the Vernon River, 10 miles from Savannah, circa 1895. Bradwell and his fellow soldiers spent several blissful months at Beaulieu before proceeding to Virginia in June 1862. (Courtesy, Georgia Historical Society, Savannah, Georgia.)

The Georgia Brigade joined General "Stonewall" Jackson's Corps in June 1862. (From *Battles and Leaders*)

Pvt Bradwell describes his regiment's band, formed in Savannah, as an integral part of the army. This illustration depicts a band leading marching soldiers past the Pulaski Monument in Savannah. (From *The Soldier in Our Civil War*)

Brigadier General Alexander A. Lawton was the first commander of what became the Lawton-Gordon-Evans Brigade. (Library of Congress, Prints and Photographs Division)

Workers pick up debris from the wreckage of a Federal train after the Second Battle of Manassas. Pvt. Bradwell recalls that the Confederates derailed one such train at Bristoe Station by throwing a crosstie on the tracks. (Frank and Marie T. Wood Print Collections, Alexandria, Va.)

Present-day photo of the stone pyramid at Hamilton's Crossing. From this location the 31st Georgia made its advance during the Battle of Fredericksburg, December 13, 1862. (Courtesy, Robert F. Koch)

Lee and Jackson plan the daring flank march that led to the Battle of Chancellorsville and Hooker's ignominious defeat. (Frank and Marie T. Wood Print Collections, Alexandria, Va.)

"The ax was about to fall with a mighty stroke" says Pvt. Bradwell concerning Federal Major General Robert Milroy's defeat at Winchester in June 1863. (Library of Congress, Prints and Photographs Division)

The Confederate Cavalry crossing the Potomac during the 1863 invasion of Maryland and Pennsylvania. (Library of Congress, Prints and Photographs Division)

Gettysburg, Pa. courthouse spire in August 1863. After staying up most of the night of June 26, 1863 as a provost guard in the town, Pvt. Bradwell slept for a few hours on a bench outside the courthouse. (Adams County Historical Society, Gettysburg, Pa.)

Confederate invasion at Wrightsville, Pa. and torching of the Columbia
Railroad bridge by retreating Federal guards. Pvt. Bradwell took a large set
of keys from one of the town's hotels as a "souvenir" of his stay. (Library of
Congress, Prints and Photographs Division)

Lieutenant General Richard S. Ewell.
(Frank and Marie T. Wood Print Collections, Alexandria, Va.)

General Robert E. Lee. (Frank and Marie T. Wood Print Collections, Alexandria, Va.)

Lee on Traveler. Says Bradwell: "...to see Lee at his best he must be seen on horseback, where he appeared to be perfectly at home." (Library of Congress, Prints and Photographs Division)

Federal soldiers at Morton's Ford depicted in a drawing by Alfred Waud. (Library of Congress, Prints and Photographs Division)

Elected Colonel of the 31st Georgia Volunteer Infantry in 1862, Clement A. Evans later commanded the Georgia Brigade as a brigadier general. (Print from author.)

Generals Alexander Shaler (*right*), and Truman Seymour. Soldiers from Bradwell's brigade captured the two Federal generals during the Battle of the Wilderness. (Library of Congress, Prints and Photographs Division)

General Grant at Spotsylvania. (Frank and Marie T. Wood Print Collections, Alexandria, Va.)

Hand-to-hand fighting at Spotsylvania. (Frank and Marie T. Wood Print Collections, Alexandria, Va.)

Captain Nicholas W. Miller, (right) Co. H. 31st Georgia, brought court martial charges against Colonel John H. Lowe. A court cleared Lowe of the charges. Colonel John H. Lowe commanded the 31st Georgia after Colonel Evans received a promotion to brigadier general. (Miller photo courtesy of A. stephen Johnson and Lowe photo courtesy James G. Lowe.

Generals Lee, Gordon, and Evans depicted in the Battle of Spotsylvania "Lee to the rear" episode. Pvt. Bradwell describes Gen. Lee's intentions to lead a desperate charge against the Federals. (Library of Congress, Prints and Catalogs Division.)

Brigadier General James A. Mulligan of the Illinois "Irish Brigade." (Library of Congress, Prints and Photographs Division)

Lieutenant General Jubal A. Early. (Frank and Marie T. Wood Print Collections, Alexandria, Va.)

Scene of the fight between detachments of the Sixth Corps and Gordon's Division, Fort Stevens, Washington D.C. (Frank and Marie T. Wood Print Collections, Alexandria, Va.)

General Gordon and Jed Hotchkiss view Sheridan's army from the top of Massanutten Mountain. (The Western Reserve Historical Society)

Major General John. B. Gordon. (Frank and Marie T. Wood Print Collections, Alexandria, Va.)

The Petersburg defenses provided formidable obstacles such as the chevaux-de-frise. (Library of Congress, Prints and Photographs Division)

Federal Brigadier General Napoleon B. McLaughlin. (Library of Congress, Prints and Photographs Division)

Lt. Billy Gwyn of the 31st Georgia. Gwyn captured Gen. McLaughlin at Ft. Steadman. (Courtesy, C.R. Gwynn, Jr.)

General Lee's return to his lines after the surrender. (Frank and Marie T. Wood Print Collections, Alexandria, Va.)

The Southern Cross
battle flag. (Frank and
Marie T. Wood Print
Collections,
Alexandria, Va.)

General
Gordon's statue
graces the
Georgia Capitol
grounds in
Atlanta.
(Georgia
Historical
Society,
Savannah,
Georgia.)

Gordon Bradwell (*left*) and his brother, Thomas, sit on the "umbrella rock" close to Lookout Mountain, Tenn. (Courtesy, Thomas M. Bradwell)

Henrietta Bradwell, Gordon Bradwell's second wife. (Courtesy, Gordon C. Bradwell)

CHAPTER ONE

1860-1861

MEMORIES OF 1860[1]

How easily impressed is the mind of the young and how lasting! Trifling events fix themselves in memory for life and remain there fresher than those of more importance in later years.

The year 1860 was an eventful period in the history of our country — the closing of the golden age ushered in by our forefathers, who won our independence and gave us our Constitution guaranteeing to the States their rights and every citizen justice in the courts. I was a small boy then, attending school with the idea of entering the University of North Carolina the next year. But politicians, North and South, were shaping my destiny for a different course, and had been doing so before I came into the stage of action; and instead of continuing my studies in mathematics and the classics, I was doomed to assist in the demonstration of military tactics under Professors Lee and Stonewall Jackson .

Among the books forming our curriculum at that time was *Mitchell's Geography*. In the back of the atlas were the statistics of the United States census for 1850, which showed that the majority of the population of the country was north of the Mason and Dixon line and that a large part of our people were negro slaves. Since this census had been taken, vast numbers of foreigners from Europe had come over and settled in the Western States and territories, all of whom were aliens and enemies to the South. These people were still coming in increased numbers, while few or none came South. It was very evident that if this thing continued, the South would have very little influence in the government, and the power which our section of the country had always exercised would pass to the North and Northwest.

War on a small scale was already in progress on the border, which the government seemed powerless to suppress. This influenced the minds of the people of the two sections against each other. Politicians

---

[1] *Confederate Veteran*, October 1923, 31:382.

and the press on both sides took advantage of the occasion to increase this bitterness. Old John Brown had been hanged by the State of Virginia for making war on her people, and this intensified the feeling of ill will already existing. All this increased the prospect of war and a dissolution of the Union. Division among our own people at home only added gloom to the perspective. Wisdom seemed to have fled from our prominent statesmen, and their eyes were closed to the impending calamity about to fall with so much force on our beloved Southland. The great Democratic party that had ruled the country almost from the beginning split up into factions over minor questions and each put out a candidate for President with the vain hope of electing him over the united opposition, when they well knew that in the previous election four years before the Free Soilers and Abolitionists came near electing Fremont, an Abolitionist, an enemy to the South and her institutions. The different factions fought each other as if there were no common danger, while we floated down stream to our inevitable destruction; and when November came with the news that Lincoln was elected, our people woke up to their folly, as if there was any cause to be surprised.

The first impression this news made on my youthful mind was "the end has come; it means war, and the destruction of our country, a radical change in our laws and institutions from honesty and virtue to corruption and venality." All of this was realized under reconstruction and carpetbag rule often after the war.

Some said: "We will fight; we will not live under Lincoln's government." But others said: "No; let us wait and see. If he violates the Constitution, we will take up arms and fight for our rights under the flag of our country, and we will have thousands of friends in the North who will fight with us." This argument might have prevailed in my state, but under the influence of the governor and most of the members of Congress and many other men of prominence, leading politicians in the different counties visited the various precincts and made an active convass for the immediate withdrawal of the State from the Union. They told the voters that Lincoln would not fight; and if he did one Southern man was equal to thousands of such men as he could put in the field, men who knew nothing about the use of guns.

One prominent speaker, Colonel S, in our county (Decatur County, Georgia) asserted that if Lincoln sent his soldiers to the South, he would muster an army of old women armed with broomsticks and drive them back out of the country. After he had finished, the wife of a prominent citizen stepped out on the platform and addressed the voters in about these words: "I have listened carefully to what Colonel S had to say, but I am afraid if we have war it will be a more serious matter than he seems to think. I am an old woman, and I volunteer now to fight it out with broomsticks; but it won't do to listen to such a foolish argument." This same Colonel S and many others like him who were so reckless in what they had to say at the time did little or nothing to support the cause either at home as citizens or on the firing line as soldiers.

Among the more conservative citizens was an old man by the name of Clay. He was truly a prophet. He was a poor man and had little to lose in case of war; but he quit his business on his little farm and followed these speakers over the country and told the people what would result from secession. He told them it meant war, for which we were entirely unprepared; that we had no trained army and no guns and ammunition; and no place where these things could be made; that we had no ships to bring these things to us from foreign countries; that our ports would all be blockaded, and we would be shut up to ourselves and cut off from all nations and finally subjugated. Everybody laughed at the old man and called him an old fool; but he was wiser than any of them, as future events proved.

A short while after the result of the election was known, I was standing in a crowd on the sidewalk in front of a store with some of my schoolmates and others and saw a tall, handsome young man going toward the courthouse square. On the bosom of his Prince Albert coat was pinned a red, white, and blue cockade. That attracted my attention, and I asked what it meant. Some one said; "That means that he is in favor of war; he is going into the courthouse now to make a speech in a meeting up there." This answer very much depressed me; it was the first move I saw for action. This young man was the brave Captain Waller, who died afterwards so nobly at Sharpsburg, Md., while leading his men with the colors of his regiment in his hand. When he fell with his body riddled with bullets, he reached up and tore the colors from the staff, rolled himself up in them, and died. If every man in the South had been made of the same kind of stuff our country would never have been overcome until the last defender was killed.[2]

Though I looked upon the result of the election of 1860 as the "abomination of desolation"—and I might say that I have never been able to see it from any other standpoint—I loved the Union. But when Lincoln sent his armies across the Potomac to kill the citizens of Virginia and burn their homes, I and my schoolmates, though too young for such service, volunteered, and those of us who were not killed remained on the firing line until the end.

COLONEL HUGH M. KING[3]

Sometime during 1859 or '60, to the town of Bainbridge, Ga., where the author of this little story lived and was spending his youthful days as a student in the schools of the town, a handsome gentleman from Columbus, Ga., or somewhere in that part of the State, came to make his home. Colonel King was an elegant-looking man, tall, and always well dressed. He allowed his full beard to grow and this, I thought, added very much to his personal appearance. He was a lawyer and newspaper man, connected in some way with a paper published there at the time by Rev. Willis M. Russel, a Methodist preacher.

He had recently married a wife who was, like himself, evidently of a noble family, but for some reason they appeared somewhat exclusive and did not mix much with other citizens. This caused some people to

---

[2] Lillian Henderson, *Roster of the Confederate Soldiers of Georgia*, (Hapeville, Ga.: Longino and Porter, 1959) 1:282. "Robert A. Waller. Private March 18, 1861. Company G, 1st Georgia Regiment, Mustered out at Augusta, Ga. March 18, 1862. Elected Captain of Company B, 8th Regiment Florida Infantry May 10, 1862. Killed at Sharpsburg, Md. September 17, 1862."

[3] *Confederate Veteran*, July 1932, 40:258-260.; Hugh M. King was mayor of Bainbridge in 1860-61. Frank S. Jones, *History of Decatur County* (Spartanburg: The Reprint Company, 1980).

talk and say their aloofness was caused by his reduced financial circumstances, that he had married his wife in spite of bitter opposition on the part of her people, and they had been disinherited. I don't know how true or false that was, but they rented a house in the suburbs of the city back of the schoolhouse in a rather lonesome place, and few people ever visited them.

In the old days it was a great pleasure for the schoolboys, with the permission of the teacher, to take the bucket and hie away to some house and bring water for the school, and, as Colonel King's house was most convenient, we usually went there. Boys were sometimes very rude when they got from under the eye of the teacher, but we always went in and got the water and out as quietly as possible so as not to disturb in any way the beautiful Mrs. King, who was always at home by herself, and, when seen, appeared to be sad and lonesome. We had the highest regard for her and Colonel King, and refrained from doing anything to give them offense. We thought it required a great bridge to span the chasm between us and Colonel King, and we respected him and his wife accordingly.

At that time people went on in their old way, following their usual avocations apparently indifferent to the future, so pregnant with great events. The muttering thunder and clouds of war that had been assembling for so many decades were now about to break and deluge our country in blood. It did not require an inspired prophet to see this. Even a schoolboy like myself could do that if he had a mind to. Our wisest statesmen were already engaged in this strife, and had been for a long time in Washington, D. C., and in Kansas a state of actual war was in progress. Every visitor to the North came back and told our citizens of the hostile feeling of that section for our Southland.

A long time before the election in the fall of 1860, it was evident that Lincoln would be elected; that neither Mr. Douglas nor Mr. Breckenridge, nor Mr. Bell had the slightest chance, yet the supporters of each of these candidates appeared confident to the last that their man would be elected; and when the result was known, all seemed to be surprised and disappointed.

Everybody in the South, even schoolboys who were not expected to be students of the signs of the times, knew that this turn of events meant war. Those at the North, except those who had worked so long to bring about this very thing, alone seemed to be ignorant and surprised.

Saddened and disappointed by an event that meant so much to them, our people were sobered and soon lost sight of the minor issue that had heretofore divided them; many declared that they would rather die than to live under a government presided over by a man who was looked upon as an avowed enemy of the South, and everybody was for war. Even the schoolboys were ready to take up arms and fight. Could they, the sons of Revolutionary fathers who had fought under Washington, Marion, and Greene for our independence, submit to live under the government of an enemy more hated than England? No, no! They would rather die.

In our town we already had a well organized military company composed of the finest fellows in the city and surrounding country. They were well armed, drilled, and fitted out in a showy uniform. These offered their services to the Governor of the State, and, leaving home on March 17, 1861, became a part of the 1st Georgia Regiment, Confederate States Army.

As soon as these were gone, Col. Hugh M. King, Col. Richard H. Whitely, and other prominent citizens went to work and organized a very fine company. This company went to Pensacola, Fla., and became a part of the 5th Georgia Regiment. General Bragg was assembling an army at that place, and after he had reviewed this regiment, he declared that it was the finest body of men he had ever seen. This regiment remained in the Western Army under Bragg, Joseph E. Johnston , and other commanders during the entire war, but Colonel King was too competent to remain in the ranks of the regiment. His talents were well known, and he was promoted and transferred several times in the Army of the West, and, in 1864, he was sent to Virginia and placed in command of all the artillery in the old Stonewall Corps, then operating under General Early in the Valley of Virginia. The artillery under him in all that strenuous campaign performed its duties faithfully and well, but again he was transferred to the West as chief of staff for Gen. Joe Wheeler, where his services ended with the surrender of Gen. Joseph E. Johnston.[4]

Years after this, he came to Alabama from New Orleans and was, when I met him here, president of a college in this state. He was the

---

[4] Hugh M. King was appointed Captain of Company H., May 11, 1861. The company was also known as Hardee Rifles. Henderson, *Roster*, 1:704.

same handsome man I had seen so often when I was a schoolboy but, of course, looking much older. He was a strict disciplinarian, and very dignified, but, strange to say, he recognized immediately the schoolboy who had held him in such reverence. Afterwards I visited him at his college home, where he talked freely with me about the past and much about his service in the army. One of these stories I must relate:

When the terms of surrender between Johnston and Sherman were concluded in North Carolina, General Wheeler sent Colonel King to inform his outpost pickets and to tell them to come in, as the war was over. He found the men some distance down the road, lying about in their temporary camp, and informed them what had been done. The men said: "Colonel, if General Johnston has surrendered, we have not. We are going to make one more raid on the Yankees before we do, and then we are willing to come in and surrender."

With this every man mounted his horse and, putting spurs to them, struck out in a cloud of dust, fell on the enemy pickets, who, unsuspecting any such movement at the time, were entirely routed, leaving everything behind. After pursuing them some distance, the Confederates returned and helped themselves to everything left by their old enemies, then rode back slowly to where Colonel King was sitting on his horse at the side of the road, and said: "Now, Colonel, we are ready to surrender."

Colonel King went back to New Orleans, where he died several years ago, leaving behind him few of that great army of heroes that, single-handed, without a friendly nation to render help, held in check the whole world for four years.

With the sons of such men multiplied now by thousands, and those of our former enemies, we can easily defy the whole world in any contest in peace or war.

IN CAMP NEAR SAVANNAH , GA.[5]

The 31st Georgia Regiment was a volunteer command raised by Colonel Phillips, of Columbus, Ga., to serve on the coast of Georgia for twelve months and to be armed with Enfield rifles imported from England. Neither of these promises was fulfilled, for, before its time on the coast expired, it was by act of the Confederate Congress reorganized and enlisted for three years, or the war, sent to Virginia, and incorporated in Jackson's army. The Enfield rifles were never furnished according to promise, and only came into the hands of the men as they picked them up on the battle fields after they had routed the enemy in numerous engagements in Virginia, Maryland, and Pennsylvania. For quite a while the men were armed only with such guns as they brought from their homes, and consisted of all sorts of firearms, most of which were absolutely unfit for use in the army. Great complaint arose among the men when they found that there were no rifles for them, and some even talked of going back to their homes when Governor Joseph E. Brown had sent a carload of pikes to the camp for the men. These were dangerous-looking weapons, with a long, keen steel blade fixed to a pole about eight feet long. Men armed only with these ancient spears could make a poor defense against an army equipped with modern firearms.[6]

The men absolutely refused to take these pikes, and the officers, seeing their discontent, did not urge them to do so. What became of them I do not know, but afterwards, when our thin line was holding our works in 1865 against Grant's heavy battalions, I thought they would have come in very handily, for they were far more formidable than a bayonet on the end of a short rifle, a weapon that was used very little in battle and killed very few men on either side. I took part in twenty-nine battles and many skirmishers, and I can remember seeing only one man killed with the bayonet. When I saw these primitive arms piled up in our camp, I realized that our country had gone to war unprepared for the great conflict.

---

[5] *Confederate Veteran*, September 1923, 31:338-339.

[6] Robert K. Krick, *Lee's Colonels*, (Dayton: Morningside, 1992), 307. "Philips resigned May 13, 1862, and became a brigadier general in the Georgia State Troops. He was a banker and died October 12, 1876."

arms piled up in our camp, I realized that our country had gone to war unprepared for the great conflict.

After some time spent in much drilling and strict discipline, a lot of old, rusty, smoothbore, muzzle-loading muskets of effete pattern, which had served in all the wars since 1776, were put into the hands of the men. They carried a ball and three buckshot, were more effective at about two hundred yards than a rifle, but were too heavy, and kicked like a young mule every time they were fired.

I must tell my own experience with one of these guns. In our first engagement in Virginia we charged a battery, and I am sure I loaded my gun and fired several times, for it reminded me of this fact every time it went off in a very unmistakable way; but when we got near up to the enemy, it kicked me ten feet out of ranks and landed me flat of my back on the ground, with blood issuing out of my mouth and nose.

When the regiment first organized in November, 1861, there were only nine companies, and some of these were quite small. A company under Captain Thornton had gone from Georgia to West Virginia some time previous, where the men had contracted measles and all but a very few, including the captain, had died. The remnant was sent to us to complete the necessary ten companies, but our numbers were small until the conscript act was passed. After this the ranks of all the companies filled up in a short while, and some of these men proved to be good soldiers, as good as those who had volunteered at first.

This act of the Confederate Congress required all twelvemonths troops to reorganize by electing new regimental officers. In this election, Major C. A. Evans was elected colonel, Captain Crowder, lieutenant colonel, and a Captain Lowe, major. These officers were much more capable for their duties than their predecessors, who had received their appointments for some political reason and knew little or nothing about military affairs. I must relate a little circumstance which on one occasion created among the men on drill much laughter at the expense of one of these political military officers. Our wide parade ground extended to a marsh to the east of the camp, this marsh forming an impassable barrier in that direction. Our lieutenant colonel, who had never drilled the regiment before, came out in his fine uniform and maneuvered the command very well for a time, until he had it faced to the east and advancing in a beautiful line. Walking backward some distance in front of the men, and not noticing where he was going, he backed into the bog and fell, while the regiment continued to advance over him. Floundering in the mud, he forgot to give the command "Right, Face," but waving his sword over his head, he made use of language too bad to repeat. This was his last effort to drill the regiment, and we never saw him again. He was a man of brilliant mind and belonged to one of the most prominent families in the State, but he had unfortunately a habit that disqualified him for any usefulness in civil or military life.[7]

Our first encampment was at Camp Wilson on the Shell road, an extension of Whitaker Street, and some distance beyond the Atlantic and Georgia, now the Atlantic Coast Line Railroad. This was a large, level field and occupied by the 25th and 27th Georgia regiments when we arrived. The former commanded by Colonel Norwood, afterwards United States Senator from Georgia, and the latter by Colonel Alexander. We had not been in these camps many days before we were invaded by measles, that dread enemy of all new soldiers, and many of our men died or were rendered unfit for further service. Other diseases thinned our ranks and for a while few recruits came to take their places. We were under very strict discipline all the time, but some men disregarded the military regulations and suffered the consequences, so that when we moved, some time in February, to Beaulieu on the Vernon River, several miles from the city, quite a number of them wore ball and chain for some misconduct. These were put to work on our new parade ground, which was full of stumps when we came, and in a short time all of these were removed and it became a lovely place.

While at Camp Wilson, when on guard, I often admired the splendid appearance of the 25th Georgia Regiment as it was maneuvered by Colonel Norwood, in his beautiful uniform and mounted on a superb horse. Sometimes they would come toward me, standing there on my post at the edge of our camp, in a long line, every knee bending at the

---

[7] Henderson, *Roster*, 3:576. "John T. Crowder. Captain October 14, 1861. Elected Lieutenant Colonel May 13, 1862. Wounded at Sharpsburg, Md. September 17, 1862. Resigned August 19, 1863"; p. 628. "John H. Lowe. Captain November 10, 1861. Elected Major May 13, 1862. Wounded at Winchester, Va. June 13, 1863. Elected Lieutenant Colonel August 19, 1863; Colonel May 19, 1864. Surrendered, Appomattox, Va. April 9, 1865. (Born in Ga. in 1834)." The humorous incident Bradwell describes about his lieutenant colonel refers to Lt. Col. Daniel Pike Hill, a Georgia Lawyer. Hill resigned his commission May 13, 1862. Henderson, *Roster*, 3:576.

same time to the lively music of a brass band. But just before they reached me, the command was always given and they wheeled off in another direction, and my fear of being run over was relieved.

A little incident which happened while we were here served to break the monotony of camp life very effectually for a short while. At midnight, when all well-behaved soldiers, except those on guard, were sound asleep, the long roll, that never-to-be-forgotten rattle that wakes a soldier to do or die, was sounded. The voice of our orderly sergeant was heard calling out "Fall in! Fall in!" In the darkness and confusion, we grabbed our clothes and got into them as quickly as possible, and, seizing our guns, we took our place in ranks. While this was going on, some of our men were so dazed by the suddenness of this rude awakening that they acted like madmen. One fellow snatched up a blanket for his trousers, but could not get into it. Our old French bandmaster rushed up and down the street, shouting all the time, "Where de capitan? Where de capitan? I die by de capitan!" We were soon trotted off to the parade ground to take our place in the ranks of the regiment there drawn up, to meet the enemy as we thought. Casting our eyes in every direction, we could not see the flashing of the enemy's guns or hear any noise of battle. Here we stood for quite a while in uncertainty, when finally Colonel Phillips appeared. Walking slowly down the line, he asked each orderly sergeant as he passed whether all the men were present, and to send all absentees up to his headquarters the next morning at 8 o'clock. We were then marched back to our quarters and dismissed for the night. The next morning at daybreak the delinquents stepped into ranks to answer to their names, ignorant of what had happened during the night. There was quite a delegation from each company to march up to headquarters that morning to receive, as they thought, a very severe penalty for their misconduct. Our good old colonel stood up before his tent and lectured the men, while others stood armed grinning and laughing at their plight; but to the surprise and joy of the guilty, he dismissed them all without punishment after they had promised him never to run away from camp again.

We were all very much improved in health by our move to Beaulieu, on the Vernon River, where we could bathe in the warm salt water. The first Sunday morning after we went to this place we were set to work throwing up a great fort in front of Mr. Jackson's residence. We pounder, cannon were afterwards mounted on it, and two fine companies of the regiment were detailed to learn how to handle the gun and man the fort. A sentinel was kept day and night walking on the parapet to look out for the approach of the enemy's ships, and another was under the fort to guard the magazine. We cut down great oaks and hauled them into position by tugboats to obstruct the river some distance in front of the fort, but the enemy never came to attack us while we were there. I have often thought what futile resistance our men with these old obsolete guns could have made against ships armed with modern long-range guns.

Spades and shovels were put into our hands that Sunday morning, and we were making the dirt fly when Colonel Phillips, to see how the work was progressing, came along dressed in his fine new uniform, a red sash around his waist, and white cotton gloves on his hands. I was working beside Mr. Costigan, an Irishman of Company E, who could smoke his pipe and sling the dirt to a great height with ease. When the colonel got within a few feet of us, Costigan, pretending not to see him, turned and threw a shovel full of dirt into his bosom. As soon as he had done this, he began to apologize to the colonel for his rude conduct, but the colonel passed on and only smiled. When he had gone, I asked Costigan why he had done so. He replied that the colonel had no business coming around where we were at "work." Costigan was a better soldier with a shovel in his hand than with a gun.[8]

Afterwards, in going into battle, Capt. Tip Harrison would call out to him in his lively way: "Mind your eye, Pat." To which Costigan would reply: "Faith, and you had better mind your own eye."[9]

---

[8] Henderson, *Roster*, 3:612. "Pat Costigan. Private November 13, 1861. Roll dated November 5, 1864, last on file, shows him absent without leave since July 2, 1864. No later record."

[9] Ibid., 609. "William Henry (Tip) Harrison. Captain, Company E, 31st Ga. Regiment;" *A History of the 31st Georgia Volunteer Infantry*, Gregory C. White, Baltimore: Butternut and Blue, 1997) 306. "Harrison, William Henry. Born March 21, 1843 in Ga. Attended U.S. Naval Academy. Enlisted November 13, 1861, 1st Lieutenant. Elected 2d Lieutenant at reorganization, May 13, 1862. Wounded in right arm at Cold Harbor, Va., June 27, 1862. Elected 1st Lieutenant, July 15, 1862. Captured at Sharpsburg Md., September 17, 1862. Exchanged, November 11, 1862. Elected Captain, November 28, 1862. Appointed Sutler in 1864. Wounded severely in side at Monocacy, Md., July 9, 1864 and captured there the following

Back of our tents we built a large commissary house, stables for horses and mules, and a chapel where divine services were held almost every night. These things being done, we were ordered to strike tents and move to Skidaway Island. We now became aware that we were overburdened with baggage, but we got there all the same and made our camp on that beautiful island in sight of the United States fleet, lying some distance out at sea. Here we had little to do except to drill, as usual four hours a day, and do picket and camp guard duty. The place was open to the sea and at times storming winds lifted our tents at night and exposed our sleeping comrades to a drenching rain. I suppose there were other troops on the island, but we never met them, and, after remaining there some weeks, we returned to our old camp at Beaulieu. We crossed over to the mainland at Isle of Hope, where the Chatham Artillery had their encampment, and we noticed with pleasure the splendid equipment of that famous battery. We also passed, on our return, the Camp of Wright's Legion afterwards called the 38th Georgia Regiment, with which we were later on to be associated in many sanguinary engagements. This was a splendid body of men and could always be counted on to the last day of the conflict. There were other well armed and equipped regiments at that time guarding the city, and for some reason the enemy made no serious effort to capture the place, though there was more or less fighting at times, in which the enemy always paid a heavy penalty for making the attack. I cannot say how many regiments were there to defend the city, but when Gen. A. R. Lawton took our (31st) regiment and five others away in June, 1862, he left a force there supposed to be sufficient to defend it against the United States fleet and land forces. The town was well fortified in every direction and never was taken until the last of the war, when the Confederates marched out and abandoned the place. Sometime after our return to our old encampment we made a new camp in a beautiful grove of large oaks just back of the Jackson residence and

November 11, 1862. Elected Captain, November 28, 1862. Appointed Sutler in 1864. Wounded severely in side at Monocacy, Md., July 9, 1864 and captured there the following day. Sent to Ft. McHenry, Md. and transferred to Ft. Delaware, Del. Released from Ft. Delaware, June 17, 1865. Died December 16, 1917."

near the fort. This place was on a high bluff overlooking the Vernon River, where the bathing and boating were fine; but camp life was monotonous, and most of us were anxious to be at the front to escape the rigid discipline to which we were subject. Afterwards, when we had our wish gratified, we longed to be sent back. Alas, how many of my comrades of that eventful period survived the war and are alive to-day!

CHAPTER TWO

CONFEDERATE SOLDIER LIFE

SOLDIER LIFE IN THE CONFEDERATE ARMY[1]

When the war broke out in 1861, I was a small boy going to school in Bainbridge, Ga. The crack military company of the town immediately offered their services to the Governor of the State and became a part of the 1st Georgia Regiment. Then another splendid company was organized and went away. After this other influential citizens raised companies, and it seemed that every available man and most of the larger schoolboys had enlisted. Those of the smaller set who had not done so now began to feel lonesome and wanted to go to the war before it should end without their having any part in the "fun."

In our little town Capt. G. W. Lewis , who had come from Tennessee a few years before, had a tailor shop, and at that time he was adjutant of the county militia. Having a desire to distinguish himself, he undertook to raise a company for service in the Confederate army. He hired a two-horse wagon and driver, a negro man to cook, secured an old tent and a couple of drums, and with these he started out on a tour of the county to induce the few who were yet at home to join his "company."

School was now out; and as we were spending a very dull summer vacation, this scribe and other boys of his age and size, attracted by the sound of the drum and the free and easy time in camp fell in and became a part of the company. We went over a great part of the county; but there were very few enlistments, and it looked as if all our drum-beating would result in failure.

At this time Mr. Augustus Bell, a prominent citizen, was also trying to raise a company, which made it more difficult for Captain Lewis; so he proposed that they unite their men and thus form a company large enough to be received in the regiment then organizing. This was done, and in November the little band, composed of small schoolboys out for a frolic, old men better suited for consuming rations than fighting, and

---

[1] *Confederate Veteran*, January 1916, 24:20-24; Paragraphs deleted from this article to eliminate duplication. Editor.

a few first-class men, started to Savannah, Ga., where the regiment was to be mustered into service. But our captain misunderstood the order and took us to Brunswick. Seeing that I could not be persuaded not to go, knowing how frail and delicate I was, and having no confidence in my personal bravery, my father finally gave his consent, after telling me of some of the hardships and suffering I would have to endure and making me understand that if I ran under fire I must not come back to his house any more, as his family had never been disgraced by cowardice. Sam, the faithful carriage driver, had hitched up and was waiting at the gate to take me and my baggage to the nearest railroad station, thirty-six miles away. A servant girl was sent upstairs to get my blanket, while my stepmother and another servant prepared my lunch. When the blanket came and the girl was told to fold it up, my father said "She shall not: let him do it. Let him learn now that he will have to fold his own blanket every day and spread it on the wet ground and sleep on it." I later realized how true was all my father had said. But I hopped into the carriage as if I were going to a picnic.

At the station I found the captain and the other men, who had trudged all the way on foot. When we detrained at Brunswick, Captain Lewis drew cooking utensils and rations for the company and said to the men: "My servant has been doing the cooking for you all this time, but you will now have to do that for yourselves. Select your messmates, about five or six to the mess." When this was done, the cooking implements and rations were issued to each mess, and we all set about preparing our first meal in camp.

While all were giggling and quarreling over who should be chosen to constitute each mess, I took my place some distance away to observe what was said and done, not wishing to impose myself on any of them, as none was any kin to me or had any special interest in me. I observed two men standing some distance from the wrangling crowd, talking quietly to each other. One of these was a Mr. A., a handsome young newspaper man; the other a Mr. T., a farmer and a somewhat older man, with a young family at home. When I had about concluded that I would be left out, Mr. T. beckoned to me and said: "We had decided not to have anybody in our mess but this Dutchman, Elbert Haendl. He can do our cooking, and we can forage around at our leisure while he does the work. But you are a good boy. I know your brother Tom and your father. "We'll take you, but will not take anybody else." This pleased me very much, and I promised to do my part. Some one proposed that we draw straws to ascertain who should cook supper. This was done, and the lot fell on Mr. T. and myself. Now, I had never cooked a meal in my life and knew absolutely nothing about it, but supposed that Mr. T., being a man of family, had some knowledge along that line and would tell me what to do. When I asked him, he said very abruptly: "Build a fire." I hadn't noticed until then that he was under the influence of liquor. Our three days' rations of meal, flour, and bacon were spread out, and Mr. A. said he did not think he could eat such coarse food; so he and Haendl set out to search the town for something better. They eventually returned with a demijohn of old black molasses that must have been ten years old.[2]

When ordered to build the fire, I hustled around and in a few minutes had collected a great pile of sticks and had a fire ten feet high, which lit up the whole camp. Mr. T. said: "That's too big a fire; put it out." I smothered the fire somewhat and asked him what next. He was standing with his coat off and his shirt sleeves rolled up, and he told me to put on our big kettle filled with water, as he wanted to make biscuits. Then he told me to put our flour in the mess pan. He said he would fry our meat. This he sliced up and put into a long-handled frying pan. The steam by this time was issuing from the spout of the kettle, and he told me to take it off and pour the water into the mess pan on the flour. This I proceeded to do, asking him to tell me when I had enough. He looked on in his drunken stupor until I had poured the last drop of the steaming hot water into the pan, and when I had done so the flour was in little hard round lumps from the size of a buckshot to that of an egg.

---

[2] In his article Bradwell refers to his companions as "Mr. A." and "Mr. T." A review of his company members reveals these men as most likely William A. Acree and Joseph H. Thomas. The *Roster of Confederate Soldiers of Georgia*, 3:643 gives the following accounts of these men. "William Augustus Acree. Private November 11, 1861. Appointed 2d Sergeant May 13, 1862; 1st Sergeant October 1, 1862; elected Jr. 2d Lieutenant December 13, 1862; 2d Lieutenant February 7, 1863. Killed at Marye's Heights, Va., May 3, 1863."; p. 648. "Joseph H. Thomas. Private November 11, 1861. Wounded at Marye's Heights, Va. May 3, 1863. Sick in hospital August 31, 1864. Paroled at Bainbridge, Ga. May 20, 1865."; Henderson, *Roster*, 3:66. Haendl enlisted November 11, 1861. He was captured and paroled in 1862. He died in Richmond, Va. in 1862 or 1863. Alternate spelling of name is "Hasndl."

When he saw what I had done, he said: "You've ruined it." I took our corn meal and poured it into the thin hot batter and tried to beat it with a spoon into the consistency of paste, but the hard round lumps remained intact. In the meantime I had put our oven on the fire and had it red-hot. Into this I poured the mixture and soon had burned a thick black crust on the bottom and numerous yellow perforations through it. Our bread for three days was a complete failure. Mr. T. put the frying pan on the fire, while I was busy with the "biscuit"; and a blaze lit into it and ran up five feet high, lighting up the whole camp and attracting the attention of everybody. The whole company began to laugh and guy him, and some hollowed: "Spit on it, spit on it." He now became furious and upset the whole thing in anger, losing our meat in putting out the fire. It was very effective, but we fasted for the next three days.

I now saw that I should have to learn to do the cooking for the mess. We stuck together in peace and harmony as one family, while the other boys were continually fighting and quarreling among themselves as long as we remained in Georgia. The next spring we were sent to Virginia and placed under Stonewall Jackson. Mr. A. made a splendid soldier. He was shot dead at my side on the heights overlooking Marye's Heights May 4, 1863. The same day Mr. T. had part of his hand shot off, but survived the war. Poor Haendl was captured, put in prison, and starved until he was a mere skeleton. When exchanged and released at Richmond, Va., where he had access to something to eat, he died and fills a grave marked "Unknown."

But I must tell something more of our stay at Savannah. Here we were drilled four hours every day and were thoroughly trained for the duties which we were expected to perform later on. But our confinement in camp and daily guard mount, dress parade, and rigid discipline grew extremely monotonous, and we all longed for freedom; so when orders came to pack up and get ready to take the train for Virginia, the officers found it impossible to exercise any kind of restraint, and we made the camp that day and night a veritable pandemonium. The younger set went wild with delight, but some of the older and more thoughtful applied for and got transfers to other commands which remained on the coast of Georgia and Florida. Each soldier that night took an inventory of his belongings, laying aside those things which he considered indispensable; and when we "fell in" the next morning, packed up for our twelve-mile walk to Savannah, we looked like a regiment of foot peddlers. We had not proceeded far in the hot sun when we began to unload. This continued until we took the train in the city.

In due time we arrived at Petersburg, Va., where Colonel Evans received orders to proceed to the Valley of Virginia. When we got there we found the other five regiments, which constituted our brigade under Gen. A. R. Lawton, awaiting us. The appearance of General Jackson's army equipment and his soldiers, who had performed such wonders, was a revelation to us, who had been bottled up in camp so long, with the greatest abundance to eat, nice floored tents to sleep in, plenty of clean clothes to wear, and no marching or fighting to do. Near our camp was a park of artillery which had lately been taken from the enemy in the desperate battle at Port Republic a few days before. The bullet marks and the blood-spattered guns showed the nature of the fighting at the hands of the Louisiana "Tigers," then commanded by Gen. "Dick" Taylor. The army horses were lean and showed the effects of hard service. The few tents we saw and the wagon sheets seemed to have been dragged through pools of mud and water. But the soldiers! How lean and ragged, yet how game and enthusiastic! And when they stood up in line on dress parade under the tattered colors, their regiments were not larger than companies. Our new brigade of six thousand men was as large as half of Jackson's whole army, and I am sure he felt proud of us that morning, a few days after our arrival, as we marched by him to join Lee at Richmond. He had spent the previous night at a beautiful country home, and he and the ladies of the household and their servants came down to the road to see his new soldiers pass by. He stood on the bank of the road dressed in a new uniform, with his arms folded; and as we passed, marching in fours, he watched each quartet with the eye of an eagle.

But I must tell you why we left the Valley of Virginia and how we appeared so suddenly and unexpectedly to General McClellan on his right wing when he and Lincoln were expecting an attack on Washington from the Valley. After our arrival Jackson made demonstrations in the Valley with his cavalry, which indicated an early advance in that direction with reenforcements which could mean nothing but the taking of Washington. Lincoln had a big army there to guard him and his capital. Jackson and Lee wanted them kept there while Jackson marched his army rapidly to Richmond to join Lee and crush McClellan. We had been with Stonewall but a few days when trains began to arrive. These consisted of stock cars, box cars, platform cars, and all kinds. We were packed inside and on top of them and dispatched about twenty miles, when we were detrained, and the cars went back for others. We kept the line of the railroad on foot through woods and fields and across streams until it came our turn to ride again. By this means we were soon at Hanover Junction and Ashland, as far as we could go by railroad. Here we could hear the distant thunder of Lee's guns, which had already engaged the enemy in anticipation of our arrival.

OUR FIRST ENGAGEMENT

While we were packed in box cars like sardines, before we reached Hanover Junction a soldier put his head out and saw a blue-coated soldier standing behind a tree observing our trains loaded with reenforcements for Lee's army. No doubt he was one of McClellan's advance pickets thrown out to make observations and report.

McClellan was begging Lincoln to send the army he had at Washington to reenforce his right wing, and, anticipating this, he had extended his cavalry pickets to Hanover Junction to meet them, although Lincoln and Stanton had never consented to do so. If this had been done, Richmond would have fallen despite the combined armies of Lee and Stonewall Jackson, and the war would have been over in 1862.

After detraining at Ashland, we started on our march to join in the fray then in progress twenty miles or more away. As we hurried on in that direction the heavy sound of artillery became "nearer, clearer, and deadlier than before." Our officers were pushing us to the limit and keeping every man in place, except those who went with our canteens to get water. One young man came back to us with his load of fresh water, and as he handed it around he said: "Boys, they've been fighting down yonder in the woods. I saw a lot of cannon left there and dead men dressed in blue lying around." They marched us until late that night in order to reach the battle field next morning as early as possible, as General Jackson had promised General Lee to have us in line at daylight the next morning to begin the grand attack all along the line on the enemy's position; but at 10 P.M. we were still miles away and so exhausted that we had to bivouac.

The next morning, when the light of the new day was making its appearance in the east, our old musician sounded the reveille as a signal to take our places in ranks and resume our march. The day was clear and warm, and our officers kept us on the move at "quick time" until afternoon, when a staff officer, who had ridden forward, returned and informed our general that the engagement had been in progress all the morning; that General Lee so far had made no impression on the enemy's works and had gotten the worst of the fighting, and to bring his men to the front at "double-quick," as we were needed there. The order was given, and we started in a trot; but many of our men soon became exhausted and dropped out.

Our ranks thinned rapidly now, and by the time we reached the place where our line was to form there were very few present. Colonel Evans halted us and gave us a few minutes to catch our breath after our long run and to allow the stragglers time to come up and resume their places in the ranks. As we filed to the left on the edge of the field to form, we found there a long line of dead Mississippians on the ground, with blankets thrown over their faces. I then remembered my father's admonition; and although dreadfully frightened at what I saw and heard, I stepped boldly into the front rank and preferred to appear brave when some of my comrades plainly showed their feelings. Colonel Evans then told us that we were now going into battle and to take off everything but our cartridge boxes and canteens of water, and a guard would be placed over our belongings until after the battle. We were new soldiers and green enough to believe this, and accordingly we made a great pile of our knapsacks. We never saw them again. The guard said the day after the fight that a quartermaster's wagon came along, and the officer with it dismissed him and took charge of the goods.

In our front as we stood here was a wide level field, and beyond this the timber in a boggy creek (Powhite) obscured from our view the progress of events; but the white smoke arising and the thunder of the artillery indicated very plainly where we would strike the enemy. Across this field came cannon balls, skipping and striking the ground and cutting up all kinds of antics. Artillery horses, with their harness flapping and dangling about them and with the blood gushing from their wounds, could be seen flying wildly to some place of safety. The bodies of dead horses and disabled caissons dotted the field and showed that the enemy had been driven that morning from this position to his chosen ground beyond the creek. During the few moments we were allowed to remain here I began to wonder why I had volunteered, against my father's and my teacher's advice, to come here to be killed like a dog when I might have remained at home in peace and plenty; but I dismissed this thought and asked the Almighty to shield me from the missiles of death and keep me from all harm. This silent prayer was answered; for, although my comrades were shot down all around me and the ground dug up and plowed by the iron and leaden hail, I escaped unharmed. I have ever since been a firm believer in God's merciful providence.

On the march that morning from our bivouac our regiment was the last of the brigade. General Lawton had ridden forward, and as the regiment arrived he threw them forward singly en echelon on our right and to the left of A. P. Hill, supported by Longstreet, who was fighting with the greatest gallantry to dislodge the enemy from his almost impregnable position at Gaines's Mill, far to our right. When we reached the scene, our five other regiments were already engaged, and the 38th, next to us, bearing the brunt of the battle, as they were in the open field and unprotected, while the other regiments were driving the enemy through the woods with comparatively small loss. Colonel Evans and the other field officers, mounted, ordered us to move forward; and as we did so he drilled us as if we were only on parade until we reached the margin of the creek, which we found to be a tangled mass of briers and undergrowth. Here he stopped us a moment to catch breath again and told us to lie down. He took a small Bible out of his breast pocket after he had dismounted and read while we rested. As we fell down a shell from the battery on the other side of the creek came cutting the air just over our heads and plunged into a marshy place back of us, lifting a great quantity of mud and weeds many feet high and spattering us with it. This shell just missed our company, and I saw its effect and felt that the gunners would make short work of us when we made our appearance in the open. Colonel Evans replaced his Bible in his pocket, drew his sword, and in his familiar voice said: "Attention, battalion!" Every man rose, and he ordered us to move forward.

We were soon through the thicket; and as we plunged into the muddy water, full of dead men and horses above, many of our men fell prostrate in it and began to drink. When we got across, our clothes and shoes were dripping mud and water. Just ahead of us, was a long line of South Carolinians, lying flat on their faces, holding the position until we should come. When they saw us they called: "Come on, boys; walk right over us." This we did, as the ground was covered with their bodies and there was nowhere else to step. A short distance up the hill we were out of the woods, where the enemy's infantry and artillerymen could see us. They immediately opened on us with their long-range rifles, while we could do nothing with our muskets, and our men were cut down all about me. The first ball struck a young soldier in Company E named Simpson, who cried in anguish: "O boys, they've shot me!" Then to my right a young man fell, then another and another.[3]

COOKING IN THE ARMY[4]

Our mother Eve perhaps baked the first hoecake for herself and father Adam soon after they were expelled from the Garden of Eden, and that duty has fallen on our mothers ever since, while fathers and sons have strolled around, exempt from this drudgery, without learning anything about preparing food for the table until forced to do so by actual necessity.

And so it was with most of us, I mean the younger set of us who volunteered for service in the earlier period of the war to get away from

---

[3] Ibid., 618. "William B. Simpson. Private March 1, 1862. Wounded at Cold Harbor, Va. June 27, 1862. Captured at Spotsylvania, Va. May 12, 1864. Paroled at Fort Delaware, Del, 1865. At home on furlough close of war. (Born in Ga. in 1845)."

[4] *Confederate Veteran*, October 1923, 31:419-420.

home and school; to have a vacation, where we should escape from discipline and have a free and easy time.

Not one of us in fifty had ever assisted in preparing a single meal, and none of us had any skill in this most common but very necessary service. It had never occurred to us when we were enlisting that we would have to do this and many other necessary things for ourselves — things that had always been done for us by others. But now these things were to be done by our own unskillful hands or go hungry.

I shall always remember the first time it was my duty to assist in preparing supper for our "mess" which consisted of three others besides myself. The rations were ample, and consisted of flour, corn meal, and bacon. To these afterwards were added, rice, pickled beef, peas, sugar, coffee, sometimes vegetables, and always hard-tack. This was a kind of cracker prepared for the army sometime previous to the outbreak of the war, and it was as hard as wood. No salt, shortening, soda, or other leaven whatever was used in its preparation, and it could be eaten only by those who had good, sound teeth; but we found out later that it could be soaked with hot water and grease in an oven and be made quite palatable. In its original state, I suppose it would keep indefinitely in any climate. Each cracker was about six inches in diameter and about an inch thick. When broken with a hatchet, or other instrument, the edges of the fragments were shiny and showed its solid composition. Later in the war the Confederate government prepared a cracker that was far superior to this.

As soon as the messes were formed, cooking utensils were issued to us. These consisted of one large sheet iron camp kettle, two iron pots, a frying pan, a "spider," or skillet, a small boiler, etc. Each man was given a tin plate, a tin cup, and knife and fork. A mess chest, with an extension top that could be opened up to form a table, was also given to each mess, and we were all then ready to begin our domestic duties in camp. All things started off well, but domestic trouble soon began and multiplied rapidly. Each member of the mess was expected to do the cooking for a day at a time, and this was done in such a careless manner by some that numerous complaints went up to the captain. Fighting and quarreling over the way in which the affairs of the messes were conducted were of daily occurrence. This state of things continued for some time, when the captain grew tired of it and told our orderly sergeant to divide the men alphabetically into messes of six or seven each. In this rearrangement I lost two of my former friends, and some came to us whose cooking nobody would like to eat. Though the youngest in the mess, I took it on myself to do the cooking, if the others would supply me with wood and water and relieve me of all other duty. The men unanimously agreed to this, and I, having had some experience in this line, assumed the duty of chief cook and bottle washer. I drew the rations, cooked our meals, placed the food on the table, and afterwards cleaned up everything, and kept things in order. While busy at this, the other men sat around the fire telling jokes, singing songs, and smoking their long-stemmed pipes, criticizing my movements all the time. But I did not mind this, and we lived in peace until we were ordered to Virginia early in June, 1862.

When we reached Virginia, there a pot wagon was assigned to each regiment of the brigade. These followed closely our line of march, and as soon as we went into camp after a long and tiresome day, men from each company rushed to the wagons to get their cooking utensils. Those who brought them always had the first use of them, and after cooking could fall down and go to sleep. Others then took them in turn, and the last who used them were expected to take them back to the wagon. Our pots were now very few and were on double duty; but sometimes our wagons did not arrive, in which case we employed our steel ramrods. We wrapped the dough around them and held it over the coals, turning it all the time so as to bake every side of it thoroughly. And we broiled our meat in the same way, when we had any, or ate it raw. An oilcloth spread on the ground served as a tray to knead the dough. Sometimes in the midst of the preparation of our scanty rations, we were ordered to snatch up everything, seize our arms and fight, or march away. On the march some of our men cooked up their rations and ate them then and there so as not to carry them the next day. I became so accustomed to eating only one poor meal a day that I can live on one now, and I rather think we all would be healthier if we ate less. Oftentimes we went days without any food whatever, but after one meal, we were all right and experienced no bad effects from our long fast.

On our retreat from the trenches in front of Petersburg to Appomattox we were days without anything to eat. On one occasion, when the enemy was making a very strenuous effort to cut our line in two, I was trotting along in a shower of balls and shells when, looking down, I saw a new frying pan thrown away by some one. I took time to pick it up and fastened it to my equipment, thinking it might serve me well in the future if I should escape from the present predicament; and it was fortunate that I did. When we surrendered, it was five days before we received our paroles, and, although we were almost starved, we lived on two pounds of beef issued to us by the Yankees. On the morning of the last day when we formally surrendered our arms and started on our march to our homes, we were so weak from our long fast that some of us could go only some two hundred yards before we were exhausted and had to stop and rest. But we gradually gained strength, and late in the afternoon reached a mill where these was a supply of Confederate corn. We found the mill grinding and turning out excellent meal. The mill house was full of soldiers when I reached it, and I had to edge my way in to where I could get my tin cup under the spout. As soon as it was full, I retired and kindled up a little fire on the dam, and in a short while had a hoecake in my frying pan that was good enough for a king. Many of my poor hungry comrades in passing asked me for the use of my frying pan, and it cooked bread for our men a great part of the night and until we reached our homes.

These frying pans were very useful to us in many ways. They were light and could be carried on the march, so if our pot wagons did not arrive in time, we could bake our bread and fry our "flapjacks" without any other cooking utensils. Indeed, I was so well pleased with them that if I should ever have to go to war again I would have one of them with me as a part of my outfit. They served us in other ways at times. They were known sometimes to turn the course of a bullet that otherwise would have gone through a soldier. The Yankees as well as the Confederates had them. On May 6, 1864, our brigade was so unkind as to make a sudden and unexpected assault on our blue-clad neighbors on Grant's right wing just at sunset, when they had kindled thousands of little fires behind their breastworks to make coffee and warm up their evening meal. So rapid were our movements that we swept Grant's entire right wing back to his headquarters, and they left their frying pans to be trampled on and knocked over. The next morning I was sent back down the captured works and saw the frying pans everywhere. But they were not the only things that favored us in battle. There was a boastful fellow in the 13th Georgia Regiment that used to carry a hatchet stuck in his belt before him so as to be independent of the company ax. In a hot fight at close range a bullet struck his hatchet and flattened itself to the thickness of a silver dollar. It did not have the force sufficient to drive the hatchet through his body, but he fell down and lay apparently dead for some time. His comrades guyed him no little, though it was no joke with him.

But I must not conclude this article without telling about Abbot. He was one of my messmates at Savannah in 1861-62, and was our company commissary at that time. He claimed to have had experience as a soldier in the Mexican War, and I am inclined to believe it from his shrewd ways of dodging and doing things to his own advantage, and incidentally to the company, and especially our mess; but not from anything he said. The night before we started to Virginia we were ordered to cook up three days' rations for the trip, and Captain Walker, our regimental commissary, was busy in our big storehouse, full of every kind of army supplies, issuing rations to the different companies. In the bustle and confusion incident to the occasion, Abbot was acting as his assistant. Now, there was a large pile of fine bacon hams stored there for the use of our officers, and Abbot was determined that every man in our company should have one of these hams for our long trip to Virginia. He got word to the men in camp to come to the commissary house and stand around in the dark near the door. This most of them were ready to do, and when Captain Walker was not watching, Abbot would pass a ham out to one of the men and tell him, without further explanation, to take it to camp. I was busy at our mess fire when the hams began to arrive, one at a time. This continued until there must have been several hundred pounds of them piled up in the street before our tents. But before Abbot got back to us to dispose of them our captain came along and, seeing the great pile of hams, made inquiry of the men who were bringing them and found that Abbot was slipping them out without authority; and he made them carry the hams all back. They were too good for common private soldiers and were kept for those higher up.[5]

We had just detrained in the Valley of Virginia when Abbot put in for a bombproof position and got it. He was put in charge of our ordnance wagon and served faithfully in that capacity until we were on the march from the Valley to Fredericksburg in the winter of 1862. On

---

[5] Henderson, *Roster*, 3:643. "James Augustus Abbott. Private November 11, 1861. Died in Charlottesville, Va. Hospital January 3, 1863. Buried there in Confederate Cemetery."

this trip he took pneumonia, was sent to Richmond, where, after partially recovering he had a relapse and died.

Since I have mentioned Captain Walker, I must say a word about him also. He was a citizen of Eufaula, Ala., and was made commissary of the 31st Georgia Regiment at Savannah when it was organized in 1861. He was perhaps the shrewdest man in all of Lee's army, and without him we would have been at our row's end at the beginning of 1864. By his wonderful management of the commissary department, he kept men and horses supplied with food to continue the contest when the country was exhausted, and all cattle, sheep and other things we had brought out of Pennsylvania were consumed. He seemed to know where every ear of corn in Virginia was to be had, and when starvation seemed evident, he always found something to issue to man and beast. When we went to Virginia he was made commissary for the whole brigade, but was soon after put in charge of that department for the division. General Lee soon recognized his ability, and from that time on to the end Captain Walker was his indispensable right-hand man. It was he who led our half dead soldiers from Appomattox to the mill where they got something to eat.[6]

Thirteen years after the war ended, I was standing on a street in Eufaula and saw Captain Walker coming toward me, with a paper in his hand and his mind preoccupied, for he was a man of big business. When he got near me, I stepped in front of him with my hat off, told him I was one of the old 31st, and asked him if he knew me. He paused a moment and fixed his eyes on me and said: "No; I don't. You boys are grown and changed so much that you don't look like you used to. But I am glad I met you; I want to talk with you; I am too busy now. Go to my office and make that your headquarters as long as you remain in Eufaula." I did so, and he told me about many very important incidents connected with our regiment, brigade, and Lee's army which have never been published. Captain Walker asked me where I was going, and when I said, "To Texas," he said: "Don't go, you can't. There are yellow fever quarantines everywhere. Stay in Alabama." I took his advice and am here yet.

---

6 Ibid., 598. "John A. Walker. Captain and Commissary November 19, 1861, 31st Georgia. Transferred July 31, 1863."

GAMBLING IN THE ARMY[7]

Young and inexperienced when I enlisted in the Confederate army, I was surprised to find so many gamblers among my comrades. It seemed that as soon as they entered the service and found themselves free from the civil law, they resorted to gambling for pastime between all duty in camp, and a great part of the night was spent in that way until our field officers ordered all lights out after a certain hour. But this did not quite put a stop to it, for during the day, when there was any leisure, there were many games of chance which could be indulged in despite our duties. One of these was the raffle, by which means many valuables, or things considered valuable, changed ownership. Many of the men had brought from home such things as watches, pistols, bowie knives, etc. The watches were out of fix, the pistols were antiquated revolvers, and the bowie knives were useful only to cut up meat in preparing our meals.

Among my comrades was a boy named Dan Bowie, a schoolmate of mine, an easy-going, lucky sort of fellow. He always took a chance in these raffles, and invariably won; good fortune seemed to follow him, even a great while after we were sent to Virginia, for there he was always favored by some one higher up and kept out of battle; but luck seemed to have forsaken him suddenly when we got back to the Valley of Virginia from our march to Washington, D. C., in 1864. We had just settled down quietly in camp when some Yankee cavalry that had followed after us from the Potomac placed a battery in position in the mountain pass overlooking our camp and threw shells down on us. One of the first of these killed poor jolly Dan. We were all ragged and dirty from our long march of four hundred miles, and I got permission to go back to the river at the foot of the mountain to take a swim with several of my comrades. We were just having a fine time in the water when,

---

[7] *Confederate Veteran*, November 1923, 31:464-475.

overhead and near us, we heard the boom of cannon. At first we thought it was our cavalry engaging the enemy, but the shells seemed to pass over us, and we hustled out and hastened to camp. When we reached it we found our men all lined up to meet an attack, which was some time developing. As soon as I reached the ranks they told me of Dan's death. He lived long enough to ask a comrade to send his belongings to his widowed mother in Georgia. As he tumbled over a photograph of a woman which he had never shown to anyone, fell out of his pocket, and the comrade who took charge of his hat and other things came to me a few days after the fight and asked me whose picture it was, saying it was the most beautiful woman he had ever seen. I recognized it as a picture of Mrs. Ware, Dan's sister. He said: "I shall write to her if I live." Soon after I had returned to my father's house after the war I went to see Dan's mother to tell her about her son's death, and she showed me the things his friend had sent her. I recognized the hat, as I had owned it myself. He had swapped me a cap for it soon after I had picked it up on the 12th day of May at Spotsylvania Courthouse. I had lost mine in that dreadful affair and snatched this one up and placed it on my head when a shell plunged into the ground and, bursting, showered me and a comrade with red mud and came near cutting our heads off. The mud stains were still on the hat.[8]

I must tell about another gambler and his "luck." Just at the outbreak of the war, a young man named Echols came to our town (Bainbridge, Ga.), and opened a barroom. He stocked it with liquors and other things usually sold in such places. There was a rich old man who used to stand around the place and wait for some one to ask him to take a drink, but he was never known to spend a cent himself. One day, when he and Echols were there alone, he asked the old man why he did not buy any drinks. This touched the old colonel in a tender spot, and he asked Echols what he would take for his whole stock. Echols named his price; and the old man took him up, paid him the cash, and sent the whole stock up to his house. Echols disappeared and I never thought of him any more until I enlisted in the Confederate army

---

[8] Henderson, *Roster*, 3:643. "Daniel Bowie. Musician, November 11, 1861. Transferred to Regimental Band June 1, 1863. Killed near Winchester, Va. September 19, 1864." Correction by historian Gregory White lists death date as July 19, 1864. Editor.

at Savannah in 1861, where I found him a private soldier in one of our Georgia regiments. He was a noted gambler and always successful. He accumulated by his operations ten thousand dollars of good money and sent it all home to his widowed mother. A great revival of religion was in progress among the soldiers, and he professed to be converted, quit gambling, and seemed to be devout and a model young man. But his good fortune deserted him, and he was killed in one of our first engagements in Virginia.

A mile or two before we reached the battle field at Cold Harbor, June 27, 1862, I was surprised to see the greasy decks of cards scattered along the way. The thunder of cannon indicated the hot time ahead of us, and the worst gambler in our ranks did not want his dead body to be found with a pack of cards in his pocket.

For awhile after the war there was no civil law, and everybody did pretty much as he pleased, and gambling was very common. On a visit to relatives at Quincy, Fla., December, 1865, a kinsman and I were strolling around the town, and in passing an empty storehouse we saw a one-armed ex-Confederate soldier sitting behind the counter with his gambling outfit spread out before him. Curiosity prompted us and others to go inside and see his "tricks." He had been there alone for sometime and nobody had offered to play. Conversing with us, he said he did not consider gambling an honorable profession, but he had lost his right arm at his shoulder in defense of his country, and since he could not work, and there was nothing else that he could do, he had taken to it to make a support. After awhile quite a crowd was attracted to the place, but still no one offered to play. I went away and left my kinsman there and had been gone some time when he came to me in another part of the town and handed me a great roll of money, and said: "Take this; it does not belong to me. Go into that store and walk by that fellow in a careless way and give him a wink. He will follow you to the back and hand him this money for me." This I did and he seemed grateful for the favor. He had fixed the game so that the other party could win and it seemed an easy matter to all the crowd looking on, but all who tried it lost. I was interested in the playing of a black Republican State Senator. He won very seldom, only enough to lead him on until he had lost his last dollar.

I knew a Confederate colonel who had by his good judgment and bravery made a splendid record under General Wheeler. From a captain in command of a company he soon became colonel of his regiment and later on brigadier general. My brother served under him, and, like all of his comrades, had the highest regard for him. When the war ended I saw the colonel frequently. He was always dressed faultlessly and appeared to be a perfect gentleman, but had no visible means of support. He had fallen back on his old profession of gambling for a livelihood. In this he was an expert and won thousands from others who were considered the shrewdest professionals. Conversing with my brother on one occasion, he asked him if he remembered a certain soldier in his regiment who was a great gambler, and told him how he broke him of the habit. This young man's mother often sent her son large sums of money, which he soon lost to much shrewder gamblers in the regiment. Knowing her and the sacrifice she was making, the colonel tried to persuade the boy not to play cards any more, but, like all other gamblers, the boy had an idea that he was very smart, and he would not promise to quit. They always cleaned him up the first night, and for days he seemed depressed and always wrote back home for more money, only to lose it again. Finally a large sum came in a letter through the hand of the colonel. He retained the package and sent for the young fellow to come to his headquarters that night. When he gave him the money he proposed a little game of cards. At first he let the boy win a good sum and this pleased him very much; but in the windup the colonel won every cent. The boy went dejected to his tent that night, and for several days remained in that condition. After he had suffered sometime over his loss, the colonel sent for him and lectured him on his conduct, and told him he did not know anything about gambling, and tried to make him promise never to do so any more; but he was too proud to do that and went away in a very sullen mood. Later on the colonel gave him the money, telling him at same time that he did not know anything about gambling and that he had won it from him to show him that he didn't know. It was a great pity the colonel did not take his own advice, for he went on in his career of gambling until he was degraded and ruined.[9]

Returning to our home from Appomattox, we first came in contact with our soldiers of Gen. Joseph E. Johnston's army in Greensboro,

---

[9] This colonel believed to be Col. C.C. Crews of the 2d Georgia Cavalry. Editor. Joseph H. Crute, Jr., *Units of the Confederate States Army*, (Midlothian, Va.: Derwent Books, 1987) 82.

N.C., and were surprised to see them everywhere engaged in gambling. I had never seen so many kinds of games of chance before. They all seemed well supplied with Confederate money, and it was changing hands pretty freely. But I suppose they were not so much to blame for this, as the money was worthless an it was a means for diverting their minds from their unfortunate situation. To their credit it may truly be said that very few of them practiced it after they returned to their homes, but they applied themselves assiduously to the task of rebuilding their homes and fortunes.

BRAVERY AND COWARDICE IN BATTLE[10]

Everybody admires bravery, even when displayed by an enemy. The old Romans considered it the highest of all virtues. Caesar, in his "Commentaries on the Gallic War," after he had almost been defeated by the Nervians, a tribe of the Belgians, says, "The Belgians are the bravest of all the Gauls," and attributed this to the fact that they were farthest removed from civilizing influences, which he thought had a tendency to weaken their martial spirit. But in this I cannot say that he is correct, for I have seen it in men of the greatest refinement and culture. Some seem to be brave by nature, while others in time of danger show by their conduct that they are absolutely wanting in this noble characteristic. But this rule will not always hold good, for I have seen men, who had allowed their fears to control their actions on some occasions, prove by their conduct at other times to be heroes; and others whom I had known to be courageous, have become utterly demoralized when there was little danger.

I have in mind now a brave soldier of my regiment, who had faced danger on the battle field time and again and always performed his

---

[10] *Confederate Veteran*, December 1924, 32:131-133.

part nobly. He was an honorable man and not afraid of one enemy in a personal affair or any number of them, yet on a certain occasion, when our army was outflanked and routed, though he fought to the last, when he saw that all was lost, he threw away his gun and other equipment, his coat, his hat, and when he passed me in his flight, was trying to get out of his shirt also. I remember other men of the regiment who were considered brave at home, and the marks on their bodies showed the scars of numerous personal conflicts. These men, under the influence of liquor, were brave and always ready for a fight. They seemed to like it and always spoiling for it, but when called on to charge the enemy on the battle field, they could not face the music. They were the biggest cowards in the army. Perhaps a little liquor just then would have given them some stamina. But I have known this remedy to have a bad effect on some who happened to have it, and caused them to expose themselves unnecessarily and suffer the consequence. We did not have it and did not need it; we had a greater stimulant to our courage—the consciousness that we were fighting for our homes and everything we held sacred; but our enemy, I am sure, employed it as a means to hearten their men in the Wilderness campaign. I am certain of this fact from the appearance of their dead, the faces of which were as black as a negro, while those of the dead Confederates were pale and natural. Many of the prisoners captured had small flasks of the stuff on their persons.

I remember on May 10, 1864, at Spotsylvania Courthouse, two days before the big battle there, the fighting lasted all day. The Confederates had very temporary breastworks as protection from the heavy lines assaulting them, but they managed to drive back every charge, although they came in massed formation, until after sunset, when the Confederates were busy preparing their evening meal behind the works, supposing the fighting over for the day. Gordon's Brigade was held in reserve that day, and when the enemy broke through the line we had just been removed some distance from the place. We were trotted back in great haste and thrown into battle without taking time to form to drive back the enemy and recover the captured works. This we did after a short but hot engagement. Although we opened on them at short range with a deadly fire that brought many of them down, the rest stood their ground and refused to move an inch—too drunk to see danger. We had to beat them back over the works with the butts of our guns.

The next morning I noticed the difference in the appearance of the dead that I have already mentioned, and on other occasions.

When we were encamped at Savannah in 1861 and 1862, our principal occupations was drilling on the beautiful parade ground in front of our encampment. Our officers selected a tall, middle-aged man for regimental color bearer. He was well drilled, and I often noticed how grandly he carried himself and our regimental colors, thinking how he would lead if we should ever be thrown into battle. But when that event did take place, he wilted, I saw him hand the standard which he had borne so long and gallantly over our heads to another's hands and retire. I never saw him again.

These color sergeants were men of wonderful bravery. They were selected for that dangerous leadership because they could be depended on in any emergency, and I always thought they were the most important men in their regiments and deserved more than anyone else. Sometimes we had several of them killed in a single engagement. I shall always remember brave Jim Ivey, color bearer of our regiment, how nobly he acted in trying to rally our men when we were surrounded at break of day May 12, at Spotsylvania. A few of us rallied around him and fought while he waved his colors and encouraged us to fight until there was no hope. What became of him I do not know, for I never saw him afterwards.[11]

There was a boy in my regiment who had been in every engagement up to September 19, 1864, when we fought Sheridan's big army at Winchester, Va. He had never been sick or wounded and was an ideal soldier. On that occasion he was carrying our colors. We had been fighting desperately from about eleven o'clock in the morning until sunset, when we had either charged the enemy or repulsed every charge; but finally our supply of ammunition was exhausted, and General Gordon mounted his horse and ordered us to "fall back, but not to run." We all started at the same time to leave the stone fence behind which we had been lying, and had not gone more than a hundred yards when I heard a ball strike some one to my right.

---

[11] Henderson, *Roster*, 3:615. "James Y. Ivey. Private November 13, 1861, Appointed 1st Corporal April 1863; Sergeant in 1863. Surrendered, Appomattox, Va. April 9, 1865."

Turning in that direction, I saw Jim Graham lying down on his face, with the colors by his side. Captain Miller, our only officer of that rank then left, called for some one to pick up the colors and carry them out, but as no one responded, he and I came to the rescue. As I reached down to pick them up in a shower of balls from the enemy, now at close quarters, he grabbed the flag and told me to get Jim on foot and bring him out. This I did with the greatest difficulty, for he was larger and heavier than I and, in the greatest danger of being killed, I finally succeeded in getting him to a place of safety.[12]

I never saw Jim again until a few years ago at the Confederate reunion at Macon, Ga., when we happened by the merest chance to recognize each other. He threw his arms around me and wept for joy, and told me his experience after I left him; how he was hauled half dead in an ambulance to New Market, Va., where he was considered too far gone to recover for service and turned over by the Yankee doctor to our surgeon, and his final arrival at home.

Our people in the South entertained mistaken notions that Northern soldiers were not as brave as our own men. We had many brave men in the Confederate army, and there were none better; the only difference was in the composition of the armies. The Federal army had in its ranks a great many foreigners, who had no interest in the struggle, mercenaries who were fighting only for pay. I have seen their officers, real Americans, display the most reckless bravery on the battlefield to encourage their men to fight. One occasion I will mention. In the battle of Winchester a few of us private soldiers from different commands were cut off and surrounded on three sides, but held the right wing of the army against every assault until near night. We were in a desperate situation where we had to make every cartridge count or be wiped out of existence by the overwhelming forces of the enemy. Every time they charged our weak line we drove them back to the cover of the woods by our accurate fire, where their officers rallied them and encouraged them by their example to try us again, only to meet the same fate.

---

[12] Ibid., 631. "James Graham. Private November 10, 1861. Wounded at Winchester, Va. September 19, 1864. At home on wounded furlough close of war. (Born in Ga. November 30, 1842)."; For another account of the Jim Graham incident, see *Confederate Veteran*, September 1907, 15:411.

How many dodgers and cowards they had among them I cannot say, but I know we had some in our own ranks who preferred to skulk and be considered cowardly rather than to face the music and the danger of being killed. There was a certain fellow of this kind in our regiment—a natural coward, just could not fight. I felt sorry for him, for I didn't love to do it myself. When General Lee went to meet Hooker at Chancellorsville, he left a few brigades at and near Fredericksburg to hold Sedgwick in check until he could finish that job, but after considerable fighting the two brigades holding the heights overlooking the town were outflanked, outnumbered, and scattered. Sedgwick then set out to strike Lee's army in the rear, but was hindered by a few men in front of him and our brigade in his rear. Early in the morning of the last day of the fighting, our regiment was deployed in skirmish formation in front of the brigade and the artillery, with a wide open field in front. A quarter of a mile beyond was a thick forest of timber, in which it was supposed the enemy had a line of infantry awaiting us. Our colonel was behind us and could see how every man carried himself, and noticing this fellow dropping back, and knowing his habit of dodging, he called him by name, and told him if he did not take his proper place in the line and do his duty like a man, he would have him shot. We were soon in the woods and this man had an opportunity to slip out, and was not seen any more that day.

Another case I will mention. In my company at Savannah, in 1861, there was a good-looking young fellow who might have been a good soldier if he hadn't lacked one very essential virtue. A false alarm one night so frightened him that he disappeared from among us somehow and went home. No effort was made to bring him back, and he joined a cavalry company, I suppose, because he thought if he ever met the enemy he would have the means of making his way to the rear as fast as possible. He was very successful in this for a long time, until complaint was made to the colonel of the regiment by the other men, who thought he ought to be made to share with them the dangers of battle. The next day, for Wheeler was fighting now every day, the colonel had two men to advance with him in battle, one on each side, with orders to shoot him if he made any attempt to dodge out. One of these men told me he never was so sorry for anyone in his life. He was pale as a corpse and half dead from fright. After this he honestly told his comrades that he just could not fight, but would willingly do any other duty they gave him to perform. Knowing this to be true, they all generously let him off. After the war was over, he was given to telling about his wonderful deeds of bravery in the army.

At Sharpsburg the Confederate army was in a desperate situation, and nothing but desperate courage saved it from total destruction. Every man in the army was conscious of this fact and acted his part accordingly. It would be impossible to mention every deed of heroism of every individual, but one instance will suffice as an example. In the third assault on our thin line that morning made by fresh troops, our brigade, now under command of Col. Marcellus Douglas, was forced to give ground. Looking back, he saw the colors of his regiment (13th Georgia) lying on the ground in a depression in front of the enemy's advancing line. He called to a boy soldier of his command, in whose bravery he had great confidence, and asked him if he could save the flag from falling into the hands of the enemy. The boy replied that he would try, dashed down in the face of the enemy, and snatched up the flag, now only a few feet in front of the enemy, and bore it away in safety, though he received two severe wounds that incapacitated him for service for a long time. Several men had already been shot down carrying these colors that day, and in a few minutes the colonel, who was suffering the loss of much blood from seven wounds, received another which put an end to his life.

Surrounded as we were at Winchester, Va., September 19, 1864, where we all thought there was no hope for any of us to escape, I saw men exhibit the most sublime courage. Every man had the protection of a big oak, or other tree, such as it afforded, against the enemy firing on us from three directions. Here some of our men lost all sense of fear and stepped out in the open, in full view of the enemy, and loading and shooting deliberately regardless of the pitiless shower of balls, cutting the ground around them, until they tumbled over dead. Brave comrades! I took a last hasty glance at their forms, lying crumpled up, as the remnant of us made our hasty dash for escape. They might have been as fortunate as we, and have lived to defend their country and its cause to the end, if they had not despaired.

THAT APPLE TREE —
AND OTHER TREES[13]

No, not that one at Appomattox, for I never saw it, if it was there; I was too busy at the time to pay any attention to it. My comrades and I were far in the advance under our noble commander, Gen. John B. Gordon, trying to cut a way through the enemy lines for General Lee and his ragged veterans to escape. But I have in mind another apple tree in the good old State of Virginia. It stood, and no doubt still stands, on ground made famous by two great battles fought there, the first in June, 1862, and the last in June, 1864. It witnessed the death of thousands of brave men on both sides; but I suppose it still stands there in the edge of the orchard around the old McGehee house peacefully bearing a fine crop of apples to feed the hungry, as if to rebuke silently mankind for slaughtering each other in war. From the appearance of the old residence, it was evidently built in colonial days, and the owner of the premises put out this tree and others of the orchard in which it stands many, many years before.

But why should I single out this tree when there are so many thousands of others which have been faithfully doing their duty to the human race so long? Is it because of its superior fruit? No; but for a little incident which impressed itself on my memory the day after we broke up McClellan's great Army of the Potomac in 1862. I visited this battle field of Cold Harbor just fifty-four years later to see the place when no sound of war broke upon the smiling landscape. There stood that very same old apple tree, green, fresh, and full of young apples. No doubt during all the years of my absence it had stood silently there year after year bearing the same kind of apples. When I came to it, I felt like raising my hand and giving it a military salute, for it had not changed in the least from the time I saw it first that morning when I found my wounded comrade and old schoolmate lying under its branches.

Yes, we had a great battle there that hot June day in 1862. I sometimes think the greatest of all the battles we fought, for our men never afterwards in all the war could have broken McClellan's lines as

---

[13] *Confederate Veteran*, July 1927, 35:262-263.

well posted as they were on that occasion. He was a master of defensive war and an experienced engineer. He always expected to be compelled to retreat and always had such a place well fortified and an ample force of splendid artillery to sweep down the Confederates as they approached. He seemed to have more confidence in this arm of his forces than his infantry. We had the grit then to tackle anything.

We were far in the rear when General Lee opened this battle, and it raged furiously the day before we reached him and all the forenoon, and much of this took place at and near this same old house and orchard before we reached the scene of the conflict. Although we were to be on the battle line at daylight, we were many miles from it at that time, and our officers were urging us to the fullest extent of our ability; but it was noon before we arrived. All along the route we saw evidences of the fight of the previous day, and the incessant boom of artillery indicated the nature of what was in store for us. But as we marched and sweated, we joked each other, indifferent to what the future had in store.

Among my comrades was a youth older than myself who seemed to have been born for misfortune of various kinds. He was a good boy, but an evil spirit seemed to have followed him. At school, when we played ball or any other game, or if we swam in the river, he was sure to get hurt. Yet he bore it all without complaining. In this battle he was shot down late in the afternoon in front of the Hoboken Battery, near the McGehee house, and left there when we were ordered to withdraw. When night spread her dark wings over the land, he crawled toward the house and managed to reach this apple tree on the outer edge of the orchard.

I knew Sol had been left with the dead and wounded, and I was anxious to find him; so as soon as day broke I applied to our captain for permission to hunt him; and under this tree I found him lying stretched out. He seemed cheerful, but haggard from his experience of the previous day. I asked him how he was, and he replied that he felt very well considering his misfortune. He said he had always been unlucky with his left foot, and yesterday, when we waded that creek, he lost the shoe from it, and the next thing the Yankees shot a ball through it. Poor Sol was picked up soon after I left him by our litter bearers and sent to the hospital at Richmond, where he died. He took erysipelas in the wounded foot, a disease which killed many thousands of our men. He was an only son of our old neighbor, Mr. David Waters, of Bainbridge, Decatur County, Ga. He sleeps in a soldier's grave in Virginia, a State he defended with his life.[14]

While I am writing about trees, I remember other trees that served me well on certain occasions. If they had not stood just where they did, perhaps I should have fared as badly or worse than my comrade, Sol Waters, and I would not be here to write about them now. One, I remember, a black locust, about fifteen or twenty feet high and perhaps six or eight inches in diameter. It stood in the open near a ditch, or natural depression, in a field about four hundred yards across. To the west of this field was a woodland, through which we had driven the enemy twice that day.

In this fighting I became mixed up with General Rodes's men. No one appeared to be in command then, as that splendid officer had just been killed and every body did as he pleased. When we reached the edge of the field mentioned, a part of the men followed the fleeing enemy, who took lodgment in the woods beyond. When they (the enemy) came to this gully, seeing that it afforded protection from the merciless fire of the pursuing Confederates, a large number of them fell down in it with their faces to the ground, so when we reached it, we found perhaps as many or more Yankees lying there than there were of us, for most of our comrades preferred to remain behind in the woods. These fellows in the ditch were quiescent, but the others kept up a hot fire on us out in the open. I suppose they could see the top of this little tree in spite of the smoke and supposed that many soldiers were collected about it for protection. It was a time when there was no necessity to load guns. There were plenty of them already lying in the ditch by the side of their owners, cocked and capped. As soon as we discharged one gun, we threw it away and jumped down and got another ready for business. But the fire from the woods was such that our number thinned out and we felt that our position could not be held much longer unless our comrades back of us in the woods would come to our relief. Looking to the left, I saw in the smoke the dim outlines of this little tree. Thinking it offered some protection, I darted to it, only to find two comrades already there. Standing behind them, we exchanged

---

14 Henderson, *Roster*, 3:648. "Soloman A. Waters. Private November 11, 1861. Wounded at Cold Harbor, Va. June 27, 1862. Died of wounds in Chimborazo Hospital at Richmond, Va. July 19, 1862."

compliments with the enemy to the best of our ability, but I was not there long before the man next to the tree fell dead without a struggle. The man who had stood behind him stepped across his body and shot away for a few minutes, when he, too, received a wound which brought him down on the body of his companion. He rolled over and soon died in great agony. I now stood over the man lying at the root of the little tree, but during the few minutes I was there the balls struck the trunk of the tree so frequently and with so much force I decided that it somehow attracted the attention of the enemy, and as they had already killed two others, I decided it was no place for me. We were over-whelmed that day (September 19, 1864, at Winchester, Va.) by Sheridan's army, and there is no good reason why we were not all killed or captured, except that he was no great shakes as a general. We were soon compelled to abandon this place and retire to our comrades in the woods, where every man had the advantage of a big oak to protect his body to some extent until late in the day, when our supply of ammunition was exhausted and they were firing on us from three directions. We then unanimously decided that we had done enough at that particular place and withdrew.

Yes, a tree sometimes was a great thing when a fellow was in a tight place. I could tell about some other incidents that I remember when a friendly oak or pine stood near to give me and others protection.

Though I did not see an apple tree at that historic place of our final surrender, I remember distinctly a small post oak under which I slept five nights while waiting for our paroles after our formal surrender. I would have gnawed the bark off that tree if I had known it would relieve the pangs of hunger. After hostilities ceased, we had two pounds of fresh beef issued to us to live on for five days, although we were wellnigh starved.

CARLOS MAXIMILIAN CASSINI, OUR OLD BANDMASTER[15]

A few years before the war in the sixties, there came to our town, Bainbridge, Ga., a tall, blue-eyed young man form somewhere in East Tennessee and put up a tailor shop. When the war broke out, almost every man fit for military service in the county enlisted immediately. After everybody had gone off to the service, our tailor took a notion to distinguish himself before the thing was over, and, as there was now little or no business in his line, he set out to raise a military company to serve on the coast of Georgia. This was an uphill business, as there were none left to enter the army except a few old men and schoolboys. But the idea of service on the coast appealed to a few, and he finally succeeded, after much effort, in getting up a small company of thirty-five or more, most of whom were unfit for active duty in war.

Among the old men in this company was one old bandmaster whose name appears at the head of this article. Born in France, he had served on board the United States Frigate Constitution, and afterward had located in New Orleans, La., where he had unfortunately been suspected of being the author of a dreadful crime, afterwards found to have been committed there by a Spaniard of similar name. He was a man of a high sense of honor, and his imprisonment for a crime he had not committed so worked on his mind that at times he appeared a little off. After he had been in prison for quite a while, it was found that a Spaniard by the name of Cassino was the guilty person, and he was relieved. But the old man never afterwards had a liking for that nationality. "Spaniard" was the meanest name he could call anyone who had been unkind to him. He finally drifted to Bainbridge, Ga., where he became an employee in Captain Lewis's tailor shop. Although overage, Captain Lewis promised him if he would enlist to secure for him, when the regiment should organize, the position of

---

[15] *Confederate Veteran*, September 1926, 34:333-334. Paragraphs deleted from this article to eliminate duplication. Editor; Henderson, *Roster*, 3:643. "Carlos Maximiliano Cassine. Musician November 11, 1861. Discharged, over-age, from General Hospital at Farmville, Va. November 20, 1862."

bandmaster, a position for which he was eminently qualified except for his age. He was a splendid musician and could teach any instrument.

Captain Lewis had no trouble in making good his promise when we went into camp at Savannah, but there were no instruments of music. After some time, a set of battered up brass horns, which had been repaired, came to us from somewhere. These were put into his hands, and he began to select from the number of rough fiddlers and others who offered their services those who should constitute his "band." It was a strange mixture, but it is remarkable how soon he trained these different characters, some of whom at first knew nothing of musical notation, to play these obsolete old instruments.

Among these was my schoolmate, poor, jolly Dan Bowie, a boy whose mother was a widow. Dan would not study when he went to school and was practically illiterate. The cymbals were put into his hands, and I was surprised to see, when Mr. Cassini first marched his band along our front, playing "Life on the Ocean Wave," how Dan clashed the cymbals together at the right time and place. He held this position, or some other, which kept him out of the firing line until his death in 1864, in the Valley of Virginia. A fragment of shell, fired from a mountain overlooking our camp, struck him on the shoulder and passed through his breast, killing him almost instantly. He tumbled over with his cymbals, which he had carried so long at his side, and begged a comrade to send his belongings home to his mother. I could tell much more about this comrade if it were appropriate here.

They all soon learned to love their old bandmaster, and the old man had a much easier time while we were in camp at this place, for they treated him with much consideration. After he had selected his men, he took them to a remote place in the forest, where they built a booth, covered it with palmetto leaves, and arranged seats in it for the men. Here he instructed them until they could play a few pieces fairly well, and at dress parade he took his position at the right of the regiment, and at the proper time they started along our front, playing a familiar piece, while some of the soldiers guyed and criticized. This was to be expected, however, as our old bandmaster didn't look a bit like a soldier. He always wore a black broadcloth Prince Albert suit and a high black beaver hat, altogether out of place in our camp. When the band reached the left of the regiment, it turned and came back down the line to the original place.

From this time on the men gradually improved in their music, as they had nothing else to do but practice while we were at Savannah. But hard times were ahead of us all. Our regiment and five others were sent to Virginia in the early summer of 1862, where we had much hard fighting and marching to do, and the old man could not keep up with us. The poor old fellow would drag along after us, sick and worn out, and say to those who were trying to help him along "I want to kill one Yank before I die." But he had to go to the hospital, from which he was discharged from service on account of his age disability. He returned to Bainbridge, where my stepmother invited him to make our home his home, and there I found him when I returned after the surrender.

What became of our old brass instruments I do not know, but in the winter of 1862-63, all the drummers and fifers in the six regiments were thrown together into one organization under Lieutenant Cox, of Company E, 31st Georgia Regiment, a splendid musician, and he remained our bandmaster to the end. It was surprising what music this numerous body of fifers and drummers could make. There was nothing like it in Lee's army. In May, 1864, on the first day's battle of the Wilderness, where Gordon's Brigade swept Grant's right wing from the battle field, a part of our regiment captured a full set of modern band instruments, with which Lieutenant Cox reorganized our original band. In marching through cities and towns, or in the grand parade, or the burial service of the dead, they always cheered us with their beautiful music.[16]

In Doles's Brigade, of Rodes's Division, there was an excellent band, but much smaller in the number of instruments. The general required them when in camp to play for hours at his headquarters every day. He said they were exempt from all duty except this, and it was little enough for them to regale their comrades in camp with their music.

There were many other good bands in the different brigades of Lee's army. Even the cavalry had their bands. Stuart was fond of music and always on the march he had a fellow riding behind him singing and playing on an old banjo.

---

[16] Henderson, *Roster*, 3:609. "Carey W. Cox. Jr. 2d Lt. November 13, 1861. Elected 2d Lt. July 15, 1862. Wounded at Sharpsburg, Md. September 17, 1862. Elected 1st Lt. November 28, 1862. Roll for November 5, 1864, last on file, shows him present. No later record."

Mr. Cassini, though a foreigner, was a true Southern gentleman of the old school. After the war he supported himself by teaching music until his death. He was never married.

A TRIBUTE TO
A BRAVE COMRADE[17]

In a humble home in the southern part of Georgia some time in the forties, two little boys were born. They were descended from those "Cajuns" (Acadians) whom the British expelled from Nova Scotia in 1755 and who settled among the people of the colonies along the Atlantic coast. The descendants of those French colonists are found sometimes in settlements to themselves and sometimes in single families throughout the Southern States; and to the present day they have maintained their characteristics and personal appearance.

The father of these little boys died when they were quite young, and their mother married again very soon a man whose brutal treatment of her children was such that, young as they were, they were forced to run away from home to escape his cruelty. Too young to form any definite plan as to what course to pursue, or where they should go, their only idea was to flee from the inhumanity of their stepfather.

In doing this they became separated, each seeking some friendly refuge among the people, drifted miles away from home, and lodged with the good people of the country, who took them in and treated them as their own children. To these friends they told the story of their expulsion from home, and this so excited the sympathy of those who gave them protection that no effort was made to return them to their mother.

In the course of time these little waifs grew up to be useful help on the farms, and their service was very much in demand. But a dark

---

17 *Confederate Veteran*, August 1923, 31:291-292.

cloud was now rising and about to sweep over the land and make many changes, destroying the lives of thousands who knew nothing of the issues which brought about this state of things. Regiments were organizing and companies forming to take part in the great war to expel the invader from our Southland; all kinds of arguments were brought to bear on every one able to carry a gun to induce him to volunteer, so as to make up the quota necessary to form a company. Many were enlisted who were totally unfit, by age or other infirmity, for military service, and after a short time were discharged. But most of the small boys who were not killed became hardened by this rough life and stuck it out to the end. Many of these looked so little like men that some one remarked they ought to be sent home to grow, that they were a disgrace to the service, and that if the Confederate government couldn't do any better in getting up an army, it had better quit then.

One of these boy soldiers was Theodore Billet, our little swarthy, dark-skinned "Cajun," who, like others, when standing at "order arms," was no higher than the muzzle of his Enfield rifle. An old wag called him "General Debility," and this new name seemed quite appropriate. But jibes did not set him back in his patriotic devotion to the cause in which he was enlisted, and his self-confidence knew no limit.[18]

In the early summer of 1862, the year of great battles, we were placed on freight trains and hurried to Virginia where this boyish enthusiasm was to be put to a test. Though sick and half starved at times, young Billet stood the trying ordeal to the end, while older and stouter men fell out of ranks and disappeared. He was with his regiment in many engagements, and had the good fortune to escape without a serious wound to return to his friends in Georgia after the surrender, where he married and reared a family.

In the winter of 1863-64 the army was stretched out many miles along the Rapidan from Culpeper Courthouse to Bolling Green. Longstreet's Corps held the left and the old Stonewall Corps the right. We had little to do during the cold months of winter but cook and eat our scant rations of beef and corn bread, and to prepare our minds for the great contest with Grant's army, which we knew would open in the

---

[18] Henderson, *Roster*, 3:644. "Theodore N. Billett. Private November 11, 1861. Captured at Frederick, Md. September 12, 1862. Exchanged at Aiken's Landing, Va., November 10, 1862. Surrendered, Appomattox, Va., April 9, 1865."

spring. This leisure gave occasion for the soldiers to get permits to visit friends and relatives, whom they had not seen in a long time, in the different commands of the army. On a certain occasion Billet had kindled a fire and was busy preparing his dinner when a visiting soldier from Longstreet's happened to pass along. Noticing Billet's peculiar features, the visitor stopped a moment and, fixing his eye on our little "Cajun," without introducing himself, ventured to ask him if his name wasn't Billet. Looking through the smoke, Billet, who had not until now noticed the newcomer, replied abruptly and indifferently, "Yes; but what's that to you?" To this the visitor retorted by saying: "I thought it was." "Why?" said Billet. "Because you look so much like a fellow in my regiment by that name." "A fellow by my name? What is his Christian name?" "Charley." "Charley Billet? That must be my brother." Billet now became very much interested, for this surely must be the long-lost brother from whom he had been parted since early childhood and had never heard a word of him. Inquiring carefully as to his division, brigade, regiment, and company, he got a pass from his captain and colonel to investigate this bit of information. With this in his pocket, he set out and tramped through many miles of camps and at last came to the identical command, and there found his brother, whom he never expected to see again in this life. We can only imagine the feelings of each as they embraced and wept. Steps were taken now to transfer Charley to his brother's command, and in a short while the exchange was made, and he became a member of our command.[19]

It happened at this time that our general (Gordon) was organizing a battalion of sharpshooters to do the skirmishing for the brigade. Every company in the entire command was called on to contribute a quota according to its strength, and none but the bravest and most reliable men were to be received. Among those of my company who volunteered for this dangerous service was Charley Billet. No braver member of this splendid command could be found. He was an example to his fellow soldiers of reckless bravery in the greatest danger. On such occasions he would mount the breastworks and wave his hat to the enemy and defy them in a shower of balls falling around him.

---

[19] Ibid., 644. "Charles H. Billett. Enlisted as a private in Co. I, 24th Regiment Ga. Infantry August 24, 1861. Transferred to Co. I, 31st Regiment Georgia Infantry May 1, 1863. Killed at Spotsylvania, Va., May 13, 1864."

From its organization until hostilities opened in May, these men were taken out of camp to target practice every day, and a prize was offered for the best marksman so that when we met Grant's army in the Wilderness and at Spotsylvania, strung out in a long thin line, thirty feet apart, they were able to hold their ground and repulse many times their own numbers or drive the enemy like a covey of partridges through the woods. Constant fighting on the front line reduced the number of the original force, and it was necessary to reenforce their ranks from our badly depleted numbers from time to time until the end.

On May 13, at Spotsylvania, the morning after the dreadful battle, General Grant had enough for the present and knew the army and the people at home would not tolerate a continuation of such a horrible sacrifice of life, and, to give his men a respite and time to forget their fearful loss, he decided to withdraw from our presence; but to deceive General Lee while he was doing this, he deployed a heavy line of skirmishers, backed up by many batteries of artillery, and opened on our decimated battalion with grape and canister.

In this engagement many of our best men who had done conspicuous service went down and among them the brave Charley Billet, unknown in history, unwept by his countrymen, and forgotten. Somewhere in Virginia, perhaps in an unmarked grave, the bones of our comrade rest, while his soul has joined the multitude of brave spirits who made the extreme sacrifice for their country. This article is written as a just tribute to the memory of a brave comrade who fell in defense of his country, whose name and deeds otherwise would never be known.

DAVID AND GOLIATH[20]

In the various companies and regiments organized for service in the Confederate army were some mighty men who prided themselves on their physical strength and looked with contempt on those younger and weaker. Some of these even said that this class of embryo soldiers ought to be sent home and given time to grow before they were allowed to stand in ranks with them.

It is quite true there were many who were young and inexperienced in war, but it was a school in which the young could learn as well as those who were older, more experienced and much stronger. Then, the younger set had more vitality to endure hardships than the middle-aged men, and we had not been in active service more than a year before we had lost a great majority of the older and more powerful comrades. They dropped out on the long, hard marches, and few of them ever returned to the ranks, and some of these did little or no execution in battle.

I have in mind now men of this class, in my own company, and one especially I will mention. He was a very brave man and an excellent shot with a rifle. I have seen him come into camps with a string of squirrels, every one of them with his head shot off. But in battle, the first and only one in which he took part, he stood in a shower of balls and shells, holding his gun, and waiting for the enemy to come out of the bushes and smoke that he might see clearly what to shoot at, and all the time abusing his younger comrades for shooting at an unseen enemy only a few feet away. There he stood until a solid shot cut his leg off and ended his career forever.

When in camps I often enjoyed the contests when these fellows ran together in a tussle, though I never saw a decision; but sometimes, when certain ones whom we were afraid to tackle, became too "bigity," and things in camp were becoming monotonous, a dozen or more of the younger set would set upon him, bring him down, and pile on him. This was always rough play, and some came out of it crippled. But all of these stout fellows were not failures. Some were splendid soldiers, and among these I must mention Sergeant Ricks, of my company. I have

---

[20] *Confederate Veteran*, November 1924, 32:419-420.

seen him perform feats of strength almost incredible. When we were engaged in tearing up the railroads, he could handle those heavy iron rails with the greatest ease. I have seen him, to show his strength, shoulder one of the iron rails that must have weighed five or six hundred pounds. He was fearless in battle and one of the best soldiers in Lee's army. Poor fellow! we lost him at Spotsylvania. He was the sergeant of our sharpshooters, and, walking calmly on the line to visit and encourage our little heroes in that dreadful fire, a ball went through his arm shivered the bone, and disabled him for any further service.[21]

But what I intended to write was this:

A noble young man, the son of a noble father, was in college about to finish his education when the war came on. As soon as he had finished, he hastened home and immediately set to work to raise a military company—young, handsome, and popular, he succeeded in this in a very short time and was elected captain. Two younger brothers enlisted under him. But his youngest brother, then only fourteen years old, was persuaded to remain at home until he should be older. The boy did not like this and, after a few months, struck out, contrary to his father's advice and that of friends, and enlisted in his brother's company, then forming part of the Confederate force holding Cumberland Gap.

Now, Dud, for that was his name, was an expert wrestler. From his earliest boyhood he had practiced this sport with the little negro boys on his father's plantation, and at school wherever he met a boy of his size he was sure to tackle him, so that by this time he had become very skillful in the art. As soon as he had become acquainted with the men and boys in the company, he began this exercise with them. He never seemed to tire at his favorite sport when off duty. Naturally very muscular, he soon developed, with so much practice, an expert knowledge of the game, and no man in the regiment could down him.

Encamped on a hill opposite was another regiment of the brigade in which there was a big fellow who was the champion of his regiment, and thought to be of the whole brigade. His command bantered the entire brigade to furnish a man to match him, but no one could be

---

21 Henderson, *Roster*, 3:647. "John M. Ricks. Private May 13, 1862. Appointed 2d Corporal May 13, 1862; 5th Sergeant February 1863. Wounded and disabled at Spotsylvania, Va. May 12, 1864. Paroled at Albany, Ga. May 10, 1865."

found to accept the challenge. This boasting was so insistent that it became offensive, and some of the men suggested that little Dud be offered as their David to meet the proud Goliath. The offer was accepted and the terms settled. These were that a large circle should be drawn where it was convenient for all the men and officers of the brigade to see the contest from higher ground all around. Dud told me after the war that when they brought him through that mass of men assembled to see the fun and set him in the ring, and he saw that big man with a heavy beard all over his face, he could not help having some misgivings; but when the man cursed Dud and asked if his regiment couldn't put a better looking thing in the ring, and told him to go back home and eat more dirt, Dud ran into him, and they clinched immediately. He told me that as soon as he threw his arms around that man he became aware that he had a man to contend with and would have to do his best to win. Around the ring they maneuvered, each trying to take advantage of the other, while each side looked on and cheered its man. Suddenly they made a mighty effort; but it resulted only in a "dog fall" — that is, neither won. No sooner had they hit the ground than both sprang up like an India rubber ball and clinched again for a decisive fall. Dud now understood his opponent's methods and determined to give him a good one for his boasting.

Again they started around the ring, each trying to get the other into the right position, for this time Dud intended not only to throw his contestant, but to throw him over his head and fall on him. At last the opportunity came, and so suddenly that the fellow hardly knew it he went over Dud's head amid the shouts of his friends. But to Dud's surprise, the man began to cry out most piteously, and when his friends ran into the ring to pull Dud off of him, they found that his leg was broken. But Dud's friends surrounded him, placed him on their shoulders, and marched around over the encampment, shouting over their victory and champion.

The poor fellow had to be sent to the hospital, where he remained several months before he recovered sufficiently to return to his command. When he did so, he hunted up Dud and told him that he never was so much surprised in his life; for when he saw the boy placed in the ring to wrestle with him, he was sure he would have little or no trouble, not only to throw him, but to throw him out of the ring.

This story I have written as I had it from the hero himself and his friends who witnessed it.

Dud made a good soldier, and, though young, his regimental commander often called on him when there was desperate fighting to do to lead the charge. In some of this fighting he was wounded, but survived to return home, where he was a prominent and highly respected citizen. He served his country honorably in war and peace and his God as a faithful member of the Church, and he reared a family of noble children to emulate his life. A few years ago he was called to report to our Great Commander. This article is written as a tribute to his memory by one of his friends who loved him.

But I must not close without a tribute to one of my old comrades who sleeps in a soldier's grave in Old Blandford Church cemetery at Petersburg, Va., where I helped to perform the last sad rites above him. "Uncle" Calvin Gurley was one of our old men. His desire to return home to his loved ones was so great that he was confined in the hospital by homesickness most of the time until we returned from Gettysburg in the summer of 1863. We were then encamped on Clark's Mountain, when he and other "hospital rats" returned to our ranks. When he came, our younger set determined to break his melancholy, make him forget his grief, and make a soldier of him.[22]

No sooner had he settled down among us than they piled up on the old man and never let him have any peace of mind or time to grieve. A dozen or more were constantly nagging at him or annoying him in every way possible. After awhile, he learned to enjoy the fun and would even at times start the "offensive," and it took ever so many of them to handle him, for he was big and strong. In all the rough play he never lost his temper more than sometimes to say, "Damn you" when he was hurt. From that time until he lost his life at the battle of Fort Steadman, March 17, 1865, he did his duty nobly. We had by this time learned to love him. The writer of this was detailed with others to bury him. The grave was on the hillside in rear of the church, in full view and under the guns of the enemy in the fort. But to their credit be it said they did not fire a shot at us while we were engaged in that painful duty.

---

[22] Ibid., 646. "Calvin Gurley. Private January 18, 1862. Killed at Fort Steadman, Va. March 25, 1865."

Our brass band played a solemn dirge while we were at work, and when we had finished it we fired a salute over his grave and left him there to rest in peace until the resurrection day.

CHAPTER THREE

1862

A STAMPEDE[1]

Perhaps many old Confederate soldiers who read this little episode will remember having had some such experience themselves, and, for their amusement and the pleasure of all readers of the VETERAN, I shall endeavor to give a graphic account of our memorable rout on the night of June 26, 1862, an incident which has never been in print and exists only in the memory of the few of the 31st Georgia men who still survive. The circumstance made a lasting impression on my mind, which the stirring events of the following day (Cold Harbor), and subsequent battles have failed to efface from my memory. This affair, which we at the time considered most disgraceful, did not seem in the least to dampen the courage of our men in the great battle to which we were hastening, but rather to stimulate them to redeem their good name, which they did so handsomely.

Although we had been in the service eight months, we had never been under fire and were untried. Our soldiering had been at Savannah until we were sent to Stonewall just as he had fought the last battle in his great Valley campaign.

When we arrived he was resting his men in camp a few days to hurl them against McClellan at Richmond.

We detrained at Ashland and set out at once on the march to join Lee's men already engaging the enemy, while the distant boom of the big guns ahead told us of the hot work to which we were hastening. We marched until a late hour of the night, and the column was halted in a deep sunken road for the men to rest until a suitable place could be found for our bivouac. We were lying and squatting about with our guns in our hands, and being very tired and drowsy, all soon fell asleep.

Half conscious, I heard a buzzing, confused noise approaching rapidly from the rear. This passed over us suddenly, knocking men about in the darkness and mixing up men and guns in the greatest

---

[1] *Confederate Veteran*, May 1922, 30:170.

confusion. Whatever it was, passed over us quickly and disappeared, so that we never knew what caused the disturbance. The men sprang to their feet stupefied, forgetting all discipline, and sought safety in flight from an unseen force. On the right of the road was a thick forest of large trees, whose branches extended over us and added to the darkness of the place. On the left an old rail fence ran along the high embankment. Up this the men rushed wildly, scrambling in the greatest confusion to get to the open field, which sloped gently about two hundred yards to a marshy swamp. Across this field the most of the men fled to take refuge in the marsh for protection from an unknown enemy.

Half asleep, I arose and endeavored to follow in the great rush to get over the fence. Rails were flying from above in the darkness, and one of these struck me on the head and knocked me senseless. How long I remained in this state I do not know, but when I regained consciousness my comrades were all gone, and I alone stood there in the road, wondering what to do. I climbed up the bank into the field and peered around in the darkness to locate my comrades, or our enemy, but I could see neither. I loaded my gun and awaited developments. The report of a pistol in the woods on the other side of the road informed me that some one was there. I then descended into the road again, and, in a minute more, Sergeant W. A. Acree (killed at my side at Marye's Heights) came from the cover of the woods and saluted me. He seemed to be utterly disgusted with the conduct of our men. Soon all returned to the road and we were marched a short distance to an open field, where we bivouacked a few hours. As I was spreading my blanket on the ground, Acree, still smarting over the disgraceful conduct of our men, stood up and made them a speech, telling them that on the morrow would be fought the greatest battle in the history of our country, and it would be seen whether they were brave men or cowards. And so it was. His words were true. Well do I remember how nobly he acted his part in that battle.

But this story would be incomplete if I should fail to relate a little joke on our orderly sergeant, George Swan. Among my schoolmates was a long-legged boy named Green Berry Moore. Nobody was ever found who could beat him in a foot race. When he was in full flight, he could clear ten or twelve feet at a bound. He was now about eighteen years old and at his best. As the men were coming back into the road to take their places in the ranks, Green Berry was in a great fit of laughter, and said: "Boys, I always thought I could run, and I was one of the first to get over that fence, and I did my best to reach that swamp; I fairly flew; but when I got there, George Swan had been there so long ahead of me, I found him there wading about knee deep in the mud and calling out: "Rally here, Company I."[2]

This little joke and the experience of the next day were too much for our proud orderly sergeant. He got some kind of a leave of absence to go home, where he turned preacher and never came to us afterwards.

Some of our men thought our herd of beef cattle stampeded and ran over us, asserting positively that they saw above them the head and horns of an ox; others thought our general and his staff officers rode over us to test the pluck of his new soldiers. One man said he was struck by a horse and knocked ten feet. Strange to say, nobody was hurt, but I am sure all were demoralized. To relate how ridiculous some acted would make this article too long.

FIRST LESSON IN WAR[3]

Meeting at the Dallas reunion, for the first time since the war, an old comrade who carried our colors on many memorable occasions and who had the misfortune to have an eye shot out at Second Manassas, August 28, 1862, my mind naturally reverted to that interesting event in our country's history and our part in it.

We had the "grit" then, but we lacked experience, which we, officers and privates, learned then and afterwards. The want of this on the part of our officers cost us dearly, and our loss could never be restored, for

---

[2] Henderson, *Roster*, 3:647. "Green B. Moore. Private November 11, 1861. Wounded at Cold Harbor, Va. June 27, 1862. Discharged, under age, November 26, 1863.; George B. Swann, 2d Sergeant November 11, 1861. Discharged, disability, at Richmond, Va. July 7, 1862."

[3] *Confederate Veteran*, October 1925, 33:382-383, 397. See *Confederate Veteran*, 34:8-9, for a letter written by Joseph Haw providing additional details to Bradwell's account. Editor.

the flower of our regiments were killed or rendered unfit for further military service.

We were well drilled in Hardee's Tactics, but had never been under fire before, and our officers, though educated in the great military school at West Point, had never commanded a brigade or regiment in battle, and it was but natural in the great confusion and noise that they should make some mistakes. Two years later there were hundreds of private soldiers who could have managed better. Indeed, the whole thing now seems to me that it might have been more wisely conducted, with greater success, and smaller loss.

But it was a game fight, though we never again in all the war exhibited such "spunk" as we did in this series of engagements known as "The Seven Days' Battle around Richmond," in which we broke up McClellan's magnificent organization, which he had so thoroughly trained to take Richmond. We did not have the fight in us afterwards that we had then, but our experience was a great schooling for rank and file and served us well on many occasions afterwards. We were brought up from Savannah and Charleston, six fine regiments, under Gen. A. R. Lawton, to assist in this great engagement.

Our regiments numbered about a thousand men each, and when we opened on the enemy the racket we made excited old General "Dick" Ewell, who was used to the noise of battle so that he rode in a gallop to General Lawton, waving his sword and shouting: "Hurrah for Georgia!"

But we were accomplishing very little at a heavy expense, as I have already intimated, at a great loss of our best men. General Lee had been fighting all the morning, losing heavily without making any impression on McClellan's line in his chosen position at Gaines's Mill and Cold Harbor, and it was now past noon and nothing accomplished except the heavy loss already mentioned. General Lawton, knowing this, and anxious to do something to the tide of battle, brought us up in a trot under the hot sun of a bright June day, through tired by a forced march from early dawn, and, as each regiment arrived, threw it forward in line of battle without any skirmishers in front to develop the enemy's line. In doing so, the first regiment encountered our own men, who, supposing they were the enemy coming up on their flank, fired into them, killing and wounding many before they found out their mistake. But the 38th and 31st, coming up last, were thrown forward and struck the enemy's extreme right in the vicinity of the McGehee house, already desperate fighting had taken place. On an eminence to the right of this house was posted the Hoboken Battery of six guns, with an open field in every direction. To the north about eight hundred yards was a woodland in which a Confederate battery had taken position, but its losses were so heavy from the fire of the Hoboken Battery that it did not function after we came on the scene. This Yankee battery was supported by infantry and was dealing out death to the Confederate lines in every direction, and especially to the 38th, when the 31st came up some distance to the left of that splendid command.

As soon as the 31st came out into the open, armed only with smooth-bore muskets, its losses were so heavy from the enemy's artillery, armed with long-range rifles, and the battery on the hill, that the men in the ranks called out to the colonel, Clement A. Evans, that we could not stand it and we must capture the battery and put a stop to the slaughter of our own regiment and the 38th. We were now having our first lesson in actual war, which served us so well afterwards at Gettysburg, the Wilderness, and on many, many other occasions, for, without awaiting the order of the colonel, since common sense dictated to the men what was necessary to be done, they dashed forward in a trot for the battery and the enemy's lines; and when they had come to within their old musket range, they opened on them with their buck-and-ball cartridges such a withering fire and yell that the enemy's line broke and fell back immediately toward the battery. Nor could the enemy be censured for this, for the noise made by our shooting and yelling and the destruction wrought by our "buck-and-ball" cartridges was enough to frighten any man, however well disciplined. The 31st, though new in the game, saw its advantage and determined to press it to rout the infantry, now fleeing back for safety, and capture the battery, and so put an end to the engagement. And this they would have done in a few minutes and saved the lives of many brave men, for up to this time our loss was comparatively small but our colonel, fearing the men in their headlong charge would penetrate too far into the line of the enemy without proper support and meet with disaster to themselves and to his military reputation, began from the rear to cry out: "Halt! Halt!" But the men paid no attention to his orders, and rushed on, driving everything ahead, like cattle. Seeing they disregarded his command, he broke through their ranks with sword in hand and ran ahead of them, still shouting, "Halt! Halt!" threatening to slash them if they did not heed. Disregarding his orders and threats, they determined to push their advantage to a successful conclusion, but, running along in front of the men from the right to the left in his frantic effort to stop the charge, he came to the center of the regiment and finally succeeded in stopping the color bearer and the company to which he belonged. Seeing this, the other companies slowed up to shoot it out with the enemy. This was most unfortunate for us, for in front of the battery was a fence and a sunken road, which gave them a splendid position, well protected from our balls, while we were exposed in the open and very near. Here we suffered our greatest loss in all the battles through which we ever passed. It was a fatal mistake, but our colonel was only human, and all men make them at times. It was very costly, but we never after this forgot how to fight. We learned that the enemy would stand and shoot at us as long as we wished to continue the game of exchanging shots with them, but that a bold charge, well organized, with good shooting and much yelling, though few compared with that of the enemy, accomplished much more than exchanging compliments with them at a distance.

But I have said we never after this had the "grit" or numbers to fight as we did on this occasion; and the reader will naturally ask the questions if so, how was it that, with greatly reduced numbers, we swept the field at Gettysburg on the first day of the battle, ran roughshod over the Yankees, killing and capturing thousands of them; and at the Wilderness, on the first day, when we drove Grant's right wing through that thick woods, capturing twenty-five hundred live prisoners besides those we killed and wounded; and the next day, when we at nightfall fell on his right wing and routed it, capturing two generals, many of their men, doubled up that great army, and would have routed the whole force if the darkness of night had not put a stop to our career? My answer is because of our first great lesson, and because we were better led. Every man was an experienced soldier, and did not have to be told what to do in an emergency. An officer in the late World War told me that our method of fighting would never do for that war; but I told him they never accomplished anything until the Americans had a force there large enough to go "over the top." It was costly but effective, and those who were not killed were soon on their way home. If they had continued to shoot at each other from holes in the ground they might have been there till now.

Then, besides this, we went forward like a cyclone, sweeping up and gathering up everything before us, and always yelling like demons to frighten our foes. This yelling was very effective. I remember on one occasion late in the war, when I and a few other comrades were surrounded after a long hard fight in a strip of woods, we considered our situation desperate, and resolved to sell our lives as dearly as possible, since we had little hope of coming out of it alive. The enemy had ten times our number, and charged us time and again in a halfhearted sort of way, but we bluffed them by the noise we made every time we repulsed them, and some of us escaped to fight it out to the bitter end. They came out into the open, waving their battle flags and huzzahing, but their advance was slow and timid, and our well-directed shots proved too much for them. If they had come forward with a wild rush, they would have killed or captured everyone of us and learned how few we were.

But I must return to my original subject and tell how that great battle of Cold Harbor ended as far as my command was concerned in it. We remained there, loading and shooting our old muskets at the enemy, while their infantry and battery slaughtered the 31st and 38th. Just as the sun was dipping down in the west on that long, hot day, and our ammunition was exhausted, we were ordered to retire under a hail of lead and iron. Glancing to the north, toward the woodland previously mentioned, we saw a sight never to be forgotten. Coming out into the open and at right angles to the enemy's line in splendid formation, were the 13th, 26th, 60th, and 61st Georgia, for our general had shifted there from our right, where they had been fighting, but accomplishing very little, and formed them there out of sight of the battery, to fall on and crush the enemy's right. They were advancing as leisurely as if they were drilling on their beautiful parade grounds at Savannah and Charleston. The men at the battery now saw the new danger and ceased to notice us any more. They turned their guns in that direction and cut wide swaths in the ranks of these brave fellows, but it made no impression whatever on them, and they marched up to the mouths of these guns which had done us so much harm, although the men stood by them to the last minute. In one moment they ceased the dreadful roar, for those who had handled them were lying prostrate in death or too badly wounded to offer further resistance, if such was possible. Too much cannot be said for these, our brave enemies.

The next day I had the opportunity to see this hill and find out who these fellows were, for I admired them for their pluck if they were our foes. I haven't the words at my command to convey to the minds of my readers the condition of things that next morning presented to my sight, and shall not attempt it, saying only that there those dogs of war stood silent while those who had handled them lay around, cold in death or suffering with dreadful wounds. But the poor horses! poor, patient dumb brutes! shot and mangled in every conceivable way, standing around or grazing peaceably on the clover as if nothing had happened, waiting only for the arrival someone to put them out of their suffering.

So many changes and improvements have been made in firearms that few of the younger generation have any idea how heavy and clumsy were the old muzzle-loading muskets with which we were at first armed. Many of these old weapons were originally flint-lock guns, but had been changed to be exploded with percussion caps. They were dangerous at both ends, for they kicked like a young mule. The next day after this battle, a comrade opened his shirt and showed me his shoulder, beaten black by the pounding he got every time his gun was discharged. Mine kicked me ten feet out of ranks and laid me flat on my back with a broken nose and blood streaming from my mouth. They threw a round ball and three buckshot and were effective at a range of two hundred yards. Every man in the regiment, who was disposed to do so, now cast aside his old gun and picked up a new Enfield or Springfield rifle, as the ground everywhere was strewn with them, and they were a menace, for most of them were loaded, cocked, and capped ready to go off if struck by anybody passing over the battle field. The night after the battle they were firing the whole time.

The capture of the Hoboken Battery was the last act in the great battle of June 27, 1862, sometimes called the battle of Gaines's Mill, or Cold Harbor. In this battleground is a Federal cemetery, in which stands an urn which contains the remains, or parts, of eighteen thousand Yankee soldiers killed in this fight and the one which took place here June 2 and 3, 1864. For years after the close of the war, the bombshells driven into the ground and lying on top of it made the cultivation of the soil dangerous.

McClellan's artillery was served on every occasion with the greatest skill. He seemed to have more confidence in that arm of the service than any other. He was an accomplished soldier and a gentleman, but overcautious.

I have written this article for the VETERAN in the interest of true history, that its readers may know the facts which I witnessed, and to present them again to the minds of my old comrades who participated in them with me. But, alas, how few of them are left! I should be pleased to hear from any or all of them now living.

I do not wish to leave the impression that Lawton's Brigade deserved more credit for winning this great battle than others; many brigades had fought that morning with the greatest gallantry before we came up, but were decimated by the fire of the enemy in their chosen position behind Powhite Creek. Too much cannot be said for the brave fellows who assaulted McClellan's center at Gaines's Mill, a position equally as strong as that held by him at Malvern Hill and Meade's at Gettysburg. The enemy occupied a hill on the east side of the creek and mill pond, made more difficult to cross by the timber being cut so as to fall into them. The hill was fortified by three lines of breastworks, one above another occupied by the infantry, and on the level at the top, overlooking the open field through which the Confederates must advance, were numerous batteries of artillery which swept the field and drove hack the Confederates in every assault they made, even though they reached the creek and pond, which they failed to cross on account of the tree tops in the water and the fire of the lines of infantry above them. This was the situation far to our right where the battle had raged so fearfully all the forenoon, and upon which General Lee had lost so many men without making any impression. The Confederates who had done this fighting were the flower of the South, and although they had failed and were discouraged, they were not to be blamed; for it does seem that they had attempted the impossible.

The writer of this account of the battle was only a private in the ranks, and trying to do his duty with his command far to the left. He was too busy to think about what was transpiring on the far-flung line to the right, for even the noise of battle there was drowned by the awful roar around him; but as soon as the Hoboken Battery was captured, news came to us that General Hood and his brigade of Texans, Georgians, and North Carolinians had stormed this position, captured the artillery, and routed the cavalry charge made by McClellan to recover his ground, and were still holding it. This was the last act in the great drama, and all McClellan's army not killed or captured on that side of the Chickahominy were now driven into the swamp of that stream and were floundering around in the darkness, mud, and water in an effort to cross over to the main force on the other side, for that stream had risen and flooded all the adjacent lowlands.

The Confederates, with their artillery, might have destroyed the fugitives in the swamp that night, but for some reason did not choose to do so.

[NOTE.—All the regiments of Lawton's brigade were armed with imported Enfield rifles except the 31st.]

FROM COLD HARBOR TO CEDAR MOUNTAIN[4]

The morning after the great battle of Cold Harbor my captain gave me permission to look for a schoolmate who had been shot the evening before. The whole field presented a fearful sight. Most of the wounded had been removed during the darkness of the night, but the dead were lying where they had fallen. My comrade had crawled some distance from where he was shot to an apple tree near the McGehee house and had not been found by our faithful litter bearers. "Poor fellow! He took erysipelas in his wound and died after he had been taken to the hospital in Richmond, where it was impossible to give proper attention to the thousands of wounded friends and foes. Perhaps there were fifty thousand, including the sick, to be taken care of by our poorly equipped medical department in the small city of Richmond. Thousands died for want of proper attention and nourishment. The

---

[4] Ibid., June 1921, 29:222-225. Paragraphs deleted from this article to eliminate duplication. Editor.

authorities, aided by the citizens, were simply deluged by the overwhelming mass of suffering men.

The enemy was now in full retreat to the protection of his fleet in the James River at Malvern Hill. He had but one route to take and that extended through White Oak Swamp, a heavily wooded, boggy section of country. General Lee sent a division to intercept him there under one of his generals; but when the broken masses of the enemy came struggling through the mud, this cowardly fellow was too timid to strike and let them pass to collect their shattered remnant of an army on the hill at Malvern, where they and their fleet mowed down our men in a dreadful slaughter. He was court-martialed for this piece of cowardly negligence and never allowed to hold a commission again. At every creek and stream McClellan left a force to hold us in check while his army dragged themselves through this dismal forest, and as our men approached they inflicted on them a heavy toll of dead and wounded, while we could do the enemy very little damage.

Our brigade took no part in these engagements until we arrived at Malvern, the last of the Seven Days' battles. Dead men and dead horses, wagons and wreckage of every kind blocked our pursuit until the once grand army reached the protection of their fleet. Here McClellan massed the remnant of his infantry and artillery to hold together some semblance of organization, while he perhaps took refuge on one of his vessels. No place could have been better suited for his purpose than this Malvern Hill. Elevated and open to the west and north, his artillery had a wide sweep over every approach from which his enemy might attack. To make the place more difficult, boggy creeks intersected the field to the west. The open field to the north did not extend very far. Beyond it was a flat, swampy forest of heavy timber, where the Confederates could form and reform as they were driven back in the fearful slaughter. Behind the hill in the James River lay the fleet with its big guns.

Who was to blame for bringing on this dreadful slaughter of our men it is not my purpose to say. I will not attempt to repeat what was said in the army about it, for much of what we heard was only hearsay, and I have nothing official to refer to. Some of the army had taken no part in the fighting at Gaines's Mill and Cold Harbor, having been stationed on the south side of the Chickahominy, while most of the fighting took place on the north side under troops commanded by A. P.

Hill, Longstreet, and Jackson. It seems that they did not heed General Lee's orders not to attack if they found the enemy at this place, but as soon as found they deployed their lines and gave orders to advance. Collected together were one hundred and fifty pieces of artillery on the eminence around the Malvern house. How many heavy guns in the fleet I have no means of knowing; but as our men advanced in the most gallant style they were mowed down, yet on they went until they reached the crest and drove away the gunners and infantry, only to be driven back by the fleet. Time and again they rallied and renewed the assault, only to be driven back, until in the darkness of night they managed to hold a part of the hill and some of the captured artillery.

Nothing at this time could exceed the bravery and enthusiasm of the Confederates. When they reached the abandoned guns, some of them mounted them and waved their hats in triumph, only to be swept away by the hot fire of the fleet. The Confederate artillery attempted to relieve the situation by replying to the guns of the enemy, but no sooner did they take position and fire one shot than a hundred guns were concentrated on them, and they were knocked to pieces and the men and horses killed.

Night was coming on when we arrived and found the whole field and surrounding swamps illuminated by the flashing artillery and exploding shells. The brigade was formed in the swamp to the north, and some regiments were sent into the field, where they did some fighting, but our regiment only stood in line in the edge of the field awaiting orders to advance. These never came, and we fell exhausted from fatigue and were soon asleep. While standing here the enemy's artillery, a few yards only in front of us, was ordered away, and when daylight came only the rear guard of McClellan's army was holding the hill. The rest of them had fled in the darkness along the banks of the James River, under the protection of the fleet, to Harrison's Landing. Orders came for our company and others to advance in skirmish formation and attack the enemy. The fighting did not last long, for the white flag soon went up for a cessation of hostilities to bury the dead and attend to the wounded. I saw many of the enemy's dead that had been killed by their shells from the fleet. Some of them were horribly mangled. The remnant of the "grand army" was now huddled up in a cove on the banks of the river at Harrison's Landing and could have been captured if Gen. J. E. B. Stuart, who found them in this situation, had only sent word to General Lee to place his guns on the surrounding hills and open on them. But in his haste, and doubtless without thought, he opened on them with his light horse artillery. This opened McClellan's eyes, and he occupied the heights and fortified his position. Thus another blunder was committed and an opportunity to end the war slipped from our hands. If this army had surrendered, as they certainly would have done, the people of the North, already tired of the war, would have forced Lincoln and his cabinet to offer terms of peace. Our scouts, operating in the rear of McClellan's army in Eastern Virginia, reported that the country was full of deserters who declared they never intended to fight the Southern people any more.

We followed McClellan's army down to a place near Harrison's Landing and formed our line in the hot, sultry river bottom, where we remained several days, long enough to be fully inoculated with the germs of malaria, typhoid fever, and dysentery—diseases that destroyed more of our men than the missiles shot at us by the enemy.

As we passed through the camps abandoned by the enemy, our men helped themselves freely to blankets and all kinds of wearing apparel, and in so doing we all became infested with those annoying pests which stuck to us to the end of the war. Up to that time we had never seen those new invaders of our soil, but we were quite familiar with them afterwards.

While these things were in progress around Richmond the government at Washington was collecting the armies of Banks, Fremont, Shields, and Milroy as a reenforcement for that of McDowell, making an army of sixty-five thousand men. These forces were strung out along the north bank of the Rappahannock and Rapidan as a protection for Washington, but now were intended for a new offensive. They were all put under command of Maj. Gen. John Pope to begin a new campaign against Richmond. There is no telling what this great boaster would have attempted if he had been let alone; but Stonewall Jackson and General Lee had their eyes on him, and before he could do anything he was the worst whipped and disgraced Falstaff that ever commanded a great army. He had had some success against half-armed citizen-soldiers out in Missouri, and on that account had been selected as commander in chief to scatter the Confederates and put down the "rebellion" in short order. His extreme cruelty to the noncombatants within his lines was a demonstration of the littleness of his soul. In a short time he was defeated at Cedar Mountain and a little later on out maneuvered and beaten in a great battle at Manassas Junction.

McClellan's army showed no signs of making any farther demonstration against Richmond, and we were marched back to that place, where we were allowed a few days' rest, after which we were sent by train and on foot to Gordonsville and made camp about four miles from that town. Here we rested a few days, and while here our brigade was transferred to Ewell's Division, which had constituted Jackson's right arm in all his battles from that at McDowell to the end of his wonderful Valley campaign. His three brigades were thinned out by their constant fighting until they were not more than half their original strength. They were Smith's Virginia Brigade, Hoke's North Carolina Brigade, and Hays's Louisiana Brigade. In the fight at Manassas shortly after this General Ewell lost a leg while rallying our regiment, and General Lawton commanded the division until he was wounded and disabled at Sharpsburg. We were always in front and opened the fighting for Jackson.

General Lee was still at Richmond with the main army under Longstreet watching McClellan, and Jackson, anxious to get some definite idea of the strength of Pope's forces, decided to strike a blow at some part of his army to find out what it could do in a general engagement. Accordingly he crossed the Rapidan on the 7th of August and on the 9th formed his line at Cedar Mountain, near Culpeper Courthouse. His line extended across the mountain and the public road leading to Culpeper on the west side. The enemy began the engagement with his cavalry, which made a grand charge, but were badly beaten. Then the infantry advanced to the attack on Jackson's left, holding the road. The fighting there was hot, and the ammunition of our men became exhausted. It then seemed for a while that the battle would be lost, for the Confederates were giving ground and fighting with clubbed guns, stones, and anything they could get. At the same time the long Federal line was advancing to envelop and outflank our extreme left. It was a critical time for Jackson, but he was equal to the occasion. He ordered a brigade under the noble General Winder to move from the extreme right of the line, where there was little or no fighting, to strike these flankers on their flank. While this movement was in progress he rushed into the midst of his retreating men on the road and, in the confusion seizing a regimental standard in the hands of a color bearer, shouted "Halt, men, and fight! Jackson is with you!" At this every man regained courage and fought around their beloved leader until a supply of cartridges came and was scattered along or the ground among the men. They grabbed up these and held the enemy at bay until General Winder struck them farther to the left and routed them. The panic spread to every part of their line, and what had seemed certain defeat was turned into a victory. But the Confederates lost the noble General Winder, who was killed at the moment of his success. Many prisoners fell into Jackson's hands, and from these he found that Pope's army was too large for him to attack without the support of General Lee. So instead of following the routed enemy, he retired peaceably the next day across the Rapidan to his old camps to await the time when General Lee should come up with Longstreet in supporting distance. Our brigade took little or no part in this battle, as it occupied the top of the mountain and the fighting was mostly to the left. From their elevated position they had a fine view of the surrounding country and could see the progress of the battle.

In connection with this I wish to relate a little story which was common talk among the soldiers for some time. In the early part of the engagement a Confederate soldier was captured and taken to Culpeper. Soon after his arrival a courier came in great haste from the scene of the conflict and reported to the crowd of anxious Federals and citizens that Jackson was defeated; that his men were on the run when he left. This created great rejoicing. But the Confederate was game and told them they would hear different news pretty soon. Then another courier arrived and was surrounded by a crowd eager to know the news. This man reported that the Confederates had made a stand and the battle was somewhat in their favor. The Confederate, though a prisoner, could not be kept silent and told them to look out for the next news and predicted that Jackson would be in the town directly. And then came another courier on a horse covered with white foam, showing that he had been ridden hard, the courier himself appearing very much excited. He reported the whole army routed and in full retreat. And soon the demoralized cavalry began to arrive, and behind them came the infantry, all in the greatest confusion and hurrying to get out of the way of "Old Jack." Our Confederate went wild with joy at their discomfiture, shouting: "I told you so; I told you so."

To my comrades who participated in this affair I am indebted for this story and also for their account of the operations of our regiment and brigade in all the battles until November following, when I returned to them. On the morning of the 7th of August, when the command marched away I was too sick with that dreadful disease, typhoid dysentery, to stand on my feet, and they left me there to die. After they had been gone some time a teamster came along to pick up whatever baggage had been left to haul to Gordonsville. This kind-hearted man found a place for me on top of his load of all kinds of army plunder and hauled me over a rough country road to town. The jolting almost killed me before we got there. He spread my blanket on the railroad platform and put me on it, then told me he had to follow the army, but he would see if he could get me into the hospital. After some time he returned to me with Lieutenant Floyd, who was there among the sick, and they told me that the doctor in charge of that institution had refused to take any more sick soldiers in, as it was already overcrowded. The whole town was full of sick men. The hotel near by and other houses were converted into hospitals, and still there was not room enough. Floyd stood in silence a while looking at me and walked away, saying he would try again. Again he and the driver came back and reported their failure to get me in, the doctor absolutely refusing to take another man. Floyd stood looking at me in silence and pity, then exclaimed angrily as he turned to go away: "It's a shame for you to die here on the platform for want of attention. They shall take you." After he had been gone some time litter bearers came and took me to the hotel, where they spread my blanket on the floor near the foot of a stairway, then brought me a pill of opium and a little later two batter cakes and some clover tea. That night I slept soundly, but the next morning I was very sick. I was then taken up and put in a freight car crowded with sick soldiers for Greenwood, a place on the rocky side of a mountain. It seemed as if we would never get to our destination.

When we reached that place I was put in a tent stretched over a rock that occupied half the ground and many more much smaller. Among these stones I lay down and remained several days with little or no attention. At last one day, to my joy, I saw a rough young fellow, whom I recognized as a member of my regiment, passing my tent. I called him. I asked if he could write, then begged him to write a letter to my father, which he did at my dictation. I told father that when he received that letter I probably would be dead, but I wanted him to come to Virginia and take my body back to Georgia and bury it beside my mother's grave back of the house. Before he got this letter the authorities took a notion to move all the sick to Nelson Courthouse, a village three miles from the nearest railroad station, and when we arrived there we were put into tents in a field near the depot. Here we remained several days, while I lingered between life and death, and I awaited the time when I should be released from my suffering. But again the authorities moved us, this time to the village, and I was put in a jury room of the little courthouse. Words cannot describe the misery and suffering in that place. Wheat straw was put on the floor for us to lie on, and this and the walls were soon alive with vermin, and little attention of any kind was given us.

When my father got my letter his private and public engagements were such that he could not leave home, and he sent my brother-in-law, B. C. Scott, who could find no record of me at Greenwood. He then went to Richmond and searched the hospitals there and then to other places without success. Finally he came to Nelson Courthouse, but there was no record there. He had just turned his back on the place and was returning to Georgia, supposing me dead, when he was seen by one of my comrades who had that day heard where I was. So he came to the jury room and looked in on the scene of misery, then called to me to stand up, as he could not recognize me. When I did so he exclaimed, "My God!" and turned away. Soon an ambulance drove up to the courthouse door, and they took me to the hotel, where I was bathed, put on new clothes, and given something to eat. Scott took me before the doctor in charge of all the sick at that place and asked him to give me a discharge. But the doctor held an official paper in his hand and told him he had just received instructions not to discharge any one, even if he had lost a limb; but he said he would give me a discharge from the hospital and Scott could take me home if he wished to assume the responsibility. This Scott agreed to do; but when we got to Charlottesville I was too unwell to make the trip to Georgia, and he got me into the house of a very nice family, who treated me with as much consideration as if I had been a son. When I was able to walk about I fortunately located our captain, who was on sick leave in the country at North Garden Station. He took me out with him, where the kind treatment of the good people and the fresh mountain air soon restored me to health.

My mind now turned to my comrades, and I longed to rejoin them to share in their hardships and dangers. Since I had left them they had fought many battles and were now (November, 1862) in camp near Winchester, Va. When I reached them they related to me their experiences in all these engagements.

NORTH GARDEN STATION, VA., 1862[5]

The cool nights of September remind me of my pleasant stay among the kind and hospitable citizens in the surrounding country about North Garden Station, Va., in the fall of 1862, where I recovered my health sufficiently to return to the ranks in Lee's army after a sojourn of several weeks. I often think, even yet after sixty-nine years, of those good people who were ever ready to do anything to relieve the suffering of a sick Confederate soldier.

In attempting to tell how I happened to be at that place, I shall be as brief as possible.

After the seven days of fighting about Richmond in 1862, there was a multitude of sick and wounded soldiers in the hospitals in Richmond and in private homes all over Virginia. There were also other thousands with the germs of disease in their systems who were unwilling to leave the ranks and go to a hospital, but kept up in hope that they would get well without medical treatment. Some did recover, but others, like myself, fell by the wayside, and it was months before we were able to do military duty, and many died for lack of everything.

So they carried me to his house [at North Garden Station] and put me on a bed in a nice room upstairs, and Mr. Lucas brought me such

---

[5] Ibid., October 1931, 39:374-377. Paragraphs deleted from this article to eliminate duplication. Editor.

food as I would have enjoyed if my condition had been such as to eat. Every time the old gentleman came up he insisted on my coming down to the table to eat and to get acquainted with his wife and daughters, telling me that I would mend faster if I would do that; but I felt too weak to go up and down the stairs, and, besides, I was melancholy and did not want to see anybody except the soldiers of my company and regiment. Finally I told him if he would help me to put on my clothes and help me up-and down-stairs, I would do as he wished.

I found them to be very nice people who had refugeed there at the outbreak of the war from Alexandria, Va. From a window near my room in this residence, I could see a little white speck on the top of a small mountain to the south, and was told that this was Monticello, Thomas Jefferson's old home. The family took a great interest in me and asked me many questions about myself and my father's family and our home in Georgia, but I never felt quite at home. I wanted to be with my comrades or at home. Then I had no papers to show that I had a right to be absent from my command. I told this to Mr. Lucas, but he could do nothing for me. I longed to see some one of my command among the thousands of soldiers coming and going every day, but never could see one, although I went every day after I had begun to convalesce to the hotel facing the railroad depot, and sat there for hours. After I had kept this is up for two or three weeks, I saw a soldier sitting in a crowd of other comrades on the steps in front of the wide piazza of the Ballard house, and I ventured to ask him if the hat he had on was his. He replied that it was not; that it belonged to a comrade with whom he was staying at the Delevan Hospital, and it turned out that this comrade was a friend of mine and a member of my company. The next day I met him, and he told me that Captain Lewis was on sick leave at North Garden Station and would be in town the next Friday to have his papers extended, and he would take me to Dr. Davis at the Delevan and get me papers. When I returned home, Mr. Lucas and all the family noticed the change in my demeanor, and I told them that I had located my captain and would get my papers all right next Friday.

When the train arrived that morning and Captain Lewis stepped on the platform, I grabbed him and told him my trouble. He said: "O, that's all right; I am going to see Dr. Davis to have my papers extended, and I will get yours for you." Returning from the office, he asked me where I was staying and how much I was paying for my board. I told him forty dollars. He said: "That's too much. Be ready when I come in the next time to go with me. I am going to take you out with me to North Garden, thirteen miles in the country, among good, kind Christian people, and your board won't cost you a cent."

The next time he came we had our papers extended, and I hastened to my friends and bade them good-bye. I have never seen them since, for when I passed through that city again, twice, my clothes were so ragged I was ashamed to see them, but corresponded with them after the war.

When we arrived at our destination Mr. Darrow was there with a horse and buggy to take me to his house. He and the Captain walked, as I was too weak to go on foot so far—five miles—so they let me ride. I found his house crowded with soldiers, fifteen or twenty at the table every meal. The Misses Sutherlands, beautiful young ladies, nieces of Mrs. Darrow, waited on the soldiers and seemed to enjoy their presence.

I had been there but one day when Captain Lewis returned to the army, and I received a note from Lieutenant Stewart, at Mr. Joe Sutherlands, to come to him at once, as he had had another hemorrhage and wanted me to stay with him until he should recover. I remained with him until November, when I returned to the army, having been out of ranks since August 7, about three months. Again, on the 13th of May, 1864, the next day after we fought that dreadful battle with Grant's army, at Spotsylvania Courthouse, I was stricken with the same trouble and was taken to the hospital at Richmond almost dead. But I rallied and returned to the ranks in less than a month, and I remained until the end.[6]

I often think of the kind people at North Garden, but I suppose there are few of the family there now, if any. Coming out of the exciting scenes of the march and the confusion incident to battle, this quiet community made a great impression on my mind. I also think of the splendid orchards of apples. The soil there seemed to be very suitable for that fruit and all others.

---

[6] Henderson, *Roster*, 3:643. "Hugh L. Stewart. 3rd Sergeant November 11, 1861. Elected 2d Lieutenant May 13, 1862. Resigned on account of phthisis, and was discharged from General Hospital at Charlottesville, Va., October 8, or 20th, 1862."

FROM CEDAR MOUNTAIN
TO SHARPSBURG[7]

When Captain Lewis met me at Charlottesville, he took me to Dr. Davis, chief surgeon there, and got a ten days' extension for me to remain in the country until I should recover sufficiently to return to the army. He took me back with him, gave me some fatherly advice, and left me. The first day after he was gone I had a note from Lieutenant Stewart a schoolmate of mine, asking me to come and stay with him as he was very sick. I found him at the house of Mr. Joseph Southerland suffering with tuberculosis. He was anxious for me to remain with him indefinitely, and all the surroundings were pleasant and inviting. After he had recovered sufficiently to do so, we walked over the fields and orchards in this quiet and peaceful retreat, and he often repeated his request that I remain with him. I always answered him reservedly in the affirmative, but felt that I owed my service first to my country. Sitting down in a quiet place one day he repeated the suggestion to me, and I told him that I had made up my mind to return to the army. He looked sadly at me, while the tears ran down his cheeks, and said: "And this is your resolution, is it?" I told him it was. He then asked me to go to the house with him, and I wrote out his resignation. I told Mr. Southerland what I had resolved to do, and the next morning he took me in his buggy to the station.

In due time I arrived at Staunton, the nearest point on the railroad to the army. Here I found a great many soldiers like myself, returning to the army from the hospitals. The authorities sent us out to the camps to spend the night. These were situated on a small mountain near the city, a wind-loved spot, swept bare by the cold north winds. A few old tents were there and some green oak wood that refused to burn. Sleep was out of the question in this inhospitable place. All with one accord, long before day, were en route for the army, ninety miles away. I made a

---

[7] *Confederate Veteran*, August 1921, 24:296-298.

solemn agreement with two brothers in my brigade that we would remain together on the march until we reached our command. Every evening before sundown we began to look out for a barn filled with hay or a haystack, where we could sleep in comfort. The weather was cold and crisp, but we made it all right to our command, near Berryville, where they had been resting since the battle of Sharpsburg. Jackson was here watching the developments of McClellan's plans, while General Lee had crossed the Blue Ridge Mountain with Longstreet's Corps to threaten any movement the enemy might make toward Richmond.

Sitting around camp fires, our men related all the details of the campaign after they had left me sick in camp near Gordonsville. As they had nothing to read and no drilling or any camp duties to perform, telling these stories and incidents connected with their marching and fighting was their only pastime. Rations were plentiful, and this, with the rest and splendid winter air, had restored our men to excellent health and spirits. Our ranks were filling up with those returning from the hospitals, and now Jackson had a force of veteran soldiers toughened by the hardest kind of military experience. All had the greatest confidence in him and he in them. General Ewell, commanding our division, had lost a leg at Second Manassas, and the command had fallen on Gen. Jubal A. Early after General Lawton, who was wounded at Sharpsburg. The brigade was after this under first one colonel and then another, all incompetent except the heroic Marcellus Douglass, of the 13th, who lost his life on the bloody field of Sharpsburg.

But I must relate the events as they took place from the battle of Cedar Mountain until my return to the ranks. After the battle of Cedar Mountain, Jackson returned to the south side of the Rapidan and rested his army in camps a few days until General Lee started on the move from Richmond to support him in a new campaign. Jackson and J. E. B. Stuart now got busy. Their activities confused General Pope so that he did not know what course to pursue or from what direction to look for an attack. Stuart raided his rear and even entered his tent after he had undressed himself and retired for the night; but when he saw Stuart enter, he blew out the candle and rushed out from under the tent into a drenching rain and, mounting a horse, escaped in the darkness half naked, leaving in his tent his clothing and official papers.

Jackson crossed the Rappahannock River at Henson's Mill, and after some fighting and by hard night marches over rough country roads and through forests he soon placed his army in the rear of Pope's. The transport wagons could not keep up with these rapid movements, and our men suffered for want of food. They subsisted on roasting ears, green apples, or anything they could get on the route. The strain was too great, and many broke down before they reached Manassas Junction.

Stuart in the meantime kept Pope employed and "in the dark as to Jackson's movements" until he had come through Thoroughfare Gap and swooped down on Manassas and Bristoe Station, where millions of dollars' worth of United States army supplies were piled up for Pope and his army. Jackson sent our division (Ewell's) toward Bristoe, while he took his main force to Manassas. Our brigade reached the station just as two freight trains from Washington were running with supplies for Pope's army, now hurrying to attack Jackson at Manassas. He had at last found that Jackson was in his rear. Having been reenforced by divisions from McClellan, he was marching north to crush Jackson before General Lee could come to his relief. The two trains were rushing at full speed, the engineer and fireman lying on their faces to avoid our balls, and would have gone by, but a lieutenant threw a heavy oak crosstie on the track and ditched the foremost engine. The other crashed into it, and supplies of every kind were scattered along the railroad track for our hungry soldiers. They were just helping themselves when Pope's men began to arrive on the scene.

The balls from the enemy put a stop to this picnic, and General Ewell formed his division in line of battle, facing Pope's whole army. He fell back in this formation on Jackson at Manassas, who knew the storm was coming and had selected his ground to meet it. He had no news from General Lee and did not know for certain that he was coming in time to save his army from complete destruction. Even the teamsters were armed and put into ranks to meet the emergency. It was a critical time for Jackson, as his army was now reduced by sickness to only about twenty thousand men. But his wisdom in selecting his own ground, the bravery of his troops, and his usual good fortune saved him until General Lee arrived with Longstreet.

Pope's advance forces fell with such weight on our men the first day that it seemed that they would be overwhelmed and cut to pieces. Our brigade was almost surrounded and beaten back in spite of all they could do. The noble Captain Forrester, of Company A, in command of our 31st Georgia Regiment, was shot dead; then Captain Fletcher assumed command. Captain Pride, his senior, now came to take command, but he, too, was shot immediately. The regiment was in great confusion and scattered in the woods, where they had been beaten back. At this moment General Ewell came riding in among them. Seeing the disorder, he inquired what regiment and, dismounting, gave his horse to an orderly, while he seized the regimental standard in the hands of the color bearer and ordered the men "to dress" on the colors. Order being restored and the fighting renewed, he turned to remount, but was shot in the knee at that moment and suffered the loss of a leg.[8]

On some parts of the line the Confederates held the railroad. Their ammunition gave out, and they were compelled to defend their position with the stones used for ballasting until a supply came. They cast these with so much force into the ranks of the enemy as they came charging up that some of them were killed and many others wounded. Jackson was holding his line with the greatest difficulty when a courier arrived to inform him that General Lee had cut his way through Thoroughfare Gap and was coming to his relief. It is said that when he received this news he arose in his stirrups and brought a sigh of relief. Looking to the rear, our men could see in the distance the regimental standards of Longstreet's men approaching. They seemed to be very tired from their forced march. It was a welcome sight. Would they take our places and drive back the enemy, who were punishing us so unmercifully? No. They marched by to take their places far to our right, and as they did so, following Longstreet, riding at the head of the column, he looked like a king leading his hosts to battle.

---

[8] Henderson, *Roster*, 3:578. "Forrester was killed August 28, 1862."; 3:650. "Richard H. Fletcher. Jr. 2d Lieutenant September 5, 1861. Elected Captain January 16, 1862. Resigned June 1, 1863. Reenlisted June 1, 1863, and detailed Acting Ordnance Sergeant. Roll for November 5, 1864, shows him present. No later record."; p. 585. "Rodolphus T. Pride. Captain October 5, 1861. Wounded at Cold Harbor, Va. June 27, 1862; 2d Manassas, Va. August 28, 1862. Elected Major July 1, 1863; Lieutenant Colonel February 1864. Wounded and disabled at Wilderness, May 6, 1864. Resigned August 19, 1864."

To Jackson's right was a hill overlooking the whole battle field. As soon as General Lee arrived he saw this advantage and had thirty pieces of artillery put there. The enemy's line was formed somewhat in the shape of the letter V. This hill stood at the point of the letter, and the artillery could enfilade both wings of their army, thus giving aid to Jackson's badly crippled divisions and at the same time cutting down the ranks of the enemy to the right. Longstreet formed his brigade in a long line, with a battery of artillery between each with orders to move up as the infantry drove the enemy back, unlimber, and open at short range with grape and canister. It was evening before all his men had passed and his formation was complete. The thunder of his guns far to our right indicated that the battle was on, and the assaults of the enemy on our weary men began to slacken. His infantry and artillery mowed down the enemy at a fearful rate and drove them back until 10 P.M.

When morning came the enemy was in full flight to the defenses around Washington. Early the next day General Lee started in pursuit, and at Chantilly he overtook the retreating enemy. They deployed their rear guard here and an engagement took place, in which they were driven back and Gen. Phil Kearney was killed. Our brigade claimed that they killed him, but other brigades made the same claim; and as I was not present, I cannot say who did it. He had many personal friends in our army who had served with him in the regular army before the war, and they sent his body into the enemy's lines.

The men of our brigade told me this about Kearney's death: A long line of United States regular troops advanced to drive them back, with Kearney riding a hundred yards in advance to encourage them on. At the first volley he fell dead from his horse near our line. This was late in the afternoon. Our loss in this engagement was very light, but at Manassas about half the men of our brigade who took part in the battle were killed or wounded. Many prisoners and much artillery and other army equipment fell into the hands of the Confederates.

Gen. A. R. Lawton now took command of the division in place of General Ewell, and Col. Marcellus Douglass, of the 13th Georgia, took command of the brigade, only to die fighting at Sharpsburg nineteen days after. No braver man ever lived or one better qualified to command. Lee, Longstreet, and Jackson were masters of the art of war, otherwise they would have been utterly defeated by the superior numbers of the enemy. It is said that Gen. Fitz John Porter, coming to

Pope's assistance with a corps of fresh troops at the time when every man in Lee's army was engaged in the Titanic struggle, was deceived by a strategem employed by Stonewall Jackson. A great cloud of dust was seen rising on a road in the rear of the army, and the cavalry reported that a heavy force was approaching from that direction. If something was not done quickly to check their advance, Lee would suffer a defeat like that of Napoleon at Waterloo. But Jackson was equal to the occasion. He ordered a cavalry regiment to cut brush and drag these in a gallop up and down a road running parallel with the one on which the Yankees were marching. This caused a great column of dust to rise, and Porter turned off and made a wide detour, arriving too late to take any part in the fighting.

Whether this circumstance had anything to do with his failure to reach the scene on time, I cannot say, but the head men of the army needed a scapegoat to bear the blame for their failure, and General Porter was court-martialed for cowardice and convicted. Perhaps politics had something to do with the findings of the court. I do not believe General Porter was a coward. He didn't fight us at Cold Harbor like a coward. He was finally relieved of this verdict during the administration of Grover Cleveland, when he was an old man.

The shattered remnants of Pope's army reached the defenses at Washington and were collected under command of General McClellan, who reorganized them. In this particular he was unsurpassed. To him the Yankees owed their final success in the war. He soon had an army of eighty thousand veteran troops, well seasoned to military service, to take the field against Lee's army, now reduced by forced marches, diseases, and loss in battle to much less than half that number. With these conditions confronting him, General Lee did not hesitate to plan a new offensive in which everything seemed to be in favor of the enemy. Trusting to his good fortune and the overcaution of the enemy, he boldly crossed over into Maryland to operate far away from his base, while the enemy had his capital and base at his back. This campaign seems to have been highly inadvisable when we consider the great risks it involved; but these were not greater than many others which he took before and after this. There can be no rules to govern a general in war. He must be his own judge when to strike and how.

Our brigade crossed the Potomac at Edwards's Ferry and marched to Monocacy Junction, about forty miles. From there, after a short rest, they went to Frederick City, where they had a small engagement with the enemy. They marched through that place by way of Middletown, Boonsboro, and Williamsport, where they recrossed the Potomac into West Virginia. They then went by a forced march to Harper's Ferry and surrounded that place on the south, while General McLaws occupied a mountain on the north side of the river called Maryland Heights. From this position he could easily force the garrison of eleven or twelve thousand men to surrender. Everything required the utmost dispatch, for General Lee was in the most imminent danger of being attacked by McClellan at a time when his divisions were widely scattered. To protect McLaws until he should force the surrender of Harper's Ferry, General Lee with the rest of the army was trying to hold Boonsboro Gap and Crampton Gap. But these forces were too weak to hold McClellan's army off very long, though the delay gave Lee time to concentrate his divisions at Sharpsburg. The white flag had gone up just as Jackson was getting ready to assault the place. He left A. P. Hill to attend to the surrender of the prisoners and secure the army equipment of every kind, when he retraced his route to Shepherdstown by a rapid night's march. There he recrossed the Potomac and at daylight had formed his lines on Longstreet's left. This strenuous campaign had reduced our brigade to a mere handful of brave spirits, and this was the case throughout the different units of the army.

GENERAL LEE AT SHARPSBURG, 1862[9]

Gen. Stephen D. Lee was one of the most successful generals of the Confederate army and an educated soldier. He commanded the artillery in the engagement at Sharpsburg, Md., and in an article on this battle which he wrote a few years before he died he declared this to have

---

[9]*Confederate Veteran*, October 1921, 29:378-80. Bradwell wrote further about Sharpsburg in *Confederate Veteran*, 21:57.

been the worst of the whole war. His opinion coincides with what my comrades who took part in it told me. The aggregate loss on both sides was greater than that sustained in any single day's fighting in the entire course of the war. Gen. R. E. Lee, with a very weak force, had a broad river at his back to cross, and in case his line should be broken it meant the complete destruction of his army. He did not want to fight at this place and under such unfavorable conditions against an army more than twice as large as his own with superior artillery, but it was not a question of his choice. Accordingly he selected the line of Antietam Creek as far as he could utilize that stream to protect his front. Some distance beyond his right was a bridge across the creek which had to be held or the enemy would cross over and cut his communications with the ford of the river at Shepherdstown and force him to surrender. This had to be guarded against by a small brigade, now reduced to only two hundred and fifty men, while the enemy was endeavoring to force the crossing with many thousands. The ground on the left bank occupied by McClellan was much higher than that held by the Confederates and afforded them excellent location for their numerous batteries of artillery. But the creek did not bend so as to protect Lee's whole front, and his lines on the left were formed in the open country from the creek across the road leading north from Sharpsburg.

As the line of the Confederates was somewhat circular, the Federal batteries on the higher ground on the other side of the creek could enfilade them on the left. The extreme left of the Confederate line was held by General Stuart with his cavalry back to the Potomac River. His light artillery, served with the most consummate skill, had no small part in saving Jackson's left, held by our division, from complete destruction, since they were in position to enfilade the lines of the charging Federals.

Jackson arrived on the scene after a forced night march from Harper's Ferry. I have heard that it was his intention to throw the weight of his little force on the enemy's right, but when he arrived he found that McClellan had guarded against this by extending his line to the Potomac. There was nothing left to him then but to arrange his line to conform to that of his foe. The Louisiana Brigade, under General Hays, was drawn up on the extreme left of the infantry, and our brigade, now commanded by Col. Marcellus Douglass, of the 13th Georgia, was formed next to them. In the rear of them, at some distance and in front of the oak grove around the little brick Dunkard Church, Walker's Virginia Brigade was formed as a reserve line. Hays's Louisianians were about five hundred in number, our brigade about fifteen hundred, and Walker's about eleven hundred, in all about thirty-one hundred in the division.

Our brigade was stretched out in a very thin line, with wide intervals between the regiments, so as to occupy as much space as possible. They were formed in open fields to the west of the road mentioned above, running north from Sharpsburg, and in front of them not more than a hundred feet was a low rail fence. From this fence to a forest to the north was a field of high corn standing very thick on the land. Lieutenant Colonel Crowder, a man destitute of fear, was in command of our regiment. He was ordered to deploy the regiment along the edge of the woods and hold his position as long as he had a man alive to defend it. This was at daybreak. He strung out his men about fifty feet apart wherever he could find protection behind a tree or other object; but these did not afford any shelter from the shells and solid shot coming from the other side of the creek. The artillery fire opened with great fury and must have been the signal for the infantry to advance. They moved forward at the same time in the woods, with several lines supporting one another, fringed in front by skirmishers to develop our position. As these came up the fire of our pickets drove them back on their advance line. So accurate was the aim of our men that they, too, were halted until the second line came up and opened on them. Colonel Crowder was shot and disabled, and so many of the regiment killed or wounded by the artillery and infantry fire that the rest were forced to flee through the corn to their friends in the main line. When they reached the fence and were getting over it—in more haste than dignity—they were guyed for coming over it in so great a hurry. Many of our men were laughing and saying, "What's the matter? What are you running for?" to which came the reply: "You'll soon see."

Then a grand sight met their eyes. The number of regimental standards floating in the morning air indicated the immense numbers of the advancing enemy. It was a wonderful sight. The remnant of our regiment formed in an apple orchard on the right of the brigade to assist in holding back the hosts of the enemy. Colonel Douglass, fearing the result of an attack by so large a force on his weak brigade, ran from regiment to regiment exhorting the men not to fire until the enemy reached the fence and began to get over it—to shoot low and make every bullet count.

On they came, crashing down the rank growth of corn, while Hardaway's Battery in rear of our line on a little hill mowed them down with grape and canister, and Stuart's light battery enfiladed their ranks. Wide gaps were torn in the blue lines, but they continued to come on until they reached the fence and began to get over in great disorder. This was the signal for the Confederates to open. The volley made them stagger and hesitate, but the second line came up, and, despite the fire of the Confederates, they came over and advanced slowly, step by step, and finally halted only a few feet in front of the Confederates, where they kept up the fight for a short while and began gradually to fall back to the fence. When they reached this, they broke in a disorderly mass toward the woods, while the Confederates helped them on by cheering and yelling.

But Colonel Douglass is badly wounded, many of his men killed or disabled, and his line is very much weakened. Though wounded in several places and feeble from the loss of blood, he still rushes from regiment to regiment exhorting the men to hold their position, to shoot low, and make every cartridge count, for he knew that this was only the beginning of the struggle.

It was McClellan's plan to throw the weight of his superior numbers on this, the weakest part of Lee's line, and cut him off from any means of escape to the Potomac by seizing the only road to the south. When the fugitives reached the woods they were met by fresh troops, and their ranks were reformed and beaten into shape for a new effort. And then, after some delay, they came into the open field again with their "huzzas," and the Confederate batteries began their deadly work, while every man in our thin ranks lay low with his gun ready to do or die; and as the enemy approached the fence they opened on them with a fire so destructive that they broke immediately to the protection of the woods. Once more the brave Douglass is wounded, but he managed to keep on foot to encourage his men; and in spite of his wounds and the entreaties of his men, he insists on remaining with them.

There is only a man every ten feet or more to resist the last and greatest effort of the enemy. Heavy reenforcements have been sent into the woods. These come forward in such numbers that the few

Confederates defending the position are beaten back step by step to the reserve line held by General Walker and his Virginians. The eighth ball pierces the body of Colonel Douglass, and he falls helpless in the arms of his soldiers. He begs them to let him die on the battle field with his men, declaring he would rather die there than in the arms of his wife at home. The brigade, now without a commander, rallied with the reserves and helped to maintain the unequal contest for a time, but these were beaten back into the grove around the church, where they held for a time, but were finally driven out.

It seems that the enemy has won, and the army will be cut off from any avenue of escape. An officer rides in a great haste toward the river, tears running down his cheeks, to find General Lee and tell him the bad news. When he meets him coming on old Traveler, he tells him that all is lost. But the General calmly points back and says: "See, Colonel, there comes Jackson with reenforcements."

There were only fifteen hundred of these. Who they were I do not know, but Jackson deployed them and moved forward, driving the victorious enemy, who were holding the grove, but without any order and in great confusion, out into the open field, across the cornfield, and into the woods beyond, where the fight first began in the morning. After so many brave officers and men had lost their lives in these three mighty efforts, they had at last been beaten back and entirely dispersed. But McClellan sends Hooker with fresh troops to renew the engagement, and General Lee at the same time sends an order to Jackson to push the offensive to weaken the pressure on Longstreet, whose line is broken. But Jackson felt too weak to obey and deemed it best to stand on the defensive, while Hooker, seeing General Mansfield and other generals lying dead and the complete demoralization of those who had been engaged, decided not to attack. He afterwards said he did not find any troops there; that they were entirely dispersed. Jackson was in no condition to renew the fight or resist Hooker if he had renewed the battle. Hooker was a good fighter, but not a very wise commander.

Our brigade took no part on this day's fight after this and that evening at sundown could muster only forty-eight men who could stand in line. The next morning they were deployed one hundred yards apart, facing the enemy, who showed no disposition to fight. Each side had had enough, and they stood there all day long watching each other like gladiators too weak from loss of blood to renew the fight. As soon as night came General Lee began to withdraw to the ford of the Potomac. Our brigade was the last of the army to cross at sunrise the next morning. After this the brigade was under first one colonel and then another, none of whom had the capacity to command in battle or the love and confidence of the soldiers that Colonel Douglass enjoyed. It is said that the War Department at Richmond had made him a brigadier general the very day he was killed, but he never knew it. If he had survived the war and returned to his native State, he would have taken a prominent part in the affairs of his country, I am sure, for the people of Georgia would have honored him with the highest offices in their gift. General Lawton was wounded in this battle and never returned to us afterwards. He had commanded the division ever since General Ewell was wounded at Manassas.

The mismanagement of these colonels was so evident that the Confederate government promoted a man whose heroic conduct in this battle was as conspicuous as that of Colonel Douglass and who, like him, had been wounded eight times and left for dead on the battle field of Sharpsburg. This was Gen. John B. Gordon, a native son of Georgia, but at the time colonel of the 6th Alabama. He was blessed with a commanding voice and a natural grace and dignity that attracted the admiration of his soldiers, a leader born to command. There was but one other officer in the whole brigade whose voice could be distinctly heard in battle from one end of the line to the other, and that was Colonel Jones, of the 60th Georgia Infantry. On one occasion when we were in winter quarters General Gordon took the brigade out into a field to maneuver. When the line was formed, he and his staff were sitting on their horses at the right of the line, which extended a half mile or more. The General called out in a voice loud enough to be distinctly heard by every regimental commander, "At-ten-tion!" then, "For-ward, march!" Some regiments moved forward promptly, but others hesitated, waiting for the colonel to repeat the command, and general disorder ensued. At this Gordon became angry and called in a loud voice that could be heard three-fourths of a mile away to know why Colonel Jones did not repeat the order. The line being once more formed, the order was repeated, and this time Colonel Jones, though at the extreme left, could be heard distinctly by every man in the ranks. So loud and clear was his voice that the whole command was convulsed with laughter. Colonel Jones was one of the bravest and coolest of our officers, and though often wounded, he survived the war and came home to assist in the restoration of our ruined country.[10]

When our brigade crossed the Potomac at the ford at Shepherdstown, a few of our men were left along the high bluff of the river as a decoy to induce the enemy to come over and pursue our army. General Lee had a trap set for them and was anxious to get even with them for what they had done for him two days before at Sharpsburg. The bluff overlooking the river at this place is very high and perpendicular, with many rocks at the bottom. The road down to the river was graded out about thirty feet wide and afforded a very good approach for ordinary travel, but for a routed army struggling to escape in a great mix-up of teams and men in a mad rush for safety, with a hostile force at their backs urging them on, it was too narrow and became choked up, leaving no avenue of escape but to leap down fifty or more feet over the bluff on the rocks below. When the Yankees came to the ford they placed their batteries on the hills on the north side and shelled the few Confederate pickets away. Their infantry and ordnance train now came across without any resistance being offered and formed their battle line with their backs to the river. In front of them was a wide open field for half a mile or more to a body of woods. No sign of the Confederates could be seen, and they moved forward in fine style toward the woods, where a line of Confederates lay concealed. When they got within a few yards of the hidden enemy, they arose as one man and fired a volley into the enemy's ranks so suddenly that all broke immediately in the greatest disorder and fled toward the river, closely pursued by the Confederates. Men, wagons, and officers on horseback rushed madly toward the ford, only to find the approach to it jammed. In their headlong flight to escape their relentless pursuers, they went over the bluff and were crushed by the rocks. Those who reached the water had a wide river with a swift current to wade under fire, while they could offer no resistance. Only a few made their escape to the other side. One year afterwards I saw the broken remains of their wagons still there.

---

10 Krick, *Lee's Colonels*, 217. "Waters Burras Jones. Born 1825. Captain, Company B, 60th Georgia, July 17, 1861. Major August 17, 1863. Wounded at Wilderness. His troops called Jones "Old Red." Colonel commanding 60th and 61st Georgia at Appomattox, but date of promotion is not clear. Died May 28, 1898."

I suppose General Lee now considered that he was even with McClellan and quietly withdrew to the vicinity of Winchester. It was a cruel revenge to inflict on his enemy, but General Lee was evidently in no good humor at this time and wanted to pay his respects to the foe before leaving him or perhaps wanted to impress him with what might be expected if there was further effort to harass his movements.

And it had the desired effect; for although it was not too late in the season for active military operations, no new offensive was begun until winter had set in. Thousands of the wounded and sick were returning now to the army, and when I got back to my command in November I found there were more men in the ranks than had been since the Seven Days' Battles about Richmond. The ground was white with snow, and the brigade had constructed temporary quarters and was once more ready for whatever General Lee or General Jackson had for it to do.

Lincoln and McClellan could never agree about how the war ought to be conducted and the object to be attained. Lincoln was an abolitionist at heart and wholly under the influence of the radical element in his political party; while McClellan was a Union man, in favor of the restoration of the seceded States to the Union with no curtailment of the rights and privileges of the citizens of those States. With him the restoration of the Union was first; with Lincoln party expediency came first. McClellan was extremely popular with the soldiers and the moderate element at the North, and at this time was a dangerous political rival for Lincoln. Something had to be done to down him, and now was the time to do it, since he had let slip this opportunity to destroy Lee's army. The Confederates were glad to know that he had been relieved of the command of the army; for while he was overcautious, he always hurt them more than any of the other Union generals when he did fight.

Lincoln put Burnsides in McClellan's place, a man more in accord with his own ideas. He was a good fighter, but he did not have the talent to command so great an army and did not enjoy the confidence of his soldiers as had their former leader. There was nothing about him to inspire enthusiasm in the army or among the people at large.

NOTE. — The soldiers who knew Colonel Douglass before the war told us this story about him, which showed his grit and unconquerable spirit. He was a lawyer in a small town in Southwest Georgia and became mixed up in a free fight between some of his clients on one side and their enemies on the other. In the beginning of the affair Douglass was shot down and in the activities that followed was supposed to be out of the fighting. Remembering where there was a loaded double-barreled shotgun, he managed to crawl on his hands and knees, and, returning with it unobserved, although desperately wounded, he opened on his enemies so effectively that he cleaned out the opposite party in short order.

Colonel Douglass was a small, fair-skinned man with light blue eyes and blonde curly hair; a man no one would suppose from his personal appearance to be the heroic soul he was. He ran for Congress on the Whig, or Union, ticket in the great campaign in 1860 against Colonel Slaughter, Democrat, who was elected and, like Colonel Douglass, was killed in battle.

Hard marching, sickness, wounds, and death had so thinned the ranks of our company from the time we had joined Stonewall in the Valley three months before that out of seventy-five men and boys we could muster only six for this engagement. These were: Lieut. Judson Butts, Ben Averett (18), Ben Barfield (18), John Cooper (50), Tom Jones (18), and Nat Sutton (18). Averett, Cooper, and Jones were killed. Barfield was slightly wounded.[11]

---

[11] Henderson, *Roster*, 3:645. "Judson A. Butts. Private November 13, 1861. Elected 1st Lieutenant March 13, 1862. Appointed Surgeon October 29, 1862. Captured at Gettysburg, Pa. July 5, 1863. Paroled at Ft. Henry, Md. and sent to City Point, Va., for exchange, November 21, 1863. Surrendered, Appomattox, Va. April 9, 1865.; 644. Benjamin F. Averett. Private November 11, 1861. Killed at Sharpsburg, Md. September 17, 1862.; 644. Benjamin F. Barfield. Private December 2, 1861. Wounded in 1864. At home on wounded furlough August 31, 1864.; 645. John Cooper. Private November 11, 1861. Killed at Sharpsburg, Md. September 17, 1862.; 646. Thomas Jones. Private April 4, 1862. Killed at Sharpsburg, Md. September 17, 1862.; 648. Nathaniel G. Sutton. Private December 2, 1861. Captured in 1864. Killed in Virginia."

THE GEORGIA BRIGADE AT FREDERICKSBURG[12]

After the battle of Sharpsburg General Lee rested his army a short time in the Valley and then took Longstreet's corps across the Blue Ridge Mountains to cooperate with Stuart's Cavalry, who were at all times in touch with the enemy. Jackson was left in the Valley with his corps to guard against any move the enemy might make from that direction, as it was not yet quite clear what plan of campaign the enemy would adopt. When it became known that McClellan had been removed and Burnsides had been put in his place, and it was seen that it was his intention to inaugurate a winter campaign by moving direct on Richmond by way of Fredericksburg, orders came to move across the mountains in support of Longstreet and Stuart.

That General Lee chose to divide his army at a distance so great between the different units and with a great mountain range intervening seems bad generalship; but he knew what his plans were and was ready to meet Burnsides in any attempt he should make. To make the situation appear worse for us our army was farther from Richmond than that of the enemy, and by good generalship Burnsides could cut our communication with our base. But he appeared to be in no great haste in his new offensive, and Jackson crossed the mountains, marching leisurely to unite with Longstreet, who had now moved south and occupied a range of hills overlooking the town of Fredericksburg and fortified them. The enemy had had time to seize these heights and did it with one advance division, but Burnsides withdrew them to the north side before Longstreet came. Here he lost his opportunity. If he had taken possession of this position with his whole army, it seems to me that General Lee would have been in a very critical situation. But perhaps he wanted Burnsides to do this very thing. If he had done so, he would have had a very dangerous and resourceful enemy on his flank and rear, while his objective was still far away.

---

[12] *Confederate Veteran*, October 1925, 33:382-383, 397. Paragraphs deleted from this article to eliminate duplication. Editor.

But I must return to our trip across the mountains and tell of incidents in connection therewith. Jackson's corps consisted of three divisions, Johnson's (the old Stonewall Division), Hill's, and ours, now commanded by Gen. Jubal A. Early. Hill's Division was in advance of ours and had orders to stop after a long march at the foot of the mountains and go into camp, as it was too great a distance to undertake the crossing until the next day. Our division was to go into camp when our advance brigade should come to General Hill's camps. But sometime that day our general got possession of that which maketh the heart of men glad and causeth him to forget the weariness of his neighbor; so when we reached General Hill's encampments he pushed on, declaring he would show General Hill how to march. The sun was now just dipping down to rest and we were very tired, but our general pushed on. The long spiral lines of our brigade as we moved up the mountain looked like an immense serpent making its way to the gap, as it was called. Above us we could see those regiments which were ahead, apparently marching in an opposite direction, and below us we could see those behind toiling along. It was dark when we reached the summit of the mountain, and we were in no condition to begin the descent; but there was no place to make camp and rest where the precipitous mountain on one side of the road rose hundreds of feet in height, and on the other was an immense chasm. There was nothing now to do but proceed, tired as we were, on our way, which proved to be more trying on our strength than the ascent. Some of our men, rather than undertake to go farther that night, found some place where they could spread a blanket and sleep; these did not return to us for many days. The rest of us pushed on, but there was nothing to be seen in the darkness but rocks, rocks everywhere. Finally, just before day, we came to a place which nature seemed to have selected to pile the surplus rocks left over in building these great mountains. Completely exhausted and unable to proceed, we fell down on these and rested a short while as well as we could in such a place.

All kinds of talk about the condition of our general could be heard among the men for some time. How true these were I have no means of knowing; but after this, even to the end of his career as commander of our division and corps, he never regained the respect due one occupying so important a position. Why General Lee, a man so opposed to such vicious habits, continued him in command I could never understand, unless it was on account of his wonderful personality. Among all the men I have ever seen in a long life I have never known another of such commanding presence. His eagle eyes and shrill, piping voice, together with his general appearance, demanded obedience and compliance on the part of his officers and men even when they held him in contempt. But no truer man ever drew a sword in defense of his country or ever was more ready to sacrifice himself in its cause.[13]

This narrative would be incomplete if I did not mention the heroic conduct of Gen. J. E. B. Stuart, commander of the cavalry, and his men. He was a man born to lead, and his conduct inspired every man under him with the same daring spirit. In winter the weather was never too severe to hinder his activities, and in summer the heat was never too great to check his operations. The nights were never too dark, but rather seemed to favor his movements. No force brought against him was equal to his stratagem and courage. His resourcefulness served him in every emergency. His confidence in his men was only equal to theirs in him. His love for his country and its cause was dearer to him than his life, which he gave up freely in its defense. His regard for his commander in chief was like that of an obedient and loving son to a father. While the infantry was held in camp snowbound, he and his men were watching the enemy's outposts or operating within their lines. Without him General Lee could never have maneuvered his infantry so successfully, for he screened his movements from the eyes of the enemy and kept him informed of their every movement. If he accomplished so much with a force so small, we naturally ask ourselves what he would have done with an army equal to the task assigned him. While Longstreet and Jackson were leisurely moving their infantry from the Valley to take position at Fredericksburg, Stuart and his men were fighting daily battles with the enemy, and nothing they did escaped his observation, for he was always on their flank and rear.

From the foot of the mountain the next morning we left our inhospitable stopping place and proceeded eastward through Madison County. As we marched through this peaceful section, removed from the scene of war, no sound of strife fell on our ears, and I felt like I could remain here the rest of my life, and indeed until now my mind often

---

[13] Bradwell refers to Gen. Jubal Early.

reverts to it as a type of that rest to which all of us old Confederates are hastening from the confusion incident to our existence here. On the right and left were smiling fields and woodlands, beautiful country homes, and grazing herds of sheep and cattle.

But we were to enjoy this only temporarily, for we were approaching the place where we were to join our comrades again in the deadly strife.

When we reached Longstreet we passed to the south of his position and made our camp ten or twelve miles to the right, near Port Royal, a small village on the Rappahannock River below Fredericksburg, where we remained several days before we were called on to participate in the great battle of Fredericksburg.

We were now under command of Col. E. N. Atkinson, of the 26th Georgia, and our ranks were once more recruited by those who had been sick or wounded until we had three thousand or more men ready for duty. I was on guard the night of December 11, and before morning the boom of Burnside's cannon in the direction of Fredericksburg could be heard. Burnsides, with a splendid army and numerous artillery, had decided to cross the river, drive the Confederates off of the heights overlooking Fredericksburg, and go on to Richmond direct from the north. If McClellan at Sharpsburg had failed in the open country to defeat a handful of worn-out Confederates, Burnsides could have no hope of success against General Lee, now with an army at least twice as large and in strong position. The town was held by Confederate pickets for some time against all efforts to drive them out; but General Lee ordered them to retire, as he wanted the enemy to come across. They then put in their pontoon without hindrance. Before the Confederates were withdrawn, Burnsides placed his artillery on the heights on the north side and at short range opened a fearful bombardment of the town, at the time full of defenseless women and children. The city was set on fire, and the inhabitants hastily snatched up a few bundles and made their way out into the freezing night to seek shelter from the merciless shelling wherever they might. No punishment by his government, not even censure, was ever imposed on Burnsides for this inhuman barbarity. The kind-hearted Lincoln, secure in Washington, took no notice of it, considering it only a slight incident of the war too small to receive attention. But Burnsides paid dearly for this in the engagement that followed.[14]

When day broke on the morning of the twelfth I was on guard near Colonel Atkinson's tent when a courier arrived with dispatches. When he handed them to the Colonel the staff officers asked him what was the news. He replied that forty thousand Yankees had crossed over up to the time he had left and the town was in flames. Orders were issued immediately to march, and we were soon on the road to the scene of hostilities.

From above Fredericksburg to Hamilton's Crossing, a distance of some six miles, there extends a range of hills, some parts of them, open but near Hamilton's Crossing they were covered with timber. At the foot of the range of hills was a railroad track, and between the railroad and the river, some three-quarters of a mile, the country was open and comparatively level. A road, bordered on each side by cedars, extended from the city about halfway from the railroad to the river. Another road branched off from this and crossed the railroad at Hamilton's Crossing. Along this elevated ridge was the Confederate position. Burnsides put in a pontoon bridge opposite Hamilton's Crossing and brought over a large part of his army at that place. Longstreet held the left of the line at Fredericksburg, and Jackson held the right as far as Hamilton's Crossing. Beyond his right was Stuart with his cavalry and horse artillery.

We bivouacked in a grove near Hamilton's Crossing about dark the evening of the 12th, and the next morning early we were marched across the railroad and deployed in line extending, I suppose, three-fourths of a mile long, as a reserve. In front of us was Gen. A. P. Hill's Division, next to the enemy now getting ready out in the open field to make their grand assault on our lines concealed in the woods. But our men, in forming this front line, made a great mistake which came near being fatal. Between two brigades was a marshy piece of ground supposed to be too boggy for the enemy to advance through, and it was left undefended. The battle opened with great fury, and the enemy

---

[14] Krick, *Lee's Colonels*, 39. "Edmund Nathan Atkinson. Born Marietta, November 14, 1834. Graduate of Georgia Military Institute. Colonel May 9, 1862. Wounded and captured at Fredericksburg. After exchange, was also captured at Fisher's Hill, released July 25, 1865. Died in Waycross, Ga., June 17, 1884."

poured through this gap, killing one of our prominent generals and routed the brigades on the right and left by attacking them on the flank and in the rear. It was now our time to advance and drive them back. How well we did this reflects no honor on our brigade or the colonel who was supposed to be in command. When the order was given to advance, if given at all, some of the regiments moved forward while others did not seem to hear it or understand what was required of them, and the whole thing was so badly mismanaged that some of our regimental commanders came near fighting a duel over it afterwards. One of them resigned and went back to Georgia. I suppose he was a fine political speaker and writer, but he was not the man to command a regiment in battle. It was said subsequently that our orders were to drive the enemy out of the woods to the line of the railroad and there stop; but if there was an order of any kind issued, we never heard it, and everybody went forward just as he pleased.[15]

When we reached the railroad and saw that Federal battery out there in the open, surrounded by white horses, every man under the leadership of Captain Lawton, brother of Gen. A. R. Lawton, rushed forward to take it, without any support on the right or left. This we did, but the gallant Captain and the beautiful bay horse he was riding both fell dead at the very mouths of the enemy's guns. We did not have a minute to rejoice over our victory, for the enemy's second grand advance, with a line that overlapped ours and threatened to envelope us, took place at this very time, and our men had to choose between a surrender or retreat under fire of the battery they had just taken, or flee for their lives back to the protection of the woods. Some were killed, others were wounded and captured, including Colonel Atkinson. Fifty-four splendid dappled artillery horses lay dead on the knoll where this battery stood and many of the enemy. Stuart's horse artillery, under the gallant Pelham, did wonders that day and aided us no little, for we were on the extreme right of the infantry and next to the cavalry.

When we got back to the woods we were completely demoralized and without the semblance of organization. Presently General Early came riding about among us in the midst of bursting shells and whizzing grapeshot. The old fellow was furious and hailed every man

---

15 When this battle started, Col. Edmund N. Atkinson commanded the brigade.

he saw, asking if he belonged to that "blankety-blankety Georgia brigade."

I have always considered this the most disgraceful affair we ever took part in during our service in the war, but the blame should rest on our commander rather than on us. All this was known at our War Department, and a man was sent to us who had the capacity to lead, the noble John B. Gordon. The very day he came to us he rode around in the camp among the men to see how they fared. When he came to the headquarters of a certain colonel he found a log, hewn to a sharp edge, fastened at both ends to trees so as to stand about four feet above the ground, on which the colonel was in the habit of placing his men in punishment for slight offenses. The general called him out of his tent and asked him what it was for. He replied that it was his "horse." The General told him he did not know his regiment was a cavalry regiment and ordered him to take it down. The ground was covered with a heavy coat of snow, and the weather was intensely cold; but we had been required by the colonel commanding to stand on camp guard all night, although we were poorly clothed. This our general put a stop to and by these acts of humane consideration won immediately our regard, which he enjoyed to the last.

If the advance of our brigade had been made under good leadership and supported on the right and left, there is no doubt that we would have destroyed the entire left wing of Burnside's army. The regiments of our right had beaten the enemy back to the public road and were very near the river, where his pontoon bridge was located. If this had fallen into our hands, the entire left wing of Burnside's army would have been cut off from any means of escape. The advance of their reserves at the proper moment alone saved them from being driven into the river or destroyed.

That night the brigade was reorganized, and before day we moved forward to occupy the front line. As we advanced through the woods, the men in the field, standing at the guns from which we had driven them the day before, saw the top of our regimental standard in the gray dawn and fired a shell at it.

The weather was cold, and many of the wounded died during the night for lack of attention. The enemy carried away all of their dead and wounded inside of their line under cover of the darkness of the night, but those left between the lines were very numerous. A

Confederate battery in the woods was almost destroyed by a shell from the Yankee battery mentioned above. A shell from it struck a case of ammunition and exploded it, killing nearly all the men and horses belonging to it. As we passed the place the men were lying around scorched and blackened so that they looked like negroes, the hair on their heads being crisped and singed.

The day was spent in skirmishing, in which there was little damage inflicted on either side. The enemy's line remained behind the protecting banks of the public road mentioned, while we rested quietly in excellent breastworks in the woods overlooking the open field, awaiting any movement on their part. Official reports say that Burnsides gave orders to renew the fighting the next day, but his division commanders refused to act, and he withdrew his army on the night of the 14th and took up his pontoons. It was well they took that view of it; for if they had fought again, we were in position to inflict on them a worse defeat than that which they had already sustained. To our left, where they charged Longstreet in mass formation, they were slaughtered by the thousands. A Confederate soldier, my brother, told me he saw a deep well filled with the dead bodies of their soldiers, thrown into it to save the trouble of burying them.

The Federal army had received a bloody defeat and had accomplished nothing under their new commander. Lincoln now began to look around for some one else to take his place and found one in the person of General Hooker, "Fighting Joe," as he was called, who was even a greater failure than Burnsides. Whoever travels on the Richmond, Fredericksburg and Potomac Railroad from Richmond to Washington will see at Hamilton's Crossing a great stone pyramid, standing on the north side of the railroad track and only a few feet away. It is constructed of blocks of stone and will last to the end of time unless it is pulled down by man. It marks the point where our regiment crossed the road in the big drive of that memorable day, December 13, 1862.

PRESENTIMENTS[16]

"I have a rendezvous with Death
At some disputed barricade,
When spring comes back with rustling shade
And apple blossoms fill the air;
I have a rendezvous with Death
When spring brings back blue days and fair."

Reading this little poem by Alan Seegar, who was killed in action during the World War shortly after the poem was written, I was led to ask myself if there really is such a thing as presentiment of some future event of good or evil, or is it only a superstition which seems to be common to all mankind? Perhaps some people worry over their surroundings until they come to believe these things will happen, and tell them to friends beforehand for facts, and when by chance the thing results as predicted, they call it "premonition." Perhaps so; but I have seen cases that led me to believe there must be such a thing, yet how or by whom is such information communicated to the mind? I will mention some cases that have fallen under my own observation.

In my company there were several young comrades who seemed to have this remarkable impression. Among them was a youth about my own age, a schoolmate of mine and a good boy. His father was a local Methodist preacher who taught him to avoid evil and to be faithful and true. Through him I was induced to volunteer for service in the Confederate army, as we were always good friends at school. After we had been in the service about seven months, he seemed to lose his usual buoyancy of mind and spirit and often said that he would never again return home. No word from any of his comrades could induce him to change his mind or modify this gloomy prediction. We experienced many bloody engagements and he maintained his place in the ranks and did his duty nobly, but at Sharpsburg, where our thin line early in the day was holding in check the grand advance of the Federals, a ball penetrated his heart. As he fell over on his face, he spoke to Dr. Butts, our lieutenant and afterwards our surgeon, who was

---

[16] *Confederate Veteran*, October 1924, 32:376-377.

in command at the time of the remnant of the company, and asked him to send his belongings home to his father. His mouth then filled so fast with blood that he was not able to say anything more.[17]

Another instance: A little comrade, often at my back or by my side when formed for battle, and always a true soldier, when on the march would often say the same thing. He stuck to it until he, too, lost his life. And then there was another little fellow, a cousin of the last mentioned, who would join in with him in the same prediction. And he lost his life, but I do not remember whether he was killed or died.

I never felt that I would be killed or would die in the army, though I had very many close calls by death in battle and by disease, but I had a dream the night after the first day's battle of Fredericksburg, December 13, 1862, that frightened me very much, and I must confess I went into battle the next morning very reluctantly. And from what happened to me a few minutes after we advanced, I have always interpreted it as a premonition. On a slight elevation out in the open field, about three hundred yards in our front, there was a Yankee battery that we (Gordon's Brigade) had captured the day before, but were unable to hold for lack of support on our right and left flanks. In retiring from it we had left fifty odd large iron gray artillery horses belonging to the battery and many of the enemy and our own men stretched out dead, including that of our own brave and much beloved Adjutant General Lawton. The enemy were sure we would renew the engagement at daybreak, and all night were standing at their guns, ready to fire at the first sign of our advance. My position in the line of the regiment was about six feet to the right of the color bearer. Straining their eyes toward the woody heights, the enemy saw in the mist of the early morning the top of our colors coming toward them. Suddenly, like a clap of thunder, I heard the report of the cannon and almost at the same time a flash and explosion in our ranks, and found myself and the comrade behind me lying prostrate ten feet in the rear, obscured from the advancing line by a cloud of smoke. Neither of us was hurt. The shell had passed between me and the colors, killing all the men and cutting a wide gap in the regiment. I snatched up my gun, lying on the ground near me and

---

[17] A review of Company I muster role reveals this individual as Thomas Jones, killed April 4, 1862. Henderson, *Roster*, 646.

resumed my place in the ranks, feeling that that was the interpretation of the dream which had worried me so much.

And now sixty years after those strenuous days of danger and hardship, my mind often carries me back over the scenes of battle and I am constrained to attribute my preservation to Divine protection. Surely Providence had other duties for me to perform for my country, my fellow men, and myself, or I should have met the fate which befell so many of my comrades. But I hope I have been as faithful in the discharge of my duties as a citizen and Christian as I was as a soldier in defense of my country.

CHAPTER FOUR

1863

THE 31ST GEORGIA AT CHANCELLORSVILLE[1]

In the spring of 1863 our encampment was near Hamilton's Crossing, about three or four miles below Fredericksburg, Va. Every three days one regiment of the brigade was detailed to do picket duty along the Rappahannock River, a mile or so away. Gordon's Brigade consisted of six Georgia regiments at this time—the 13th, 26th, 31st 38th, 60th, and 61st. Afterwards the 12th Battalion, formerly of the artillery, was added. When General Hooker, who now commanded the Federal army, decided to begin active operations, the 13th Georgia was on picket along our front. Other infantry pickets extended ten or fifteen miles above and below Fredericksburg, and then the line was extended much farther by the cavalry, so that General Lee was always fully informed as to any movement made by the enemy. Hooker's plan of campaign was perfect; and if he had carried it out, it would have resulted in the capture of Richmond. He sent a force twenty-five thousand strong under General Sedgwick, one of his best generals, to cross the river at Hamilton's Crossing; while he, with the main army, over a hundred thousand in number, crossed the river fifteen miles above Fredericksburg. The 13th was one of the best regiments in the brigade; but it could offer little resistance to Sedgwick's army, and after some fighting it fell back and gave the enemy an opportunity to put in their pontoon bridges without opposition. As soon as this was done Sedgwick's whole force came across, formed a line parallel with the river, and fortified their positions with excellent breastworks. Behind these they remained very quiet and at first did not seem disposed to make trouble.

The wooded hills about a mile back from the river were well fortified by General Lee, and in these our brigade was led when the

---

[1] *Confederate Veteran*, October 1915, 23: 446-447. For another account of this battle see 30:257-260.

news came that the enemy had crossed. A fine old road runs from Fredericksburg down the river. This road had a cedar thicket on each side which almost shut out the view from our breastworks. Through a few openings our men could see the enemy busily engaged building their breastworks and mounting their guns. The 31st Regiment, commanded by Col. Clement A. Evans, was ordered to occupy the road and observe the movements of the enemy. Our position was only a short distance from the breastworks of the Federals, and we had nothing to do but watch them at work. They did not have any skirmishers out to annoy us, and at first we had a fine time peeping up over the bank of the road, which afforded us ample protection. Some of the men felt so secure that they made little fires in the road and behind the cedar brake toward our men and began to warm their breakfasts, for this was early in the day. Suddenly there was a volley of artillery from the Confederate position in our rear, and shrieking shells brought every man to his feet. This was the beginning of an artillery duel with a Federal battery a short distance in front of us. The Confederate artillerymen cut the fuses of their first shells too short, and they exploded just over our heads and scattered fragments and shrapnel all around us, but did us no harm. The Federal guns in their redoubts in our front now began to reply. Some of our men watched the effect of our shells as they fell in and around the enemy, while others observed the solid shot from the Yankee guns as they plunged into the red dirt in front of our works. When the firing was at its hottest, Lieutenant Acree threw up his hands and exclaimed: "That was a good shot!" A shell from our battery cut a Yankee in the redoubt in two. We were in great danger from our shells all the time and were glad when the shelling ceased.

At this time Lee and Stonewall Jackson were making it so interesting for General Hooker and his big army at Chancellorsville that he changed his plan of battle. Orders came to Sedgwick to abandon his efforts at Hamilton's Crossing and to unite his force in our front with that at Fredericksburg and drive away the small force left by General Lee to defend the heights above the town and march direct by the plank road to Lee's rear. This Sedgwick did, and after the loss of a great many men he succeeded in overwhelming the few defenders. The road to General Lee's rear was now open. One small brigade only, under General Wilcox, was in Sedgwick's front to oppose his advance. The thunder of the guns at Chancellorsville told to friends and foes alike that a great battle was in progress there. Early's whole division, which constituted the forces at Hamilton's Crossing, was now in the rear of Sedgwick, who was slowly driving Wilcox ahead of him.

When it was known that Sedgwick had captured the heights at Fredericksburg, our command was marched in that direction late in the afternoon. About sundown we came to Colonel Cutts's battalion of Georgia artillery deployed for battle behind a hedge about a mile from the plank road, his guns all pointing in that direction. The artillery had no support, and we were formed in the rear of Cutts's guns and ordered to lie down. Every one of his artillerymen was in his place ready for action when we came. In front was a level field three or four hundred yards wide extending to a piece of woods. We had hardly taken our place in the rear of the artillery when we saw a smart-looking officer coming toward us, riding at a lively pace from the woods. When he got within fifty yards of his guns, he commanded them in a loud tone to commence firing. This his men responded to by firing from one end of the line to the other in rapid succession. We now naturally expected to see the enemy's line advance or that they would open on us with their artillery posted in the woods; but when we rose up we saw General Gordon coming out of the woods on his horse toward us in a full gallop. When near enough to be heard, he commanded in a loud voice: "Cease firing." To this the artillery paid no attention, and the General rode to the rear. After some words between him and Colonel Cutts, the latter gave the order, and the guns ceased. It seems that General Gordon and Colonel Cutts were both reconnoitering in the woods to ascertain the enemy's movements. Colonel Cutts came up on the enemy, rode away, and ordered his artillery to fire on the woods, not knowing at this time that General Gordon was there. The latter had not seen any Yankees there when the artillery opened and was of the opinion that it was held by our men.

Darkness now came on, and we slept on our arms in line of battle. Nothing happened to disturb our rest; and when day broke we were called to arms, and our regiment was deployed in front of the guns, so as to cover the ground occupied by the other five regiments. The order was given to advance, and our long line did so in fine style. I remember this advance distinctly and how nobly Mark Everett, of Company E, carried our regimental colors through all the fighting of that memorable day. Although we were expecting the enemy's line in the woods to open on us every moment, the regiment crossed the field and entered the woods in front with a formation as perfect as if it were on parade. When we entered the woods we saw a number of United States army wagons loaded with army supplies turned bottom up. The mules, tangled in the harness, were still hitched to the wagons. They raised their heads and snorted as they saw our men coming toward them. Our litter bearers saw that the hind gates of the wagons were off and, peeping in, found that the teamsters had gotten in there for safety. The line made no halt here, but kept right ahead through the woods. No enemy appeared until it reached the opening beyond. Here there was a plain view of the enemy's trains on the plank road, guarded by a line of men on each side, all hastening on toward Salem Church, where Sedgwick's army now was. The land sloped from the woods about a thousand yards to a mill creek near the road. On the high ground beyond this was the plank road, on which the enemy was traveling. The sight of the enemy in plain view and the knowledge that they were in General Lee's rear inspired our men to make the most of this opportunity to do them all the harm in their power. The regiment advanced at double-quick down to the creek, which was about fifty yards wide and dammed up below where we were to cross. Some one plunged in and found that it was fordable, and in a short while the whole regiment was in the water. The aim of the enemy was bad, and we got across without losing any of our men. The ascent on the other side was steep, and, our clothing being wet, we climbed up the hill with difficulty. When the men got to the top, they opened fire on the enemy in reply to their sharp fire, to which we had made no response till now. This threw the teamsters and guards into great confusion. Some attempted to whip up their teams and go on, others tried to turn around and go back to Fredericksburg, while many abandoned their teams and tried to escape on foot. Much valuable property fell into our hands, and the guards fell back uphill toward some old Confederate entrenchment's occupying a very commanding position above Marye's Heights. Colonel Evans now reformed his men for the purpose of driving them out of these also.

While here our men, looking back over the ground over which they had just come, saw the other five regiments far to the rear. The color bearers were waving their flags and the men and officers their hats, but we could not hear what they were saying. They saw us when we captured the trains and dispersed the guards, and we supposed they meant that they were coming to our support. Colonel Evans ordered the advance, and we drove the enemy's sharpshooters ahead of us until they took refuge in the entrenchments on the hill. We thought these were held only by the men we had been fighting, and we advanced with confidence until we were within a few feet of the works, when a whole line of infantry rose and fired a volley. Strange to say, we did not suffer any loss; we were occupying lower ground, and their balls went over our heads. Colonel Evans ordered the men to lie down; but some, under the lead of our color bearer, Everett, wanted to mount the works. After remaining here for some time without losing any of our men, Colonel Evans gave orders to fall back forty or fifty steps. Here the enemy could see us, and we suffered some loss.

After we had been here some time under a very heavy fire of infantry and artillery, some one saw fit to send the 13th Virginia Regiment to assist us. This regiment was very much reduced in numbers, but came up the hill in the open in gallant style. The enemy's fire was thinning their ranks with fearful rapidity. When they reached our men on the left, they called out to them to get up and help them drive the enemy out. To this our men replied in language more forcible than polite and informed them that what our regiment had failed to do they would be very far from doing. They advanced only a few steps more when they broke and fled for protection under the hill. Their loss must have been considerable. Why a little handful of brave men were thus sent into the jaws of death without any hope of accomplishing any good the writer could never see. They lost more men in five minutes' time than we did in the whole engagement. Everett had stuck his flagstaff in the ground, and its folds waved in the smoky breeze of battle in full view of the enemy, only a few steps away.

At length, seeing that he was losing valuable men here where he was without support and without hope of accomplishing anything, Colonel Evans ordered a retreat. This had to be made under fire and in full view of the enemy to another line of earthworks some distance downhill. When the order was given, it was obeyed forthwith and without loss. There we remained until late in the afternoon, when we were ordered to the left, where, with the other regiments of the brigade, we joined in the general advance and drove the enemy from his position on the heights into the river swamp, from which he crossed the river during the night and made his escape. The entire loss of our regiment in this day was perhaps not more than forty or fifty killed and wounded. The other regiments of the brigade suffered less, as they were not so much exposed.

CAPTURE OF WINCHESTER, VA., AND MILROY'S ARMY IN JUNE, 1863[2]

This town seemed to have been a favorite place for the two armies to meet and fight, from the number of engagements that took place here in the sixties. It occupies a central position in the northern end of the great Valley of Virginia, and from it roads radiate in every direction—to the fords of the Potomac, to the gaps in the mountain ranges, to the east and west. The great Valley pike passes through it from north to south. It is situated in a fine grain country, which helped to feed both armies until it was completely devastated and ravaged by fire and sword in the fall of 1864 by Sheridan and Custer. But in spite of this, the people remained true to the South to the last. After Jackson left the Valley in June, 1862, only a small cavalry force remained there, and the Federal General Milroy made Winchester his headquarters and held it with a force of six thousand five hundred infantry and cavalry. They had little trouble to keep in check the few Confederate scouts operating there, and a practical period of peace prevailed for twelve months, until "Old Jube Early" broke in on them so rudely and unexpectedly in June, 1863. The officers and men had sent north for their wives and sweethearts, and were boarding them at the hotels, boarding houses, and in the homes of the citizens of the city.

---

[2] Ibid., September 1922, 30:330-332.

To the west of the town is an eminence commanding the city and surrounding country in every direction except on the west, where there were some good positions for artillery. Milroy's main fort stood on this hill. To protect this from any attack from that direction; he had one of these fortified also.

He had every reason to believe himself secure, as his position was well-nigh impregnable. In the midst of the great fort stood a tall flag pole, from the top of which floated in the breeze a United States flag thirty feet long. From this secure place Milroy exercised his authority over the defenseless Southern people in a manner so arbitrary as to secure for himself the ill will of everybody. But now the moment had arrived, and the ax was about to fall with a mighty stroke and break up this happy state of affairs with General Milroy and his army, for General Lee had planned to invade Pennsylvania, and Winchester was on his route. This place must first be captured and the way made clear of all enemies before the grand advance could be made.

After the Chancellorsville battle, our brigade made camps in an oak grove near Hamilton's Crossing. The situation was elevated, and we could see the enemy's couriers riding to and fro carrying orders and the men drilling near their camps every day. We spent the rest of the month of May in these camps, having an easy time. Rations, such as they were, were plentiful, and everything was made ready for the march. On June 1, we made great heaps of logs on the side of our camps toward the enemy, and when night came we set fire to these and quietly marched away. No doubt the enemy on the other side of the river was puzzled to know what these brilliant fires on the hill meant.

We traveled only at night for some time, camping only a short time before day, lest our movements should be observed by the enemy's scouts and signal men. When we had been gone several days and were entirely out of sight, we made rapid day marches by the way of Culpepper Courthouse and Front Royal, where we crossed the Blue Ridge into the Valley. The weather was hot and the roads dry and dusty. This dust, worked up by the wagon trains and artillery, settled on us until we were as brown as the dust itself. General Gordon, riding along by us, said in a loud voice: "Boys, if your mothers could see you now, they wouldn't know you." Some of us were limping along on blistered feet, and the General greatly endeared himself to us by his conduct on this occasion. Getting down from his horse, he mounted a private soldier in the saddle, while he fell into ranks with a gun on his shoulder and trudged along with us.

We reached the summit of the mountain late in the afternoon and, looking down to our left, we could see a black cloud below us, the flashing lightning in it, and hear the rolling thunder, while it was hot and dusty with us. When we reached the plain below and made our hasty bivouac, we found the ground covered with pools of water. Orders came from General Early to cook up rations for the next day and be ready to move at four o'clock in the morning. Long before that hour we were on our way to Winchester, for everything depended on a rapid march.

During these days, on the east side of the Blue Ridge, Stuart, with his cavalry, was so entertaining the Federal cavalry that he completely screened the movements of our infantry and mystified the enemy as to what his activities meant. With his poorly equipped force and inferior numbers, he was more than a match for the enemy, who lacked nothing in this respect, fighting hand to hand in some of the greatest cavalry battles of the war. Stuart was a great leader and fought for the love and excitement of fighting. His men caught the spirit of their great commander and emulated his example. He never sent his men into danger, but was always found in the lead and in the thickest of the fighting. He did not seem to need discipline to control his men, for all followed him, charmed by his manner and ever ready to do his will.

At Front Royal, the three divisions constituting Ewell's corps took different roads. While Early's division marched direct to Winchester, Johnson's and Rodes's divisions took routes leading to the north of that place so as to cut Milroy off from any means of escape to the fords of the Potomac. As we moved forward over the ground made memorable by the battles fought here the year before, the old veterans who took part in these engagements under Stonewall pointed out to us the place where he struck Banks and routed his army and won his first great victory. About noon our line was formed for battle in fields and forests, for Milroy had gotten wind of our approach and had come out of his fortified position at Winchester to meet us, supposing we were only a straggling band of Confederates. For a short time the fighting was fast and furious, but the enemy could not stand against charge and yelling, and they broke immediately for the cover of their fortifications.

In this engagement we lost some of our best men killed. We pressed the enemy back to the city and hastened to invest it on all sides; but this necessitated leaving great spaces in the line unoccupied. The 31st Georgia Regiment occupied the left of the brigade, and its left rested near the Valley pike, south of the town, in full view of the fort, while the other regiments were strung out to the eastward. General Hays's Louisiana brigade extended from a point near the pike westward. Their skirmishers were two or three hundred yards in advance of us up the road toward the fort, while we had none out in our front. Ours were engaged with those of the enemy in another direction, where they were driving them from one block to another toward the fort. Some of the patriotic women of the place, rejoicing to see our troops, lost their lives in bringing food and drink to our men. I suppose they were inspired by their eagerness to see, after so long a time, our soldiers whom they loved so well.

And now, while we lay here in the open field under the bursting shells from the fort, we saw one of the most splendid spectacles I have ever seen. The sally port toward us was open and out of it rode squadron after squadron of well mounted cavalry, with their shining swords drawn and other equipment reflecting the bright sunshine. They formed so as to occupy the entire width of the pike, intending to cut their way out by a sudden and overwhelming dash through our lines. After some delay, the order was given and the start made. Here they came. The rattle of their steel scabbards, the clanking of their spurs, and the noise of the iron shoes of their horses as they struck the hard surface of the pike were awe-inspiring, but doomed to result in an ignominious failure. In their headlong drive down the long slope they came in range of Hays's Louisianians, who poured into their ranks a few well directed shots that emptied a half dozen saddles and drove the rest back in a disorganized mass into the fort. We were holding our guns in readiness for use at the proper time, but were disappointed by the too great haste of our brave Louisiana comrades.

At nightfall of the second day of the investment, a detail was called for to approach the fort and dig redoubts under cover of darkness. Among those sent were myself and a comrade of the same company. Picks and shovels were furnished us and the work to be done laid off. We labored at our task until the small hours of the night and had just finished it and thrown ourselves down on the clover to snatch a few short moments or rest and sleep, when we were startled by a great rumbling noise like the sudden moving of many trains. The sound came from the north side of the fort, and some one suggested that the enemy had rushed out of their fortification and escaped. This proved true in part, for they had massed all their forces on that side and rushed down the hill upon our drowsy soldiers so unexpectedly that they made no resistance. They (the enemy) had now reached the roads which led to the Potomac, confident that they had made their escape, only to be disappointed later on. All the army equipment, consisting of wagon trains, artillery, and sutler wagons, followed the infantry and cavalry. But they had not progressed very far on their way when the head of their column came in contact with Rodes's and Johnson's pickets, and consternation prevailed in the minds of the drivers to such an extent that they detached their teams from the wagons in hope of making their escape on horseback.

Orders came to us that we might cease work on the redoubt and return to our command. When we had done so, we found them already on the march to the fort, which we approached and found deserted. As we entered it, General Gordon came galloping in from somewhere on a large black United States army horse which we all called "Old Milroy," supposing him to belong to the commander of the fort. The General rode up to the flag pole in the center of the fort and, hauling down the colors, detached them from the rope and placed one end of them on his saddle. Remounting, he put spurs to his horse and sailed out of the sally port ahead of us, while the "Star Spangled Banner" floated out thirty feet behind on the morning air. We followed leisurely the course the enemy had gone, and after we had advanced a few miles from the city, we found long lines of wagon and artillery trains standing in the road. To the east of the road was a strip of woodland and beyond this a field of clover, in which hundreds of United States army horses and mules were peacefully grazing. Our column halted a while at the baggage wagons, and the 1st North Carolina regiment of infantry rode up to us mounted on captured horses and mules and announced that they had served in the infantry heretofore, but now henceforth would serve as cavalry. They made us jealous of their good luck, but our envy was not well grounded, as they were made to turn over their mounts almost immediately to the quartermaster of the army and resume their places in the ranks of Jackson's foot "cavalry."

In the grove just mentioned an unusual sight met our eyes. All the bright colors of the rainbow, all the finery displayed in the most fashionable shops of a city seemed assembled there in that strip of woods. What could it mean? In a few minutes they started toward us, two and two, led by a grayclad soldier. When they reached us, we found they were the wives and sweethearts of our enemies, who, in their haste to follow the army, had put on their most costly attire and mounted the army wagons and horses in an effort to escape. As they passed us all were in tears and excited our sympathy by their hasty inquiries as to what had become of Lieutenant or Captain or Colonel So and So. Of course, we could give them no satisfactory answers, and all were marched back to the city and finally sent back through the lines to their friends in the North. The whole army, except General Milroy and the cavalry—about fifteen hundred men—fell into our hands. We were greatly disappointed in not getting the General, as he was very obnoxious to the citizens of the Valley on account of his harsh treatment of them in their defenseless condition under him. According to General Lee's report, we captured four thousand prisoners and a corresponding number of small arms; twenty-eight pieces of superior artillery; about three hundred army wagons and many horses, together with a quantity of ordnance, commissary, and quartermaster's stores.

In this operation the enemy was expelled from the Valley. This must have wound up the military career of General Milroy, for we never heard of him afterwards. We lost about one hundred and fifty valuable men of our brigade, among them the gallant Captain Hawkins.[3]

---

[3] Henderson, *Roster*, 4:157. "Capt. Charles Hawkins was from Company E, 38th Ga. He was killed leading the company in the charge at Winchester, Virginia, June 15, 1863."; Bradwell concludes this article with the following request: "I have never seen any account of the part taken by Rodes's Division in the capture of this army, and only a partial account of Johnson's in the VETERAN for May, 1921, by T. H. Lauck, Leander, Tex. He mentions the capture of one thousand prisoners at Stephenson's Depot. Who captured the balance? In the VETERAN for February, 1921, is an article under the heading, "Heroic Defense of a Bridge at Stephenson's Depot, Va." The author does not mention the number of prisoners taken and describes only the operation at the bridge. I should be glad to hear from any of my old comrades who took part in this capture."

CROSSING THE POTOMAC[4]

After the capture of Milroy's army and cleaning up the Valley of Virginia of all Federal forces, we marched leisurely to the fords of the Potomac and crossed over into Maryland on what might be called a summer picnic excursion, which did not end until we reached the Susquehanna River at Wrightsville and Harrisburg, Pa., and returned to Gettysburg, where, to our surprise, we found that General Lee had followed us with his whole army. Some parts of our (Ewell's) corps crossed the river at Williamsport, but Gordon's Brigade forded it at Shepherdstown.

On a bluff on one side of the road leading down to the ford was our military band playing "Dixie" and "Maryland, My Maryland," while many of our soldiers from that State sat on their horses on the opposite side near General Gordon and seemed greatly pleased as we plunged into the blue water waist deep, delighted with the prospect of our driving the enemy out of their beloved native state.

The river at this place is wide, with a strong current; but we made the landing on the other side without an accident.

We then marched straight toward Sharpsburg and passed through the old battle field where, the previous September was fought the most desperate engagement of the entire war.

We continued our course through Hagerstown and were soon across Mason and Dixon's line in Pennsylvania. Less than a mile from the state line we made our camp for the night; but before we broke ranks General Lee's order was read forbidding us to trespass on private property under pain of death. Some of our soldiers were inclined to disregard this order of our noble general, since the enemy ravaged our Southland without hindrance by those over them, and thought we ought to pay them back in kind, since we were in their country.

---

[4] *Confederate Veteran*, October 1922, 30:370-372. Paragraphs deleted from this article to eliminate duplication. Editor.

Compare our conduct in Pennsylvania with that of Sherman in Georgia and the Carolinas, and Sheridan and Custer in the Valley of Virginia, and decide which side was the more humane.

In every regiment, I suppose there were some who were unworthy and even a disgrace to the service. In my company was a short, stocky fellow of German descent, who was always among the stragglers in the rear when there was any fighting to do and ahead us of when we were on the retreat. This knock-kneed, slew-footed fellow was a natural thief, always drunk when he could get liquor to drink, a consummate coward and dodger; but when under the influence of spirits a very dangerous man. Some wag dubbed him "Old Webfoot," and the name was so appropriate as to stick. Near the public road and just a few feet from the State line stood a very substantial residence, evidently the home of well-to-do people. "Webfoot" fell out of the ranks of the stragglers when he saw the house and entered it, demanding in his abrupt manner something to eat. The folks treated his request with contempt, refusing to give him anything; whereupon he went through the dining room and pantry, taking the best of what he found. Not satisfied with this, he examined the premises and found concealed in the basement, under a quantity of hay, a span of splendid dappled iron-gray horses, very suitable for artillery service. This he reported to our quartermaster, whose duty it was to impress horses for the army, and in a short while the horses were led out and inducted into the Confederate service.

We marched the next day without any interruption and made our camp near a village. The next morning the captain sent me and a comrade ahead of the column to fill the canteens with water. We stopped in front of a beautiful residence, with a grassy lawn in front, and hailed. An old gentleman, dressed in blue overalls, with a wide straw hat on his head, came out, apparently very much frightened. We spoke to him respectfully and asked if we might fill the canteens at the pump just over the fence in the yard. But the old fellow's mind was so preoccupied with the apprehension that his factory on the other side of the street would be burned that he paid no attention to our request and would talk to us about nothing else. We assured him that it would not be molested, but this did not satisfy him, and we left him in a state of extreme doubt and fear. No doubt he judged us from his own standard of right and wrong. I saw but one private enterprise destroyed in this campaign in Pennsylvania, and that was the iron works of Thad

Stevens, a member of the United States Congress, one of the bitterest enemies of the South, and an advocate of every extreme measure enacted before, during, and after the war.

In crossing the mountainous part of the country we found the few people we saw to be rough and ignorant, living in little log shacks; but the men were not at home; they had business somewhere else at that time. When we reached the open country it was quite different. Our route lay through a lovely country of well tilled farms, nice towns, and villages. We, the infantry, were kept close in ranks, while the quartermasters and the small cavalry force with us were busy collecting horses, cattle, and sheep for the use of the army; but we were not allowed to appropriate anything to our own use.

Passing in front of a lovely home, which reminded me, from its style of architecture and the grounds in front, of a Southern residence, I rushed in at the front gate, through which others were passing, and went into the spacious hall through the open front door, thinking to find hospitable people who would give me something to eat; all doors were wide open. I found a lady, trembling with fear, in a room to the left, with three little children clinging to her. I think I never saw anyone so badly frightened as this woman was at the sight of our men coming into the house in a great hurry, all asking for bread and milk. She excited my sympathy, and I stepped up to her, supposing a kind word would dismiss her fear, and told her not to be afraid, that the soldiers did not mean to do her any harm, but only wanted to get something to eat; but the poor creature was so overcome by her feelings that she did not seem to hear me. I was disposed to stand by her side until the whole army passed, but I knew that would not do, so I hastily snatched up from the dining room such as I found convenient and left her and her little ones there to themselves, knowing that they would not suffer any violence at the hands of our men, for there was not a one in our whole army mean enough to do such a thing.

The day we marched into Gettysburg was cold and raw, although it was June, and a drizzly rain falling. The brigade entered the town from the west and marched to the public square, where the head of the column turned down the main street to the south and halted while our military band took position on the principal corner and played "Dixie" and many other selections; but none of the older citizens showed themselves. The younger set, however, of both sexes, considered it a holiday and turned out in force. They were anxious to know when we were going to burn the town. Crowds of these youngsters hung to us everywhere we went, asking this same question. Our only answer was that Southern soldiers didn't burn towns.

The 31st Georgia Regiment was selected to do provost guard duty in the town, and we were up a great part of the night. Worn out by the long march of the previous day and tramping over the town until a late hour, wet and chilled to the bone, I made my way to the courthouse and threw myself down on a bench to spend the few remaining hours of the night in sleep. At early dawn the rattle of the drum called us to ranks, and we set out on the march to York.

This place was much larger than Gettysburg and the inhabitants did not shut themselves up in their houses through fear of us, but were so anxious to see us and converse with us that we had some difficulty in forcing our way through the city. It was Sunday morning, and everybody was dressed in his very best. So great was the pressure that our officers marched us through the town in single column of twos. Handsomely dressed women extended their hands from each side, anxious to have a word with us; but our officers hurried us along as rapidly as possible. Among the men I saw several who were suffering from wounds, but these kept themselves well to the rear and did not seek to come in contact with us. The people of York were the most refined and intelligent folk we met in the State and reminded us of our friends at home, both in manners and personal appearance. They did not seem to be a bit reserved, and if we had not known where we were, we might, from their conduct, have supposed ourselves in Dixie.

We continued our course to the east and in two days more reached Wrightsville, on the Susquehanna, where we met the first hostile demonstration since we had entered the State. The river at this place is very wide and rapid. A long bridge spanned the stream, and from the bridge the town extended up a long and rather steep hill, and consisted of a row of wooden buildings on each side of the street.

Other brigades of Early's division went to the Susquehanna at Harrisburg and captured thousands of State militia (some say five thousand), and would have taken the State capital could they have crossed the river. We remained at Wrightsville until the next day at eleven o'clock in the morning, when we were ordered to return to York. From that place we marched rapidly to Gettysburg, where we were surprised to learn that General Lee had followed Ewell's Corps with the rest of the army.

At York General Early had made a demand on the merchants for a large sum of money as indemnity for destruction of property in Virginia. When they were unable to pay the amount imposed, he seized a large quantity of such goods as the army needed. We arrived there in the night, after a hard march from Wrightsville, and bivouacked. The orderly sergeant detailed me and a comrade to go to the quartermaster and draw rations, and our part of the goods coming to our company. It was surprising to see the amount and variety issued to us, and to get it all to the men consumed a great part of the night, and we found many of them lying about fast asleep, and could not waken them to take anything. We finally fell down ourselves and had hardly closed our eyes in sleep when we were called to ranks, half dead from fatigue, to resume a hard march to Gettysburg. Even when our men awoke they paid no attention to the great piles of supplies we had brought them, and marched away, leaving their portions for anybody who might find them. Among the rations I remember were two hindquarters of very fine beef, a barrel or two of flour, some buckets of wine, sugar, clothing, shoes, etc. All this for about twenty men. I suppose the rest of Early's division got things in the same proportion as our company, all of which would have required quite a train to transport it.

My comrade and I had been up the greater part of three nights in succession, to say nothing of the hard marching, and, as the hot sun arose, we found it impossible to keep up with the regiment, then hurrying toward Gettysburg. Both of us were scorched with fever and had to follow slowly with the stragglers. Before noon the boom of cannon ahead of us indicated that an engagement was on, but the brigade had left us far to the rear and by the time we reached the place where it struck the enemy, it had driven them through forest and field, through the city, and from every position where they had attempted to make a stand. The remnant not killed or captured took position on top of a great elevation overlooking the town and began immediately to fortify it. So few were left our men did not bother to attack them that evening, but heavy reenforcements arrived during the night, and they were able to hold their strong position. To the left of our brigade our men captured parts of their line the next day, but could not hold the ground against superior numbers. Our brigade lay in line of battle in the suburbs under shell fire from the artillery and the enemy's sharpshooters on the heights above them, while our skirmishers in the upper rooms of the houses in the town kept up a hot fire on the enemy's line, returning shot for shot. Some of our brave comrades, exhausted by the fatigue of the past few days, lying here under fire, fell asleep despite the noise of this great battle, and in this condition they were killed, and thus never awoke to know their fate. When my comrade and I reached the place where the brigade struck the enemy, we walked over the ground for some distance to see if we could find any of our comrades among the dead and wounded. We saw some dead Confederates and some hopelessly wounded, but none we knew. The enemy's dead were everywhere as far as we could see toward the town. From the prisoners we learned that the brigade struck them just as they had arrived from a forced march to assist those parts of their army that A. P. Hill and General Rodes of our corps were driving toward the city, and just as the enemy had formed in line and were stacking arms to take a minute's rest, our brigade opened on them, mowing them down at a fearful rate. This threw them into a great panic, from which they were never able to recover, although they made several attempts to hold positions between that place and the town. The brigade, under General Gordon's splendid leadership, drove them like cattle, while Hill and Rodes, to our right, were doing the same thing. Ten thousand of the enemy were lying wounded or dead on the battle field and the sun was still shining in the heavens. Gordon did not want to halt at the town, but was anxious to drive the enemy from the heights, which he could have done at this time so easily, but was not allowed to do so by his superiors. It is said that he was so mortified at their refusal that he cried: "O, for Stonewall Jackson!" If they had only hearkened to Gordon that afternoon history would have been quite different. That night, when Meade arrived, he would have found the Confederates holding the high ground and in position to destroy his army. Gordon's ability was never appreciated until it was too late for him to accomplish anything.

When our men were driving the enemy's broken ranks toward the city, certain individuals of the enemy exhibited acts of heroism worthy to be mentioned. The color bearer of a New York regiment was a hundred yards in the rear of his men, waving his flag and begging his comrades to stand and fight. Certain soldiers in my company noticed him and cried: "Shoot him! Shoot him!" and one of them threw up his gun and fired, bringing down the flag and killing the brave fellow. Seeing what he had done, he said: "O, I am sorry I killed that brave man; I ought to have shot one of those cowardly rascals yonder running away."

THE BURNING OF WRIGHTSVILLE, PA.[5]

The paragraph on page 225 of the June VETERAN in regard to the "burning done by Confederates in the Gettysburg campaign" turned my thoughts back to the circumstances surrounding the burning of Wrightsville, Pa., about which, after reflection and refreshment of memory, I decided to write, so that every lover of the truth might see the spirit which animated the Confederate soldiers while they were in the enemy's territory and compare it with that which the Federals exhibited in devastating with the torch the beautiful Valley of Virginia and many other parts of the South. No one in our command was disposed to commit outrages on the people or their property, but we were restrained from acts of violence of any kind by strict orders from General Lee himself which were read to us as soon as we crossed Mason and Dixon's line. Of course some of our boys stole a chicken or a pig now and then, but that was no more than they did in Virginia and everywhere the army went; but I never heard of our men burning towns or private houses.

The only two instances of burning that I witnessed was when our military authorities had old Thad Stevens's iron works burned. The other was the burning of Blair's beautiful new residence near Washington City in the summer of 1864, when we under Early visited

---

[5] Ibid., August 1919, 27:300-301. Paragraphs deleted from this article to eliminate duplication. Editor.

that city and caused a great panic there. The house stood in the rear of our brigade as we lay facing their works, perhaps a quarter of a mile, and our men went there for water. It has always been a mooted question as to who set it on fire. Some say it was fired by the shells shot at us by the Federal batteries; but I am sure that was not the cause of the fire, for whoever operated those big guns aimed them at the moon or some imaginary enemy high above our heads, and every one of those huge missiles passed far above every object and exploded miles in the rear. As they passed over us they made a noise like the passing of a railroad train, and some one remarked that perhaps the "Melish" were shooting at our wagon trains far in the rear. Some say it was fired by General Early's orders in retaliation for similar outrages committed time and again in Virginia. But I am told that he denied this report. It may have been the work of some Virginia soldier whose home had been destroyed to let Mr. Blair, who was a member of Lincoln's cabinet, feel a little of what the Confederates had suffered for a long time.

From Winchester we went to the fords of the Potomac, then on to Gettysburg, which we entered in a raw, drizzling rain. One of the first things that attracted our attention as we rose over a little hill in the suburbs of the town was a fellow in his back yard waving his hat frantically and shouting at the top of his voice: "Hurrah for Jeff Davis! Hurrah for Jeff Davis!" Our men looked upon him as a sneak and a coward who wanted to curry favor with us, and they replied to him in language too inelegant to print, but among other things told him to go and get a gun and fight.

We were now marching toward Philadelphia, and the next town on our route was Wrightsville, on the Susquehanna. Beyond that river was Lancaster, the residence of James Buchanan, ex-President of the United States, and we were all eager to visit the old gentleman in his home and shake hands with him; but in this we were disappointed by the Pennsylvania "Melish," who burned the bridge across the river and thereby put a stop to our further progress toward the Quaker City. The town of Wrightsville was situated on a hillside sloping down to the river, which was spanned at this place by a wooden bridge.

Before we reached the town on our march from York, a mile, I suppose, from the place, we were traveling leisurely along without any evidence that the enemy was anywhere near, for we had not seen an armed man since we were in the State, when, looking forward toward the head of the column, I saw the regiment in front deploying at right angles to the road across a field of rye now headed out and up to their shoulders. Soon the entire brigade was in line, and Capt. Warren D. Wood, of our regiment, was ordered to deploy his own company (F) and two other companies and to develop the position of the enemy. In front of us was low ground for some distance, and on the rising ground on the other side could be seen a line of excellent earthworks. Captain Wood and his men moved forward in skirmish formation about one hundred and fifty yards, when the fun—the old-time familiar crack of rifles—began. This was immediately responded to by the popping of muskets and the whiz of balls over our heads. Every one exclaimed: "Musket balls! Melish!" [6]

In the meantime two pieces of twenty-pound rifle cannon were taking position just back of our line on rising ground. These now opened on the enemy's works. A buzzing and confused noise arose, as if some great event was taking place over there, and in a moment we were ordered to advance to the enemy's works, which we found abandoned, and from there to the town the enemy had divested themselves of their equipment in their hasty flight. We had just crossed their works when we heard a great explosion, and, looking toward the town, we saw the timbers of the bridge rising high into the blue sky and almost immediately the black smoke rising from the burning bridge and buildings in the village. We hastened on unopposed and found the merchants in the business part of town near the bridge rolling their goods out into the street and the greedy flames eating their way from house to house up the street on the north side. Without orders, everybody went to work to assist the citizens in their efforts to save their goods and to subdue the fire; but in spite of our labor the conflagration continued to make headway until our pioneers came with kegs of powder. These were placed under the buildings most exposed to the fire, and our officers ordered some of our men to put on their bayonets and force our soldiers back up the street out of danger of the explosion. When this took place the houses were knocked to pieces and collapsed. By this means the town was saved from destruction, caused either by the blowing up of the bridge by the Federals to prevent our

---

[6] Henderson, *Roster*, 3:620. "Warren D. Wood. Captain October 27, 1861. Wounded at Fredericksburg, Va. December 13, 1862. Died of wound November 25, 1863."

following them or by some of them under orders who set it on fire to thwart the Confederates in their advance through the State.

It was late at night when the fire was subdued, and, being tired and worn out by long marches, I decided to slip away from the great crowd to some quiet place and lie down for a few hours' rest. Falling in with a comrade, I made the suggestion to him, and accordingly we left the crowd for the suburbs. Coming to a neat residence, we decided to go in and spread our blankets on the floor of the piazza, for it was now raining. But before doing so we took a seat on a bench to get our bearings, nothing as well as we could in the darkness of the night what were the conditions of the place. As soon as we were seated we heard a multitude of voices inside speaking in a low tone, for the house we found was packed full of women who had gone there to spend the night. They had heard our footsteps as we came in, and some one mustered up courage enough to come to the door. Opening it a few inches, she asked me timidly when we were going to burn the town. To this I replied that Confederate soldiers didn't burn towns; that was done by their soldiers. After this, questions were repeated and answered in the same way about a dozen times I suggested to my comrade that we couldn't sleep there, so we went down the steps and spread our blankets on the pavement in the rain, where we spent the rest of the night oblivious of all the trying scenes of war until the rattle of the reveille roused us from our slumbers at first dawn. We hastened down town to find our captain and the rest of the company.

On the south side of the main street, opposite the burnt section and next to the foot of the bridge, stood a large sign in front of the hotel on which were the words in large letters, "Henry Hunt's Hotel." Here we found Captain Lewis installed in the office as provost marshal, and our men were lounging around in full possession of everything. In the panic Hunt had abandoned his business and placed the river between him and us. Captain Lewis was in full charge of the city, and men of our company were the guards. He had put one of his most trusted men in the cellar, where Hunt had a large and well-selected stock of liquors, to keep our men out, but they had little difficulty in getting as much as they wanted. Hunt left a large bunch of keys in the office, and a certain wag of a soldier took these and carried them through all the subsequent marching and fighting, even to Appomattox and to his home in Georgia.

FROM GETTYSBURG TO THE POTOMAC[7]

It was afternoon when we reached the field hospital, where we found our surgeons and their helpers amputating limbs and dressing wounds. The sight of piles of arms and legs in fence corners and the scent of fresh blood were enough to disgust every soul with war and cause one to forget the splendid sight of our beautiful lines advancing and driving victoriously the enemy from the field and the thunder of our guns. Scorched with a burning fever, I spread my blanket on the ground with no protection from the July sun shining from a clear sky, and begged my comrade to get me a drink of water to quench my thirst. This he refused to do, saying he could not find any. He sat down by my side, and I continued to beg him for water. Finally he snatched up a canteen and went away grumbling and apparently in a very bad humor. After quite a while, he returned with some hot, muddy water he had found somewhere that was hardly fit for a horse to drink, and gave it to me. He had had great difficulty in finding this poor stuff in a pool in the dry bed of what had been a stream of water.

And then, while lying there in this condition, pandemonium suddenly broke loose along the front lines. The whole earth seemed to quake under the unbroken roar of artillery and exploding shells. At first the enemy replied vigorously to the Confederates, but the deadly accuracy of the latter soon knocked them out and silenced their guns. When the Confederates ceased firing, piles of the enemy's dead men and horses were lying around their batteries, and the ground was literally covered with fragments of shells. General Lee lacked but one thing to complete the utter destruction of every living creature on the summit of that ridge, and that was an adequate supply of artillery

---

[7] *Confederate Veteran*, November 1922, 30:428-429, 437.

ammunition to last another hour or two. A few were still alive and able to meet the advance of our infantry against an impregnable position, where one man on their side was equal to ten on ours.

One proof of this assertion is the number of the enemy's dead and wounded found lying on the ground after this short artillery engagement, as seen by our men who were captured in the assault. Federal prisoners taken after this when questioned as to the reason General Meade did not follow the Confederates more vigorously to the Potomac, replied that he could not do it; that his horses were all killed and his army too badly cut up to assume the offensive.

In the first day's engagement the enemy is supposed to have lost ten thousand men. Take this number from the total loss, and you see Meade's loss in this short period of fighting was thirteen thousand, only a few of whom were killed by our infantry after the first day's fighting. From this it will be seen that a few more hours of such artillery fire would have scraped the crest of every living defender, so that when the Confederates advanced they would have found the ground held only by the dead and wounded.

The Federals fought no better at Gettysburg than they did anywhere else, but their splendid position won for them a victory where valor did not count. Where they fought in the open country the first day, it was like First and Second Manassas, the Wilderness, and wherever they met us in the open field. Their Dutch and other foreign soldiers were driven from every position they tried to hold against the irresistible advance of our Southern Anglo-Saxons. No troops of any nationality can resist, in an open field, well disciplined Anglo-Saxons, and especially those from the Southern States of the American Union. Their steady courage, animated and enthused by their defiant yell, and the deadly accuracy of their fire will always break any line not well protected by earthworks or other obstacles too formidable to overcome; and even such positions as these they sometimes swept over and captured, though held by a superior force, as at Gaines's Mill, in the hard-fought battle of Cold Harbor, Va., on June 27, 1862.

Our failure to win this (Gettysburg) great battle may be attributed to three chief causes: First, neglecting to take possession of the heights overlooking the town in the evening of the first day, when the enemy was utterly defeated. Second, the lack of a sufficient supply of artillery ammunition to complete the destruction of Meade's army. Third, widely separated attacks at different times and places on the well fortified crest, where the enemy could reenforce from an inner line and retake any position captured by our men. To the left of Gordon's Georgia Brigade, Hoke's North Carolina and Hays's Louisiana Brigades, of Early's Division, captured the heights, but were not supported and were finally driven back. Again, Johnson's Virginia Division captured a most important point and was forced to retire. From either of these our artillery could have swept the enemy's line from the rear and destroyed their army while our other forces were engaging them in front; so that Meade gained a victory by a succession of blunders on the part of the Confederates and the insurmountable position the enemy held.

Orders came to the field hospital for all the sick and wounded who could travel to follow the ambulance and wagon trains, and we set out for the Potomac River. These trains were forty miles in length and were accompanied by a multitude of stock collected in Pennsylvania for the use of the army. The enemy made a few weak efforts to capture this rich plunder, but were easily driven off, and all arrived safe at the fords of the Potomac, which we found too full to be forded for some days. This vast aggregation went into camp to await the time when it could cross over into Virginia, while General Lee, with the army, far to our rear, was coming on slowly in the same direction without any hindrance by the enemy.

And now I must describe a little incident in which I saw more blood spilt than in any other engagement in the whole war; when my comrade and I reached the bank of the river, he had recovered from the fever, but I was still quite sick. He stretched a little dog tent and spread a blanket in it on the ground for me to lie on. Pretty soon an order came for every convalescent and teamster to go to the ordnance wagon and get a gun and ammunition to defend the camp. Looking toward the north, I could see in the distance small white knots of smoke in the blue sky, made by exploding shells, and hear the boom of cannon. A division of Yankee cavalry had some how ridden around Lee's army and were coming in haste to capture our entire train of army impedimenta. Every man obeyed the order, and the quartermasters deployed their men in the woods around the camp just as the enemy arrived and began to make dispositions for the attack. A few shots were exchanged, when the sudden arrival of one of General Stuart's Confederate brigades, who were riding hard in their rear all day, rode in sight and opened with artillery on some of them huddled up in close formation on their horses in a lane flanked on each side by a high, close plank fence. The few shots fired were so accurate that the road was blocked with dead men and horses. Not knowing what force was in the woods in front of them and with a vigorous force in rear of them firing into their backs, they decided it was about time to abandon the idea of capturing the rich plunder General Lee had collected in Pennsylvania; so every man of them struck out to save himself, if possible, and the fight was over. My comrade came back to me with gun in hand, laughing, and said: "Those Yankees would have gotten us if Stuart's men hadn't arrived just in time to help us." We had some curiosity to see what caused their sudden stampede, and walked out a few hundred yards up the road, and there found the men and their horses lying in pools of blood. It was a shocking sight.

In the meantime a pontoon bridge was constructed over the raging stream and an ample supply of ammunition was brought over to the army which had now arrived and taken position at Falling Waters, some miles back from the river. General Lee had "faced about" and was awaiting the arrival of Meade, who had followed him timidly at a great distance. When his advance came in sight of our army, they deployed their lines and threw up formidable earthworks and showed no sign of hostile intention. The river subsided slowly and the army was withdrawn to the south side of the stream, some crossing on the pontoons, but our brigade, the last to cross except that under the noble Pettigrew, waded the stream up to their armpits. I should not have been able to make the crossing in my feeble condition, against the strong current, but our surgeon, Dr. Judson Butts, took me up behind him on his horse and landed me safe on the other shore. All the brigade got safely over in spite of the deep water, while a lively little battle was in progress below us between General Pettigrew's men and the enemy for the possession of the bridge. In this engagement a small squad of Yankees rode up to where General Pettigrew was standing by the roadside and fired a volley at him and his attendants, mortally wounding the general, one of the most accomplished officers in the whole army. The whole South mourned the loss of this splendid soldier.

The entire army and the vast accumulation of baggage and army supplies had now crossed over the river safely with little or no loss, and General Lee was once more on the soil of Virginia and near the source of his supply of ammunition. The enemy made no effort to follow us, and we marched away peacefully, while a Confederate battery on an elevation on the south side of the river shelled the woods on the other side. After marching south a few days, we crossed the Blue Ridge and finally took up a position on the south side of the Rapidan, where we had a long period of perfect rest and peace, for General Meade, for some reason, did not care to renew hostilities. This condition continued until late in the fall, when General Lee assumed the offensive and drove Meade back to the defenses at Washington. If Meade had remained in command of the United States army, the war would have continued the balance of his life with no results of importance; but Lincoln saw fit to put Grant in supreme command, whose policy was for a long drawn out contest to wear out the Confederates, already exhausted by years of war, in which they had lost the flower of their military force and the resources of the country had been reduced to the lowest point. If he had been a Robert E. Lee, a Stonewall Jackson, or a John B. Gordon, with the men and means at his command, he would have surrounded and captured our little army in less than a month. Either doubting the capacity of his officers and the valor of his men, or fearing the efficiency and resourcefulness of his adversary, he preferred not to risk anything, but to make front attacks in mass formation to wear out his enemy by a slow process, in which he finally accomplished his object by losing as many men as his opponent had.

In one respect, Grant was superior to any of his predecessors who had commanded the army before him, since he was never dismayed by the appalling loss inflicted on him by the Confederates, but always brought up reserves to fill his depleted ranks and renewed the fighting without showing the least sign of discouragement. In another respect he was more resourceful; if one plan failed, he was ready to try another and was never disheartened by any failure. He had counted beforehand the cost of winning the war, and stuck to his program until he made it a success.

———————————

MINE RUN–
A GHOST STORY[8]

After the battle of Gettysburg Lee's army returned to Virginia and took up again its old position south of the Rapidan. The enemy did little or nothing to break the monotony of camp life; and the Confederates had time to rest and recuperate until late in the fall, when General Meade, then in command of the Federals, decided to try General Lee once more. Why he came to this sudden conclusion at that time has never been explained, but perhaps it was because the term of enlistment of a great many of his men would soon expire, and Lincoln was urging him to do something before that should happen. He chose to make the crossing at Morton's Ford—named, I suppose, for old Dr. Morton, who lived on the public road only a short distance from the river in a large two-story house surrounded by a grove of large oaks, the grounds of an acre or more enclosed with a plank fence. On every side the house was surrounded by an open field. A row of negro houses extended from the road and residence some distance toward the south. Farther south the land was high and covered with a heavy growth of timber.

Previous to this time a short distance back in this forest General Lee had fortified his position well with excellent breastworks and was only too glad to know that his opponent had chosen this place to fight, as he was anxious to pay him back for Gettysburg. From the higher ground he could see every movement made by the Federals in the open fields, while his force was concealed by the forest.

When our brigade arrived on the scene a hot skirmish battle was in progress, and I came near getting a ball through my head. We were shifted from one place to another and finally placed in the trenches on both sides of the public road leading down to the ford. After skirmishing with the Confederates two or three days, General Meade decided that the time was not propitious for a big battle and began to withdraw his forces to the north flank. To protect his rear he left a

---

[8] Ibid., October 1918, 26:445-446.

strong guard at the Morton residence and negro quarters until all the army should get safely over the river.

Gen. John B. Gordon, who was then in command of our brigade, discovered that there was a ravine which started near the left of our brigade and extended toward the river and in the rear of the Morton house. He accordingly decided to attack the enemy in front with a line of skirmishers and, while their attention was occupied with this force, send another consisting of three companies of our regiment under Captain Shorter down the ravine and, coming up from the rear unexpected, capture the whole force, whose number he greatly underestimated. As soon as Captain Shorter started Captain Lewis was ordered to hold his company in readiness to go to the relief of our men if there should be need for them.[9]

The fighting was pretty hot about the negro houses when Captain Shorter started, and when he arrived on the scene he and his men emerged from the ravine and advanced in the twilight toward the Morton residence. The enemy discovered their presence, but Captain Shorter and his men continued to advance in spite of the hot fire from the house and from the shade trees in the yard until they reached the yard fence. The Federal fought stubbornly; but the Confederates under Captain Shorter by superior marksmanship finally cleared the premises of all except their dead, which lay at the root of every tree, in the rooms, hallways, and piazzas of the house, and outside in the chimney corners. The only man of the three companies to receive a wound was Captain Shorter, who had a finger shot off.

When the engagement was at its hottest, Captain Lewis was ordered to march his company down the road to assist Captain Shorter; but when we arrived there we could see nothing of the enemy, now fleeing in the darkness toward the river, but the flash of their guns and could hear the whistle of their bullets about our heads. Captain Lewis ordered us to lie down in line of battle under the trees and told Sergeant Warn to post a man in front as a vidette at a small outhouse adjoining the road. Now, the man selected for this duty was a brave and vigilant fellow named Knight, but he was somewhat superstitious. Near by a

---

[9] Henderson, *Roster*, 3:578. "Charles S. Shorter. 1st Lieutenant August 29, 1861. Elected Captain August 28, 1862, transferred to Engineer Corps October 14, 1864. Captured at Burgess Mill, Va. April 2, 1865. Released at Johnson's Island, June 20, 1865."

wounded Federal soldier lay groaning in agony. Only a few minutes elapsed until the light flashed from Knight's trusty rifle. He quit his post and came trotting toward us, saying in a low voice: "Captain, I have killed a ghost. It's white and as big as a cow." This caused great amusement among the men, but Jack protested and said that any of them could see it lying out there in the field. Captain Lewis told him to go back to his post; but he refused to do so, saying he couldn't. Sergeant Warn and a young fellow named Bell went to the corner of the house and saw the "ghost," sure enough. Warn left Bell there and came back laughing and said there certainly was a white object lying out in the field, but it didn't appear to be as large as a cow. It seems that Bell had been on post but a few minutes when he was approached by an officer wearing a sword, perhaps searching for some one lost in the fight. Each fired at the other simultaneously and at short range. The ball from the officer's pistol struck the root on which I was sitting, but did me no harm. We were all keen to see the ghost; and when day broke, a little white, shaggy poodle dog lay there with its head split wide open. No doubt it was old Dr. Morton's little pet, which he had taken away with him before the fight began, running rapidly across the field when it fell a victim of Jack's deadly rifle.[10]

If any of my old comrades should see this and remember the fight at Mine Run, I should be pleased to hear from them.

----

[10] Ibid., 646. "John J. Knight. Private February 25, 1862. Wounded in leg, necessitating amputation, and captured at Winchester, Va. September 19, 1864. Released at Point Lookout, Md. June 5, 1865."; 649. "W. T. Worn [or Warn]. Private November 11, 1861. Appointed 1st Sergeant May 1863. Wounded in 1864. Admitted to General Hospital #9, at Richmond, Va., wounded, January 9, 1864, and left hospital January 10, 1864. Wounded at Wilderness, Va. May 6, 1864. Surrendered, Appomattox, Va. April 9, 1865."

HOW IT STARTED[11]

Perhaps General Lee never knew how hostilities between his forces and those of Meade began in the late fall of 1863, culminating in a campaign which lasted until cold weather put an end to it and resulted in much fighting and the driving of the enemy back to their defenses at Washington. A little incident which I will relate grew to such a state that General Lee decided that "Mr. Meade" and his people were bad neighbors, and since he would not come out and show his hand, Lee decided to make him do so by assuming the offensive himself. No doubt General Lee thought the intense picket fighting along his whole front was only to cover some move on the part of Meade, who was always ready to do what was unexpected and then withdraw without a general engagement. This picket fighting along the front was a favorite ruse with General Lee himself when he wanted to cover some important move and hit the enemy a hard blow, and he became suspicious. Accordingly he swung our corps, now commanded by General Ewell, around by a wide detour which took us through the country by the way of Madison Courthouse and Warrington, where we overtook the rear of Meade's army. The skirmishers of our brigade were thrown forward and pressed the enemy, killing and capturing a great many raw recruits. Some of these fellows, when ordered to throw down their guns, were afraid to do so lest they would have to pay for them or be punished by their officers.

After we came back from Gettysburg we made our camp along the south side of the Rapidan and did picket duty along that stream while the enemy was perfectly peaceable and for a long time made no demonstration whatever. New clothes and shoes were issued to us, and many of those who were left sick in the hospitals when we started to Pennsylvania had come back, so our ranks were very much strengthened. The old enterprising spirit of our men returned, and they became impatient for something of an exciting nature which offered them a chance to share in the rich plunder of the enemy.

As already stated, our pickets were posted at wide intervals along the river, while the enemy posted his men some distance from us in

---

[11] *Confederate Veteran*, February 1922, 30:65, 78.

squads of six or eight at each place. They were too far from us to carry on any conversation and were perfectly peaceable and might have remained so if it had not been for the desire of certain men in my company to raid one of their posts which stood in full view on the other side of the river, though at a distance from us. The whole regiment was stretched out in a thin line and extended perhaps a mile or more. A part of the line held by the company was elevated, and we had a good view of the open field opposite us, in which there was a grave enclosed with a picket fence. At this place the Yanks had one of their posts, and after stacking their guns, they took off their blankets, well-filled haversacks, and other equipment and hung them up where we could see them. A public road crossed the river at this place, and to the right of this on the other side of the ford our view was obscured by a thick woodland.

The sight of this plunder exposed to us was more than some of our hungry soldiers could stand. Ever ready for any enterprise, however dangerous, so it afforded a chance to raid the enemy, they begged our captain to let them cross the river in broad daylight, enter the woods, and surround and take the whole thing. They explained to the captain how easily they could do this by entering the woods below the ford, where their movements would not be seen, and so maneuver as to get into the enemy's rear. But the captain was unwilling to assume the responsibility for this offensive without the consent of the colonel at a time when there was perfect peace along the whole front of the two armies. They begged and teased him no little to let them go, but he still refused. Finally he told Lieut. Charles M. Compton, a man equally as reckless as the others, to take a squad of men from the company and cross the river and reconnoiter; if he should find it feasible he would report the matter to the colonel, and with his consent he could make the raid that night.[12]

Among those who volunteered was a fifteen-year-old boy, one of the most reckless of the company. This boy spoiled the whole game by his precipitate haste. Compton and his squad forded the river unobserved

---

[12] Henderson, *Roster*, 3:645. "Charles M. Compton. Private November 11, 1861. Appointed 4th Sergeant May 13, 186; 2d Sergeant December 13, 1862. Elected Jr. 2d Lieutenant February 7, 1863. Wounded at Wilderness, Va. May 6, 1864. Captured at Winchester, Va. September 19, 1864. Released at Fort Delaware, Del. June 17, 1865."

by the enemy and entered the woods. They had not gone far when they observed a house, which we could not see from the other side of the river. This house faced the public road and field in front of which was the picket post. As soon as they saw the house, all with one accord decided to approach it from the back way and get a good dinner, apparently unmindful of their mission. The family occupying the house went to work immediately to set before them such a dinner as they had not seen for a long time, for they were true Southern people. Without posting a guard to keep watch outside while they enjoyed the feast, all sat down and were helping themselves when a little girl came running into the dining room and said: "La, ma, just look up the road at the Yankees coming! The road is full of men and horses." Compton and his men hastily grabbed up their guns and rushed out of the back door unobserved by the enemy. He hid his men behind the front yard fence and in the shrubbery, hastily telling them to hold their fire until the cavalry should come up quite near, and not to fire until he gave the order to do so. The Yankees were riding in fours leisurely along the road, not expecting any trouble, when they rode into this ambush. Meade had decided to relieve the infantry pickets with cavalry, and these men were coming to take their places. When the Yankees were about one hundred yards away, little Rube could wait no longer and pulled down on them. It was now too late to mend the matter, for the cavalry broke in the greatest confusion and scattered in a stampede over the field, firing back as they ran. Compton and his men fired at them as they galloped away, and Sergeant Ricks brought down a big German trooper, who fell in a ditch. Ricks ran out into the field and managed to get him on his horse. The man was shot through the thigh and seemed to be suffering very much when Ricks brought him to us.[13]

And now began a picket fight at long range in which much ammunition was spent by the Yankees and little or no damage was done to us. This fighting spread from us to the right and left until it extended along the whole front for many miles and lasted several days.

General Lee was at a loss to know what Meade meant. Finally he decided to assume the offensive. This resulted in Meade's hasty retreat to the defenses around Washington and many small engagements until

---

[13] Ibid., 649. The 14 year old boy was Reuben J. Windsor. Captured and paroled in 1862, he was killed at Winchester, Va. July 24, 1864."

cold weather put a stop to all activities and both armies went into winter quarters in December, 1863.

Lieutenant Compton was wounded at the second day's Battle of the Wilderness, when our company captured General Seymour and General Shaler. After this he was captured by the enemy at the battle of Winchester, Va., September 19, 1864. Sergeant Ricks was totally disabled for further military service at the battle of Spottsylvania Courthouse. Little Rube was killed by my side at the battle of Kernstown, Va., where our men killed the Federal General Mulligan and routed his army. He lost his life by exposing himself unnecessarily and contrary to orders. He was a brave boy and loved the excitement of battle, but was heedless. He had run away from his widowed mother and come to us when only fourteen years old.

THE GRAND REVIEW[14]

I wonder if any Confederate soldier who took part in this review will see this article. If so, I am sure he will remember this event, and I would be glad to hear from him. But, alas, how few of those heroes of a hundred battles who stepped so proudly before their grand old chief that day survived the campaign of the following spring and summer!

> "On Fame's eternal camping ground
> Their silent tents are spread."

In the winter of 1863-64, after the Gettysburg campaign and that in which we had driven Meade's army back to the defenses around Washington, D. C., General Lee's army was strung out for many miles

---

[14] *Confederate Veteran*, January 1923, 31:16-18. Paragraphs deleted from this article to eliminate duplication. Editor.; The grand review took place on September 9, 1863. Gregory C. White, *A History of the 31st Georgia Volunteer Infantry*, (Baltimore; Butternut and Blue, 1997) 102.

along the south side of the Rapidan River in winter quarters. To the north of our (Gordon's) camp, about two or three miles, was a large field one and a half miles or more square, on the east side of which was quite an elevation, affording a splendid view of the whole field. There was not a tree or shrub anywhere to obstruct the landscape. Nature seemed to have designed the place for the occasion, and the quick eye of our general caught the inspiration and ordered a review of our (the old Stonewall) corps, I suppose for his own pleasure and to cultivate the martial spirit of his men; for all of the army who chose to attend were free to do so. The weather was perfect, and all the brigades constituting the three divisions marched to the appointed place on time and took their position in line. Our division, then commanded by "Old Jube" Early, occupied the front. Gen. R. E. Rodes's division stood to our rear about two hundred yards, and General Johnson's (the old Stonewall) division, the same distance to the rear of Rodes's. The lines were perfectly straight and parallel, extending each a mile or more east and west. To the right of each brigade stood the military band or other musicians belonging to that command. When the lines were all formed, General Lee, mounted on his fine dappled iron gray horse, rode to the brow of the hill above mentioned and sat motionless, while his staff officers, all mounted, took positions on his right and left. In rear of these, his mounted bodyguard formed a line, while a large company of observers, consisting of soldiers, women, and citizens, occupied the space farther to the right and left.

At the proper moment, General Lee rode down the hill toward the right of the front division, with his adjutant general by his side, while his numerous staff and bodyguard followed. At the head of the column he was joined by General Early, and all set out in a gallop down the line to the extreme left and then back again in our rear, where he was joined by General Rodes in a ride down in front and up in rear of his division, and then again by General Johnson, where the same thing was repeated back to the grand stand on the hill, having completed a ride of six miles without a single misstep or break in gait.

I think I never saw a horse perform his part so beautifully as did old Traveller on this occasion, or a rider sit more gracefully in the saddle. But to see General Lee at his best he must be seen on horseback, where he appeared to be perfectly at home. The same can be said of Gens.

Joseph E. Johnston and Beauregard. They looked like kings when mounted.

And then the various regiments broke up into platoons and marched around the field by our old commander, sitting bare headed and motionless, except to acknowledge the salute of each officer as he led his command in front of him. This all consumed a great part of the day, and at the close we returned to our camps.

A little circumstance in this connection, which afforded the men in ranks much amusement, must be mentioned: *The Fingal*, a British blockade runner, came into Savannah just before the Yankee fleet bombarded and captured Fort Pulaski at the mouth of the harbor. The vessel could not escape to the ocean any more to continue in the business of blockade running, and General Lee, who was in command at that time of the forces at Savannah, commissioned two of the officers of the ship in the Confederate service. Lieutenant Burns was assigned as a sort of supernumerary officer in our 31st Georgia regiment. He had no special duties to perform, and was a kind of "free lance," to go and come when he pleased and to fight or not as he liked. But there was no truer or braver soldier in the army than Lieutenant Burns, for he was always with us when the fighting was thickest, with a gun in his hand doing his duty as a private soldier, until shot down in battle at Second Manassas, when he fell with his knee shattered by a ball, the litter bearers placed him on a stretcher to remove him out of any further danger. As they were taking him away, he asked the men how the battle was going and when told that we were holding our line against the powerful assaults of Pope's army, for Longstreet had not as yet come to our help, he lit his pipe and replied: "I don't care a farthing if I lose my leg if we win the day." When he was well and discharged from the hospital, he got a cork leg and returned to General Lee for further service as one of his staff. The quartermaster of our regiment furnished him with a beautiful and spirited young mount for this occasion, but Lieutenant Burns was more expert at climbing ropes on board a ship than riding a horse in a grand parade. Doubting his ability to ride with the other staff officers, he chose to take his place in the rear of the bodyguard. For a while he followed the flying horsemen and stuck to the saddle very well, but before he got to the extreme left, he was far behind, as his cork leg became detached and began to fly about in the air in such an ungovernable way as to excite every one to laughter, and, since he could not control his horse and his false member at the same time, he was compelled to halt at the left of the division until the review was over. Poor, brave Lieutenant Burns! I wonder what became of him. Some years after the war I saw frequent mention of him in the papers, but this generation has forgotten his heroic, unselfish sacrifice in our behalf, as well as that of many others who sleep somewhere in unknown graves. But the Righteous Judge will requite them at the last day.

A few days later General Lee, on the same ground, reviewed General Stuart's cavalry corps, consisting of three divisions, whose ranks were very much depleted by constant contact with the enemy and hard service. This was very evident from the appearance of the men and their horses. The wonder is that their general, with so poor a force and equipment, could perform such achievements against such overwhelming odds. Surely Stuart and his men were little less than superhuman. But how proudly rode "The Knight of the Black Plume" that day before his chief!

After this General Lee reviewed A. P. Hill's corps at the same place, but we did not think they made so fine a show as ours (Ewell's). I cannot say whether General Lee reviewed Longstreet's corps, as they were more distant from us toward Culpeper.[15]

------

[15] Bradwell includes the following note at the end of this article: [NOTE — Will some veteran who participated in this, one of the greatest cavalry battles of the war write it up for the readers of the VETERAN? I cannot do so myself, as I did not take part in it and would have to depend on "hearsay," though I passed through that part of the ground where the fighting was hottest two days afterwards with my regiment and saw dead horses and other evidences everywhere over a great extent of country.]

CHAPTER FIVE

1864

MORTON'S FORD, JANUARY 4, 1864[1]

This place was the scene of two severe engagements of a minor character during the war of the sixties, in which Gordon's Georgia Brigade was the participant on the side of the Confederates. It was here General Meade left his rear guard when he suddenly declined to fight at Mine Run. General Gordon attempted to capture this force late in the evening of the last day of the fight, but his plan, though well conceived, resulted only in a severe fight, which lasted till late in the night, and all of the enemy escaped except those who were killed. After this, General Lee, supposing that winter had put a stop to all aggression on the part of the Yankees until spring should open, issued an order allowing one man from each company in every regiment to have a twenty-four-day furlough, beginning with the most meritorious who had never had a leave of absence. I was among those who got one of these furloughs and was therefore absent at home in Georgia when the second engagement took place, and this account of it will be as it came from my comrades.

General Lee had left the army and gone on a visit to his family at Richmond, and General Gordon had gone to Culpeper Courthouse, many miles away from his command. Col. Clement A. Evans, of the 31st Georgia, was the senior officer of the brigade and in command. This brigade had gone into winter quarters a few miles back from the ford and were the nearest troops to our pickets stationed there. Everything seemed to indicate a quiet, peaceable time for the rest of the winter; but hostilities suddenly broke out again. Why the enemy came over and began a new offensive could be accounted for only on the grounds that somebody at the head of the movement, under the potent influence of Christmas cheer, decided to end the war then and there without further delay.

---

[1]*Confederate Veteran*, November 1925, 23:412-414.

Orders were issued to build a bridge that night at the ford. This was done, or half done, for the bridge of round poles did not reach the southern bank of the stream, and the drunken soldiers who crossed on it had to jump to make a landing. To the surprise of the Confederates, early on the morning of January 4, firing at the ford attracted the attention of our men, and pretty soon news came that two brigades of the enemy had driven off our pickets and had crossed over and were formed in line of battle. Hasty orders were issued and the men were started in a trot to meet the enemy. When they came in sight of them, Colonel Evans saw that he had quite a large force to meet. They were drawn up in line beyond Dr. Morton's house, while their skirmishers held the grove around it and the negro quarters across the road to the south. These were constructed of brick and were only four or five feet apart and, being in line with Dr. Morton's residence, afforded a safe position for their pickets.

The Confederates advanced in the open under fire to within a short distance of the enemy, where they found a gully or depression in the land that gave them protection. There they stopped and maintained an exchange of shots until late in the afternoon, when Colonel Evans brought up a battery and opened fire on the houses. At the same time the skirmishers advanced with a yell and captured the position, driving off the enemy and killing and capturing quite a number of them. But this was only the beginning. They reenforced their troops and made several efforts to retake the position, advancing boldly to within a few feet of the Confederates, where many of them, rather than risk the chance of being killed in a retreat back to their own main line, rushed into the houses and surrendered. Not satisfied with this failure, they now advanced a solid line of battle, but with no better success.

It was now very dark, and, through some misunderstanding, the Confederates on the right withdrew; the enemy discovering this, swung around in the rear and flanked our men out of their position, capturing one man who was in Dr. Morton's house and unaware of what had occurred. But Colonel Evans had sent a new line of skirmishers in to take the place of those who had been fighting all day. The enemy, somewhat sobered by their bloody defeat, decided not to renew the engagement and put an end to the war that very night. Before morning all who were not drowned in trying to cross the river on their bridge constructed of poles, killed, or captured, were on the other side of the

Rapidan. One hundred and seventeen of them lay dead in front of the negro houses, and one hundred and fifty prisoners stood up in line. No one knows how many lost their lives in crossing the river, but General Hayes, who was in command, told W.H. Bland, who fell into their hands, that he lost five hundred men. Our loss in this affair was only four men—one killed in the rear by a stray ball, one captured, and two wounded.

General Lee had now arrived from Richmond, and as he rode along in view of the prisoners on his old iron gray horse, these men made many complimentary remarks about him. One would say, "O, if we had such a general;" and another, "What a splendid looking man!" "He is the noblest man I ever saw."

I want to say here tnat all our men in this affair were sober, not because they were all prohibitionists, but to demonstrate how inefficient a drunken man is.

This wound up all active hostilities until we broke up camp and marched off to the Wilderness on May 4, 1864, to meet Grant's army on the 5th and 6th of that month.

I should add that the principal part of this fighting was done by two companies of not more than forty men of the 61st Georgia Regiment under the brave Captain Kennedy. When he routed the enemy out of the houses, he pursued them some distance and wanted to continue the drive, feeling sure he could push the whole outfit into the river, but was ordered to return and hold the position taken.[2]

[NOTE: The General Hayes who figured in this affair was afterwards President of the United States and a good man. As such he filled the office acceptably to the people of the South by withdrawing all military forces from the States.]

---

[2] Ibid., 23:413-414. Bradwell then quotes a letter from W.H. Bland, of Baxley, Ga., on December 20, 1897, to G.W. Nichols, telling him of his experience after his capture in this fight. For the text of this letter, see the appendix §2.

BATTLE OF THE WILDERNESS[3]

Gordon's Brigade, afterwards commanded by Gen. Clement A. Evans, spent the winter of 1863-64 at Clark's Mountain not far from where the fighting began in May, and we did not have far to march to reach the battle field when the campaign opened in the spring. I suppose there were less than twenty-five hundred effectives in the entire command [Brigade]. During the winter we suffered very much from lack of proper food and want of clothing, and we knew from reports that came to us that we would be called on in the spring to make greater sacrifices than ever before. We were told that General Grant had assumed command of the mighty army under Meade, whom we did not fear, and had brought from the West, where he had been operating, corps of victorious troops who boasted that they had never turned their backs on the Rebels, and when the campaign opened they would show us and their comrades of the Army of the Potomac how to fight. We knew that without these we were already overmatched in numbers, equipment, and everything to make an army efficient; but we consoled ourselves with the reflection that we could die if necessary for our country and, that Divine Providence was on our side, while we had a leader in General Lee who, we felt, would be equal to the occasion.

The Federal army, though north of the Rapidan, was as near Richmond as the Confederate army, which was scattered along the south side as far as Culpeper C. H., thus giving Grant opportunity to cross that stream and place his forces between us and our base at Richmond. It seemed strange to me at the time that General Lee would so dispose his forces in the face of the great odds against us, but he knew Grant and what his plans were, and he wanted him to do the very thing he had in his mind, intending to fall on him in this wilderness, where he least expected it and where his superior numbers and numerous artillery could do him little good. General Grant had made every preparation for the coming contest, but waited until the ground had sufficiently hardened from the winter rains so he could

---

[3] Ibid., December 1919, 27:458-459. For another Bradwell account of the Battle of the Wilderness see 16:447-448.

maneuver his heavy artillery trains without difficulty. Accordingly on the 4th of May he crossed the river and set out for Richmond. So far everything was lovely for him; but A. P. Hill, with a part of his corps, and Gen. R. E. Rodes, with his division of our corps, fell on his long lines passing through this thickly wooded country with such vigor that the advance was checked. Fighting of the severest character now began, and Hill and Rodes had a little more than they could do to hold their own.

In all the previous battles in which we had taken part we were warned by a heavy cannonade and skirmish fire, but in this instance we broke camp and marched leisurely from our winter quarters, without hearing the sound of a gun, to a place four or five miles from where we were thrown into battle. We marched leisurely from where we bivouacked that night, and about eleven o'clock, while marching along a public road leading into the thick woods, I saw the regiments ahead deploying to the left and right. Rodes was at this time having a hot time of it some distance in front and to our right, and many of his wounded were coming out. General Lee and General Gordon, who knew the critical situation, had had an interview in which Lee told Gordon that everything depended upon the success of the fight our brigade was to make; that if we failed he would have to retreat, a thing he could not afford to do. And as the line stood there a moment, formed and only waiting for word to move forward, Gordon rode along the entire front of the brigade, seeming as one inspired with burning words of eloquence. With hat in hand he passed along, his face fairly radiant as he spoke to his men in these words: "Soldiers, we have always driven the enemy before us, but this day we are going to scatter them like the leaves of the forest." With these words and many others which I did not hear he raised the fighting spirit in his men to the highest pitch, and as he rode around our right and behind the line he cautioned us not to crowd to the right or left, but to maintain our line as we advanced and not to fire or raise the Rebel yell, a thing for which we were noted and at this time were on the point of doing, but to reserve our fire until we struck the enemy and then to rush on them and not let them rest a moment until we had driven them off and won for General Lee the ground he was so anxious to hold. And did we? Let us see.

The word was now given and repeated by every officer and private. We swept forward through the thick undergrowth, slowly at first, until we struck the enemy, only a hundred yards or so away, when pandemonium broke loose. Their line crumbled immediately under our first volley as our men rushed over them, and I could see them to the right, left, and in front throwing up their hands and surrendering by scores. We were now somewhat disorganized, but moved on as if nothing had happened and were soon on another line, reenforced by fugitives from the first; but this offered little resistance, as we rushed over them and scattered them also. Without allowing them to stop and take breath, we pressed them back on other lines, every one of which seemed demoralized by our rapid advance and the multitude of fugitives coming to them.

The fighting began about noon, and in the great excitement incident to the occasion time passed so rapidly that it seemed but an hour when we struck their last reserves just as night was coming on. Just how many of these lines we encountered and broke that evening I cannot say. By this time our regiment was advancing in detached squads, with a man here and there, having veered to the right of the brigade some distance and out of touch with them. As we approached these reserves they opened on us with a startling volley that did us no harm, but made every one of us seek cover. This was the hottest fire we had experienced the whole afternoon. Looking to the left, I could see no one. On the right there was a squad, but I could not see any of our men.

I was now in a dilemma as I stopped behind a tree. Here I was alone in the face of a strong line of Yankees, under a heavy and continuous shower of balls, and not a comrade in sight. The little tree offered very little protection, and I did not want to be killed here by myself, where no one could ever know what became of me. Glancing to the right, I saw a gray-clad figure rise up as if out of the earth and dart toward the enemy and disappear just in front of them. Then two more did the same thing, and others followed them until perhaps thirty or forty had gone. It occurred to me that they had found some place of safety there, and I resolved to go too. Holding my head low, it took me less time than it takes to tell it to pass over the intervening space. There I found my comrades lying in a gully only a few feet from the enemy, secure from all harm. The ground between us was level, and our fire, from what we saw afterwards, was very effective. Lieutenant Colonel Pride was the last man to jump into the gully, and as he did so he ordered us to rise and charge them; but we knew better than to undertake to do this, as the enemy outnumbered us twenty to one. Only one man responded, and he was shot down immediately. Standing by the side of the colonel, loading my gun, I heard the sound of a ball striking him in the stomach. This ball passed through his body and came out at his back between the buttons of his military coat. His ruddy face became pale immediately, and he reeled and fell. Some of our men grabbed him and ran out with him. Strange to say, he recovered, but was nevermore fit for military duty.

Soon after this the firing of the enemy suddenly ceased. We all jumped up and ran out to the front. There a sight long to be remembered met our eyes. It seemed that every shot we fired took effect. A line of their dead lay there, and the pine straw was sprinkled with the blood of others who had gone away wounded. They left in their retreat the drums and instruments of a fine silver cornet band, the heads of the drums having been shot out.

In advancing through the thick forest our regiment became separated far to the right, and night was now spreading a mantle over the scene. Colonel Evans hunted us up and found us there, while firing was going on far to our rear on the right and left. After winding about there for some time, he took a straight course which led us to where the other regiments had collected. As we came up to them they were on their tiptoes shouting to us, saying: "Boys, this beats Gettysburg (which we had always considered our greatest victory). We've captured twenty-five hundred Yankees, including a full Pennsylvania regiment, with their colonel." I can't vouch for the numbers, as we came to the rallying place last and did not see the prisoners; but General Lee had been there and, taking off his glove, shook hands with General Gordon, congratulating him and making him a major general to date from that day. He had ordered rations to be brought up and issued to our men, but in this our regiment did not participate, for in a few minutes after our arrival we were ordered away to help our "Louisiana Tigers" hold their part of the line. Sometime during the night we were relieved and rejoined the brigade.

Thus ended the events of the ever-memorable first day's battle of the Wilderness. In another article I will tell about our experience in the second day's fighting, which was not less exciting and was equally successful and which should have resulted in cutting General Grant's army off from the ford of the Rapidan, by which he brought up his supplies and reserves. Had our superior officers allowed General Gordon to make the fight earlier in the day, as Gordon begged to do, seeing that he had all the advantage, there is no telling what the consequences might have been.

SECOND DAY'S BATTLE OF THE WILDERNESS MAY 6, 1864[4]

I will continue my narrative of the battle of the Wilderness by telling of the part we had in the next day's activities—a day in which the fortunes of our country hung in the balance quite a while; and had it not been for the withholding of permission for General Gordon to throw the weight of his own brigade, supported by every man that could be spared on the left of our line, on Grant's exposed right until it was too late in the day to have a decisive result, Grant's defeat would have been more complete than that of Hooker near that place a year before. Their right wing completely crushed and routed, followed closely by the yelling Confederates, would have produced consternation in the men holding the center. These in turn would have given way when they saw themselves attacked on two sides at a time when their left was giving ground before Longstreet and A. P. Hill. From what I saw on this occasion and afterwards, Gordon possessed more military sagacity than all his superiors except General Lee himself, though all of them were slow to see it and to allow him a chance to demonstrate his ability. Grant, of whom so much was expected, defeated and his great army destroyed at that time, would have been more than public sentiment at the North could have borne, and some kind of a peace quite different from that which we got at Appomattox would have been arranged.

---

[4] Ibid., January 1920, 28:20-22. Paragraphs deleted from this article to eliminate duplication. For another account of the second day of the Battle of the Wilderness see 16:641-42.

Our brigade spent the night after this great fight in noisy rejoicing over its splendid achievements, passing the word in loud shouting to the next brigade to the right that they had whipped everything. This was communicated to the next until the news went from brigade to brigade to Lee's extreme right. The word came back to us, by the same means from every part of the line, of the same import. So great and continuous was the noisy demonstration that the enemy decided we were receiving reenforcements from the coast, but this was only bluff on our part to affect the morale of our foe. When day dawned each side had constructed breastworks out of logs and everything lying about on the ground. Ours consisted of logs and dirt dug up with bayonets and cast up with tin plates and our naked hands. Those of the enemy contained also the dead bodies of their own men, besides army blankets, knapsacks, and anything they could find in the darkness of the night. These two lines ran parallel to each other for miles through this wilderness and about one hundred or one hundred and fifty yards apart. As to the dead being used in the construction of the enemy's defenses, I do not pretend to say this from what I heard, but I make this assertion from what I actually saw on the third morning of the fighting after we had routed them from their works.

Not a match was struck and not an ax was used on either side in building the works, on account of the proximity of the two armies. Those in command of Grant's extreme right made a fatal mistake in leaving that wing exposed and entirely unprotected. Their line extended to an open field on the west. This field was crossed from north to south by a deep ravine not more than a hundred yards from the end of their works, giving the Confederates a convenient place to form a brigade of troops at right angles to their line and out of their sight. The Confederate line ended opposite that of the Federals, but was concealed by thick woods, which gave them protection in reconnoitering the position of the enemy.

This was the situation on the morning of the second day of the fighting; and our brigade, under our noble Gordon, except the battalion of sharpshooters under Captain Keller, was kept in reserve and shifted from point to point whenever it was thought they might be needed to restore the line if it should be broken. This battalion was strung out in a very thin line, thirty or forty feet apart, wherever each man could find protection for himself in front of the other brigades composing the division (Early's). Opposite them, the enemy had a heavy line of skirmishers, five men on each post. This battalion of Confederates was composed of select men from every company in Gordon's Brigade, the best marksmen and the most fearless, well trained for this special duty. They were armed with short Enfield rifles, and when strung out thirty or forty feet apart they could hold any advancing line in check. From what I saw in going over the ground the next morning, very few shots fired by them were ineffectual. In front of them at every post occupied by their opponents, as far as I went, were lying from one to five dead men. Prisoners told us that they were compelled to reenforce their skimishers several times during the day with new men to take the places of those killed and wounded.

It was fortunate for General Grant and his army that General Gordon was held in check by his superiors and not allowed to make his great flank movement earlier in the day, when Longstreet and A. P. Hill were striking sledge-hammer blows on his left and driving him back in confusion. At the eleventh hour permission was given to make the movement, just as the sun was going down, and it was a complete surprise to the enemy. His right wing was routed and driven back on his center, and the darkness of night alone put a stop to the progress of the victorious Confederates when they were only a short distance from Grant's headquarters.

Just before sundown we were shifted to the extreme left in the rear of the works held by the Virginia brigade of our division to await orders. While here I noticed General Gordon taking with him General Early on foot to observe the enemy's position. They soon returned, and Gordon took with him General Ewell, who commanded the corps, over the same ground. Then Gordon appeared again with General Lee. He showed him also the great advantage he had over Grant's men and explained to him what he had been begging to do all day. They were not gone long until they came up out of the thick woods to where an orderly was holding old Traveler. General Lee rode off and disappeared from our sight. He had at last seen his great opportunity, and now orders came to strike. We were told to move to the left with our heads low and not to make the least noise. When we reached the ravine we moved up into the field and formed the entire brigade, with the sharpshooters deployed a few feet in front. All orders were given in a whisper. The sharpshooters were to advance up the steep hill at the word at double-quick; we were to advance at quick time and not to fire until we had passed over these brave fellows, who were to fall flat after the first volley. This last order was not well carried out, as everybody in the main line knew we had the enemy entirely in our power and were eager to begin the fray.

The order to advance was now given, and the skirmishers ran up the hill and were on the enemy, then cooking their evening meal on thousands of small fires, secure, as they thought, behind their breastworks. Poor fellows! None of them suspected the bolt that was about to strike them. Suddenly, and only a few yards away, the long line of gray-clad soldiers appeared and opened on them seated in groups about the fires with their guns stacked back of their works. Never was lightning from the clouds more unexpected, and confusion reigned supreme. About this time the main line came on the scene, and so anxious were they to open fire that they disregarded the orders and poured a deadly volley into the confused enemy, endangering very much the lives of our sharpshooters, who fell on their faces, shouting back to us not to shoot until we had passed over them. No attention was paid to this; and we were at their works. The regiment to which I belonged was on the extreme right of the brigade, and my company formed the right of the regiment. It so happened that the most of the company was on the right of the enemy's works. The enemy, rolled up in a confused mass behind their defenses, supposed we were the only troops making the attack and, seeing us in the dim light of their fires, opened on us with a heavy fire. All the company leaped over to the left side, and I found myself the only survivor remaining on that side. Thinking perhaps the fire on the left side, where my comrades had gone, was less severe and afforded some hope of life, I jumped over among the men fighting there. No sooner had I done so than two or three of my comrades fell dead by my side, and the fire from the great mob, only a few feet in our front, was too hot for us. It was like the old saying about jumping out of the frying pan into the fire. So I again crossed the works, while my comrades moved to the left, but at the same time advancing on the enemy, who continued shooting in the direction of their abandoned works. The other regiments to the left were now sweeping on through the forest almost unopposed, shooting at the fleeing enemy whenever seen, like sportsmen driving game through the woods, with little or no loss to themselves.

When I landed on that side (I cannot say now with what dignity that maneuver was made), I found an oak tree standing there to shelter me from the rain of Minie balls passing through the air. Behind this I took my stand and opened fire on my opponents, a short distance away, but out of sight on account of the thick undergrowth. I had been here but a short while when Col. Clement A. Evans came running up to me in great excitement and told me that I was firing into our own men and for me to move forward. I could not do this, alone as I was, without being killed or captured; but I veered to the right as I went forward and was soon out of range of the enemy's fire, which was directed down the breastworks. They were wasting a great deal of ammunition at this time while the whole force of Confederates was sweeping onward in their rear.

I now made my way through the forest, illuminated only by the flashing of guns and the explosion of Confederate shells, looking for comrades with whom I could unite to assist in the fighting. Finally I saw a small gray-clad soldier standing behind a tree, from which he was shooting toward the enemy's works. I asked him what command he belonged to, and he said: "Hays's Louisiana Brigade." Ah! then, I felt that I had found a friend I could rely on. I told him not to shoot over there any more, as he might injure our own men. He replied indignantly: "They are Yankees." This was true, but I was not sure of it. I told him I was going to see, and he said he would go too. So we started and were soon standing on the breastworks. Out in the woods we could see a great number of men in much confusion. Not knowing exactly who they were, we went in among them and found from their uniforms and their foreign accent that they were Yankees. The fire from the Confederates was cutting them down around us, and the brigade looked like an army of fireflies in the forest as they advanced in a long line through the woods. My comrade stuck close to my side, and I whispered: "They are Yankees. Let us run out." We elbowed our way to their front and bolted. For the first hundred yards of our retreat out of this situation I suppose we struck the ground a few times, but we gradually slackened our pace until we came to a long line of Confederates brought up to assist our brigade if needed. They were sitting and lying about on the ground and kindly allowed us to pass on when we told them that we had just made our escape from the enemy. Following the line of works, we soon saw ahead of us a number of small fires kindled out in the field where we first made the attack, around which were Confederate soldiers and Yankee prisoners. As soon as I reached the opening I met a comrade who informed me that our company had captured two generals—General Seymour, of New York, and General Shaler—and their fine horses. Pointing to a small fire, he said: "There they are." And my curiosity led me to draw near and see them and hear what they had to say. General Seymour was talking to his captors as familiarly as if he had been one of them. He told them it was only a matter of time when we all would be compelled to come back into the Union. He was a tall, handsome young officer with a very pleasing address. General Shaler was short and thick-set and seemed too mad to say a word, gazing sullenly at the little fire before him, while his fellow prisoner chatted with our men, all of whom took a great liking to him. These two generals in the confusion as our men were sweeping through the woods rode into our company, supposing they were their own men. They were made to surrender and dismount. In doing so General Seymour patted his fine dappled iron-gray on the hip and said: "Take good care of him, boys; he is a fine animal." Just at this time Lieutenant Compton, who was leading the company, was shot in the ankle. His men put him on Seymour's horse and went to the rear with their prisoners.

I had heard General Seymour make only a few remarks when Col. Clement A. Evans rode up and told me to take all of our brigade back into the woods to the firing line. I was puzzled to know how I should do this, since I had been separated from them and did not know where they were. But my comrade volunteered to show me the way, and I soon had them all in line, some two hundred of them, and on our way. Just before we reached our destination the Yankees opened with a great volley on our men ahead of us. I ordered all to fall on their faces, which they were very prompt to do, and as soon as the shooting had somewhat subsided I told every man to break for his place in the line.

When day dawned I was sent to the rear on some errand and had an opportunity to see the captured works of the enemy and their dead and wounded, who had not as yet been picked up and sent to the field hospital. I also was surprised to see the great number of little fires and suppers that were in course of preparation, some of which had been knocked over in the scuffle of the night before. I returned by way of the line held by our skirmishers the day before and observed the deadly effect of their fire, plainly demonstrated by blue-coated corpses lying at each post held by the enemy.

Our foe retired from our front some distance during the night and fortified their position, and our sharpshooters, ever ready to renew the fight, were pushed forward to develop their new position. All that day they kept up the fight, bantering them to come out and try it again with us, telling them how we had beaten them the previous two days; but they kept close in and replied only feebly. Grant had decided not "to fight it out on that line if it took all summer," but was endeavoring to extend his left wing to occupy a position at Spotsylvania C. H. between Lee's army and Richmond. All that day the brigade lay quietly in the woods, resting and waiting for orders, which came at midnight for us to move to the right; and at dawn the next day, the 8th, after a hard night's march, we found ourselves at Spotsylvania, where other troops had already arrived and were engaged in building earthworks.

SPOTSYLVANIA, VA.
MAY 8 AND 9, 1864[5]

We left our works in the Wilderness about midnight and marched in the darkness through woods, fields, and across streams, by roads made by the feet of those who had gone ahead, and at daylight we found ourselves at a line of Confederate soldiers who were hastily constructing breastworks of poles, dirt, and everything they could lay hands on. We threw ourselves down behind these for a rest, but were soon called to order and marched to the right to assist in fortifying our position. As far to the right as could be heard there was the incessant noise of the pick, the shovel, and the ax. There were no idlers in Lee's army that day, for

---

[5] Ibid., February 1920, 28:56-57.

the desultory skirmish in front warned every man to do his best and to get ready for the bloody work which all knew to be impending.

Grant had determined, after his three days' experience in the Wilderness, not to fight it out there, but to bring up his fresh legions from the other side of the river as reenforcements for his badly decimated army and get between Lee and Richmond. But when he found that he had been outmaneuvered in this, he decided to carry his point by throwing his overwhelming numbers on our weak lines (now sadly depleted by constant fighting), scatter our forces, and go on to the Confederate capital and thereby end the war. When we consider the great disparity of numbers, this seems reasonable enough, but the few defenders were men who were true and tried veterans fighting for everything held dear in life and were ready to die, if need be, for their country, while a large part of their foes were foreigners—Germans, enlisted to get the big bounty offered by Lincoln, and many other foreigners who fought only under military discipline. The front attacks were extremely costly in human life, but then that was nothing, as multitudes were coming over from Europe continually to take the place in the ranks of those killed, and they knew they could afford to lose ten to our one and in time win the war. No attempt was made to attack our flanks, as that involved some risk. General Grant followed this policy until the end, but could have defeated Lee's army at any time if he had attacked both our right and left at the same time with a large force while we were occupied by superior numbers in front.

The day (May 8) wore on with skirmish-fighting and an occasional attack in force on some part of our line as Grant had not as yet gotten all his army in position to make his grand assault; but nowhere did he break our thin line. Our brigade, having made a great reputation under Gordon, was relieved from building breastworks as soon as we had completed them and was shifted from point to point in reserve wherever there was danger of the enemy's breaking through, and for that reason it did very little fighting this day. I cannot say what losses the Confederates sustained, but, as they were protected by their works, I do not suppose they amounted to much.

The next day (May 9) was one of bitter fighting, a day of slaughter. Our enemy came up in heavy lines, supporting each other time and again, only to be mowed down and driven back without making any impression until about sunset, when they made a sudden attack at one point where our men, thinking that their foes had had enough for the day, were preparing to eat their evening meal. So unexpected and determined was this charge that they crossed our works the length of a North Carolina brigade, killing some of them with bayonet and driving the artillerymen away from their guns. This is the only place I saw during my entire experience a Confederate soldier where any one was killed with the bayonet.

We had been held in the rear of this part of our line for some time that evening, but before this unfortunate event took place we were led off some distance to the left and were resting on an elevated place in an open field. General Gordon and Col. Evans, next in command, had ridden away, I suppose, to see how the fighting was progressing in front of where we then were, there being no field officer present except Lieutenant Colonel Berry, of the 60th. Looking back in the direction from which we had just come, we saw a courier coming toward us as fast as his horse could run. When he arrived he asked hastily where General Gordon was. No one knew, and he rode off to find him. Glancing back in the same direction, we saw another courier coming at full speed, his hat off and his hair flying about his head. When he arrived he made the same inquiry and received the same reply. But now we saw an officer of General Lee's staff coming toward us riding at the same pace. When he reached us he made the same inquiry, and, receiving the same answer, he spoke to Colonel Berry and told him that General Lee's line was broken and ordered him to take command of the brigade and follow him. He turned his horse's head and trotted back in front of us, saying repeatedly: "Come on, boys; come on." Ahead of us on the left was a straggling piece of woodland through which our works extended and to the right a short line of works out in the field behind which were crouching our sharpshooters and others who had taken refuge there when the line was broken.[6]

About one hundred and fifty yards in the rear of our line of works ran an old road parallel to them. We entered the woods by this road, trotting along in fours, following Col. Berry, when suddenly just as I stepped over the body of a dead Confederate soldier he wheeled to the

---

6 Krick, *Lee's Colonels*, 52. "Thomas J. Berry. Graduated U.S. Military Academy, 1857. Lt., U.S. Cavalry, 1857-1861. Served on Lawton's staff. Major, 60th Georgia, September 19, 1861. Wounded at Second Manassas. Retired, Jan 3, 1865. 'Could not help sometimes taking a little too much whiskey.'"

left and shouted: "Here they are, men!" In an instant we turned, and, to our surprise, there stood in the twilight not more than a hundred feet away a blue mass of Yankee soldiers apparently indifferent to our approach. We instantly brought our guns into position, and a line of fire flashed along the regiment as we closed in on the enemy. Stupid under the influence of liquor, they retired slowly and sullenly, while our men beat them with clubbed guns back to the breastworks, which they defended obstinately for a while. I ran up to a piece of artillery where the fighting was hand to hand and where it was impossible to distinguish friend from foe on account of the darkness except by the flash of a gun. In the midst of the confusion some one cried out: "Get away! Get away!"

Seeing that one place was as safe as another, I stood still when the sudden flash and boom of a cannon and its recoil to my feet told me what it meant and that our artillerymen, who had come back with us, had turned the gun around while our men and the enemy were fighting for its possession. Our men beat them out of the works, and they retired to another line built by our men and afterwards abandoned when they first came to this place. Those intersected our line like the two sides of the letter V. Behind these they took refuge and from the volley they maintained I suppose there were thousands of them. In all my experience in war I was never under a heavier fire. It seemed as if a hand or a head above the protection of the works for a moment would be pierced by a Minie ball.

Word was passed down the line for three regiments of our brigade to mount the works and charge the enemy out of their den. My! thought I, how is it possible for living men to face such a fire? Yet every man responded. Some fell back dead as they mounted the works, but the rest swept forward and in ten minutes had cleared the enemy from our immediate front, and the firing along the entire line suddenly ceased for the night. How glad I was that my regiment was not called on to make this desperate dash into the very jaws of death I cannot express in words. Many of those brave spirits who put duty to their country first sacrificed their lives on its altar that night.

Word now came for the other three regiments to assist in holding the position just won, and we were deployed along the works, which we found to be well constructed. As soon as we were settled in them the orderly sergeant ordered me and a comrade to mount the works and to take position in the open in front to guard against a sudden assault by the enemy. Standing there in silence, I listened to the beautiful music of the various bands along the enemy's line, while our men in the rear spent their time in jeering and bantering them to come out and try it again, saying: "You may play your bands over there, but we whipped you yesterday and again to-day and will do it again tomorrow."

It had indeed been a bloody day. The enemy had not spared human life in their endeavor to break through our lines. We were not on the front line, but were told by those who were that they charged sometimes in lines fourteen deep; but this must have been an exaggeration. The fighting lasted all day and accomplished nothing but the slaughter of thousands of our enemy, who threw themselves recklessly time and again against our defenses, only to be driven back in an engagement in which every well-directed Confederate bullet must have injured some one in so great a mass of men. The commander of the Federals, perceiving the bad effects of this dreadful affair on the minds of his men, ordered his army bands to the lines to dispense their sweetest music, to divert, if possible, their thoughts from the great disaster.

A man even so callous as General Grant saw that he must hold his hand and refrain from so great a sacrifice as a matter of policy, and the next two days (May 10 and 11) he spent in skirmishing and maneuvering for some advantage, to find some weak point in Lee's line where he could concentrate and make a bold rush through it with his overwhelming numbers while we were too weak to assume the offensive. During the night our brigade was withdrawn from the captured works. The full moon shone over the battle field as we returned and presented a sight never to be forgotten. Corpses lay everywhere and in every position. Few prisoners were taken on either side. Our loss in killed and wounded was negligible except at this particular place. The next morning I was struck by the appearance of the dead. The faces of the Confederates were pale, while the Federals were as black as negroes. I asked the reason and was told that it was because the Federals were drunk when killed. Those who were in the front line said they could smell the scent of liquor when the wind blew from the Federal lines. I cannot vouch for this, but I am sure, from the way they acted, that their men were drunk when we struck them that evening.

I have never seen an official statement of Grant's loss in this day's engagement, but I am sure it was as great as that he sustained in the three days' fighting in the Wilderness and consisted of killed and wounded. It must have been as great as that he sustained on the 12th of May or equal to that at Cold Harbor, on the 3d of June, where Northern historians say he lost fifteen thousand.

In a future article I will tell what happened to us on the 12th of May and how the utter rout of Lee's army was averted and the day resulted in a drawn battle by the good management of some of our officers and the desperate valor of Confederate soldiers and how Grant's army was so badly used up that he withdrew to rest up.

SPOTSYLVANIA, MAY 12, 13, 1864[7]

As I have already said, General Grant doubtless saw that his army had had enough of the great sacrifice of human life, and, fearing its effect on the population at the North as well as upon the army, he decided to try another method by which he hoped to be more successful. Accordingly on the 10th and 11th of May, 1864, there was only desultory skirmishing and a careful examination of our position as far as it was possible to make it. This disclosed to him that one part of our line curved like a horseshoe and was held by a mere skirmish line of defenders. These stood thirty or forty steps apart. The men holding this section of the line were General Johnson's division, all brave and true veteran soldiers, who had won many victories under their able general and his brigade commanders; but their ranks were too thin to hold so long a line of defenders against a determined attack. Behind this semicircle, at some distance to the rear, three regiments of our brigade occupied a short line of works as a reserve. The 31st Georgia occupied the right of the line of reserves, and Company I, under Capt.

[7] *Confederate Veteran*, March 1920, 28:102-103.

G. W. Lewis, held the right of the regiment and consequently was the first of the reserve line to be attacked when the front line was overwhelmed and captured. The previous night was dark and rainy, making the leafy covering of the earth as soft and noiseless as a carpet to the feet of an advancing army. Under this favorable condition the enemy moved up their front line during the night as near General Johnson's position as possible without detection, with instructions to make a bold rush at four o'clock in the morning and capture the position.

Johnson's men, now worn out by fighting seven days and nights almost without intermission, although apprehensive of a surprise, were overcome by fatigue and at this hour were drowsy and half asleep. When the great rush came those who were awake seized their arms, only to find that the rain had wet the percussion caps on their loaded guns so that they refused to fire. The enemy was so near and the attack so well timed that it was almost a complete success. General Johnson himself and two of his brigade commanders, fighting in the darkness and confusion with guns in their hands as private soldiers, were compelled to surrender. A few escaped to the rear, but the bulk of the division fell into the hands of the enemy as prisoners of war. I was told that brave old General Johnson refused to surrender the gun in his hands until they took him and his generals in an army ambulance to General Grant's tent, where he surrendered it to him.

So far all things were well with the enemy and might have resulted in the complete rout and destruction of Lee's weak and sorely tried army. Johnson and his division were captured, and a wide breach in General Lee's line was open through which Grant could pour his thousands. These came up and rushed in to hold the captured position.

But at this critical moment a higher power intervened, and nature spread a mantle of fog over the forest so thick that it was impossible to see an object more than thirty feet away. The few fugitives who escaped capture fell back past the small reserve, and we then knew that our front line was broken. There was little or no shooting on the front line to indicate any fighting, and this alone informed us of the disaster.

I am not superstitious, but I must admit that there are some impressions made at times on the human mind which I cannot understand. Lying in the ditch behind the breastworks at the right of the company and regiment, I awoke out of a troubled sleep with something of a dreadful sensation bearing heavily on my mind. So strong was this impression that I jumped up and began to fold up the blanket under which I had been sleeping, and while doing this I called to Lieut. D. J. McNair, who was still sleeping, to get up and call the men to attention, for I was sure some great trouble for us was impending. He got up immediately and ordered all the others to do so. At this moment some of the fugitives from the front line made their appearance to our right and rear in the dense fog. Lieutenant McNair ordered them to stop, but they were bent on making their escape and went on without giving heed to what was said to them. A moment later, looking in the same direction and only a few feet away, I saw the blue uniforms of the enemy and the distinguishing corps badges on their caps. I brought my gun into proper position and fired at them. They now knew that they were on the flank of our reserve line, and they opened on me and Lieutenant McNair, whom they could see standing up side by side. This volley hastened the movements of every man in the company and regiment. Two balls passed through the breast of McNair's coat, but did not injure him. Our men, seeing themselves outflanked, showed no sign of panic in this sudden attack on our flank and rear; but every man was game and ready to fight if only Captain Lewis, who was in command of the regiment, would get up and form them in line to face the enemy. This Lieutenant McNair urged him to do, but he only drew his blanket about his body more tightly and lay there in the ditch, while we fought over him and around him without any order or system. While we checked the advance of the enemy near us, those farther in our rear continued to advance, at the same time calling to us in language more expressive than chaste to throw down our arms and surrender. This I was determined never to do as long as there was one chance in a hundred to make my escape; and this, I must say, seemed to be the sentiment of all except our captain, who up to this time had shown himself a good and faithful soldier. Poor fellow! I suppose he had lost heart when he knew the situation and thought it useless to make an effort to extricate ourselves from this hopeless predicament. We stood our ground for some time, holding back the enemy; but seeing this to be useless while others were cutting us off from the means of escape, we fell back on Company E, color company of the regiment, where our gallant ensign, Jim Ivey, was waving our old tattered battle flag and calling on the men to form on him and fight. This we did for a time, but, no one being in command to direct our efforts, we were compelled to fall back on the next regiment, which was also fighting without any commander. We fought with these until we saw our last opportunity to escape going to Fort Delaware. When we knew this, we did not stand on the order of our going, but bolted toward the opening in the rear.[8]

When I was a schoolboy I was notably swift on foot and was always chosen in all games that required good runners, but on this occasion I think I broke all previous records until I got out of the woods to where I saw General Lee coming with a little band of ragged soldiers. I was hatless but in this respect was not alone. A few of our men still stood their ground and had to fight their way out through the enemy's line, while others pretended to be dead or wounded and finally escaped. It would make this article too long to mention their experience. The enemy did not hold this ground long until they were driven back by the small force just mentioned. They were formed deliberately in a line which could not have been over a hundred yards long, and General Lee, riding his dappled iron-gray horse, intended to lead the charge; but a soldier stepped out from the ranks, took his horse by the bridle, and led him to the rear. The General's countenance showed that he had despaired and was ready to die rather than see the defeat of his army. Those brave fellows—I do not know who they were—moved forward in good style and struck the enemy in the woods, driving them back over some of the ground from which they had driven our three regiments a few minutes before, but were too few in number to accomplish much. In the meantime, while these events were taking place under my observation, more important movements were going on under the direction of General Gordon, with the other three regiments of our brigade and our sharpshooters. Why he left us there without any one in command, to be surrounded and beaten back, I could never understand. As it was, we accomplished nothing, while the other three regiments and some other troops struck the enemy at another point in their rear and saved our army from utter defeat. But we never succeeded in recovering all the line taken from General Johnson in the early morning. The enemy brought up heavy reenforcements and

---

[8] See Henderson, *Roster*, 3:615. Bradwell gives an excerpt of a letter on Jim Ivey's life in 32:325.

charged our men time and again, exhibiting the greatest bravery, only to be repulsed every time.

The fighting lasted from about day, when Gordon struck them, until 10 P.M. without a moment's intermission. Two days after, when General Grant had withdrawn, our men went over the ground in front of the works to see the result of the fighting and found the enemy's dead lying in heaps in front of the works. The timber in the woods was cut and marred by rifle balls. Grant had left without making any effort to have his dead buried, leaving them there just where they had fallen. Whether they were ever buried I cannot say. This battle, so favorably begun for the enemy, was a complete success for them at first and threatened the destruction of Lee's army. But it failed and resulted in a drawn battle, in which their dead and wounded far exceeded our loss, for three reasons: First, because of the dense fog mentioned above in which the enemy could not maneuver troops advantageously in the area covered by a thick forest just won from us; secondly, the lack of some bold leadership; thirdly, because of General Gordon's remarkable diligence and foresight in hastily assembling a small force and making an attack on the enemy's flank before they had time to reform and fully understand the situation. When the fog cleared away and they had brought up their reenforcements, Gordon had already retaken most of the line, and it afforded the Confederates opportunity to aim more accurately at their splendid lines as they advanced so gallantly to recover the advantage they had won earlier in the day.

If I should attempt to mention the many deeds of heroism exhibited by our men that day or the narrow escapes from death of my comrades and myself, it would make this article too long; but we came out of it all; and while some fell on the battle field afterwards, those who remained fought it out to the end.

The next day (the 13th) General Grant, ever resourceful and never despondent, opened along our whole line with a skirmish fire and an artillery engagement which indicated an intention on his part to assault our whole line. But this was only bluff. He was only doing this to keep our forces expectant while he removed his army away from the dreadful shambles to relieve their minds of his disastrous failure. In this fighting we lost some of our best soldiers, killed or permanently disabled.

I must now refer to myself and tell why I took no part in the subsequent operations of the army for nearly a month. That morning I became violently sick with that malady which destroyed the lives of so many of our men, brought on by continued fighting day and night, poor food poorly prepared, and eating this at any hour whenever there was opportunity to do so. Standing in the breastworks with my comrades, I called the attention of the lieutenant commanding the company to my condition, but he had no authority to excuse me. Later on Col. J. H. Lowe came along the ditch, and I told him the same thing; but he brushed by me and told me the same thing and asked with some warmth where was the assistant surgeon. Of course I did not know, and I concluded I would have to die there in the ditch. But after a second thought he came back to me and said he had no authority to send any one away from the line, but if I was willing to undertake to go to the field hospital with his permit he would give me one. In my desperate condition I was willing to do anything, for remaining there was certain death. I put my gun down and started, but could go only a short distance, when I became so exhausted that I was compelled to lie down. Mustering all my strength, I again managed to get on foot and start again. I repeated this several times until I came to a disabled provost guard standing in the road. He demanded my papers, which I gave him while lying exhausted on the ground. He told me he was sorry for me, seeing how sick I was, but that he could not let me pass; that I would have to see the doctor in command of the line of guards and directed me to his tent, about a hundred yards away from the road. After resting awhile, I managed to get up again and start. When I got to the doctor's tent I fell down as he came up to me, abusing me for everything mean and cowardly. After doing this he went back to his tent and remained awhile. Lying there in my helpless condition, I cannot describe my feelings, especially since I knew I had always done my duty faithfully. After a while he came to me and told me to show him my tongue. For a while I hesitated whether to do so or not, but as I had no choice, I finally did, and he bade me go. When I reached the hospital I found our regimental surgeon, Dr. Judson. Butts, who gave me some brandy and laudanum, which relieved me very much. The next day he sent me and all the sick and wounded to Guinea Station, from which place we were sent to Richmond. When I regained consciousness I found myself in Camp Jackson Hospital. The army in the meantime was beating its way toward Richmond, and on the 2d and 3d of June, while lying on my bunk, I could hear the constant boom of cannon. I knew by this that our men were engaged, and I felt it my duty to return to the army as soon as possible. This I did before I was well and remained with it on the firing line until the last shot was fired at Appomattox.

COLD HARBOR, LYNCHBURG, VALLEY CAMPAIGNS, ETC., 1864[9]

I had been confined to my bed at Camp Jackson nearly three weeks from the time I left my comrades at Spotsylvania, and the army had beaten its way toward Richmond. The thunder of the guns of Lee and Grant seemed to call me to the help of my friends, but I was too weak to respond. The nurse told me after I had gained some strength that I might walk about the aisles of the ward for exercise, and I took advantage of this to go to the spring near by. In going down the narrow path to it some one in the crowd slapped me on the shoulder and accosted me in a familiar tone. Looking around, to my surprise there stood one of my comrades who had been at Camp Jackson some time and had recovered sufficiently to return to the army. He expressed great surprise at seeing me and began to abuse the place and everybody connected with the management of it, saying no gentleman would remain there; that he intended to return to the army immediately and insisted that I must go too. This I could not do, but I promised to comply with his wishes as soon as I had gained strength enough. This did not satisfy him, and he demanded a date when I should leave with him. I told him I would do so the next Wednesday. When the day arrived I was still very feeble, but, remembering my promise, I went to the doctor and asked for a discharge from the

---

[9] *Confederate Veteran*, April 1920, 28:138-139.

hospital to return to my command. Standing up before him in his little office in the yard, with nothing on but the two garments given me by the nurse, I no doubt presented a very poor appearance for a soldier. He looked at me with surprise and said: "You are not well enough to go." I insisted, and he finally consented to let me go if I was willing to take the risk.

I soon joined my comrades and others, who agreed to help me along if I should break down. Although I had fever that night, the next day we reached our comrades, whom we found in the breastworks at Cold Harbor. I gradually grew stronger, and from that time I was on the firing line until the end without the loss of a day. Sitting behind the works, they related to me their experience after I had left them and told me what part they had taken in the great battle of Cold Harbor, fought a few days before my return. In front of our line some two or three hundred yards away could be seen across a level field several lines of works. No one could be seen in them, but no doubt they were occupied. These works were captured by our brigade in the battle, and in this way:

While the fight was in progress on the right of Lee's army, where the main attack was made, the Federal force holding these forts for some reason kept their heads down, and no sign of life could be seen in them. General Gordon, either through curiosity or to make a diversion to relieve the pressure on the right of the army, decided to move forward his command. Accordingly the brigade, which had during my absence been reenforced by the 12th Georgia Battalion, was formed for battle and moved forward across the open space until it came within thirty feet of the enemy's works. Suddenly a whole line of infantry arose and fired a volley. When their heads popped up our men fell flat on their faces immediately, and not a man was hurt. Our men with their loaded guns jumped up and were on top of their works in a moment before the enemy could reload, shooting and bayoneting them without mercy. This was too much for them, and they broke for their reserve line, followed closely by our men, who entered this new line with them.

Frightened by this demoralized mass of friends and their foes all mixed up, they made little or no resistance and fled to their third line. Thinking they had gone far enough, our men stopped their pursuit at this line with the loss of but one man of our regiment. But not so with the 12th battalion. These soldiers, sent to us from Charleston, S. C., had a wonderfully exaggerated idea of the prowess of our brigade from what they had heard of our fighting. I don't know what the orders were, but these fellows, fighting on the right of the brigade, after they had driven the enemy out of two lines of their works, assaulted the third line. Taking these also, they continued to press on the fleeing enemy, and in their ardor of pursuit lost some men. Their commander, Lieutenant Colonel Capers, was badly wounded in the early part of the engagement and never again returned to his command. Some said our new soldiers never stopped in their charge until they went on to Washington. When these brave fellows came to our brigade from Charleston, where they had been holding the pile of bricks in Charleston Harbor which was Fort Sumter, each company contained from one hundred and twenty-five to one hundred and eighty-five men and was as large as one of our decimated regiments. They were the flower of the fighting population of Georgia and showed the same fighting qualities to the end. If any difference ever arose between any two of them, and this was often the case, their comrades would cry out: "Fight, fight!" At this all would run together and form a circle around the two and compel them to have it out with their naked fists. After this the incident was supposed to be forever closed. When they first arrived and began to detrain, our ragged veterans looked at these splendid fellows in their neat gray uniforms and decided they were "pets" and had very little confidence in their fighting quality; but after Cold Harbor they never entertained a doubt that they would stand the test. In every engagement in which our brigade took part they showed the same dash and courage as in this their first fight in Virginia.

But now a dark cloud was rising for Lee's army from the west which threatened to sweep down on Richmond, capture the city, and force the Confederate army to surrender. It was a desperate situation and lacked only bold leadership to succeed; but our old general was equal to the occasion. General Hunter, the Federal commander, was a very timid man and had an exaggerated idea of the numbers and resources of his enemy. No sooner had our two small divisions (Gordon's and Rodes's) faced him at Lynchburg than he beat a hasty retreat to the mountains of West Virginia without a fight, although he outnumbered us three to one. When Lee's army was grappling with Grant's there was only a small force in the Valley to protect it, and Hunter came out of the mountains of West Virginia and had his own way, destroying and burning that beautiful section of country. After doing this to his satisfaction he crossed the Blue Ridge unopposed and marched to Lynchburg, which place was undefended except by a few old men too weak in number and equipment to offer any resistance. Here he paused and began to fortify his position as if he were face to face with a formidable foe. Grant dispatched Sheridan with ten thousand well-equipped cavalry to ride around the left of Lee's army, tear up the railroad to Gordonsville, and proceed to Lynchburg, where he expected him to unite with Hunter. But all this resulted in an ignominious failure.

A week after the great battle of Cold Harbor we were lying peacefully behind the breastworks there with no idea that we were about to enter upon a great campaign in an entirely different direction, which would eventually take us to the defenses at Washington and in sight of the Capitol.

We were withdrawn from the defenses and placed in camps in the rear of the army, where we were allowed to rest two days. We then set out on the march and soon reached the railroad, which we found to be completely destroyed by Sheridan's army. When we reached the vicinity of Trevilian Station dead horses were everywhere in evidence, and the whole country showed the effects of the battle that had been fought there a few days before between Gen. Wade Hampton and Sheridan. This, I suppose, was the greatest cavalry battle fought during the war and was a complete victory for the Confederates. When General Lee heard of Sheridan's movements, he sent General Hampton with his cavalry, perhaps not more than thirty-five hundred men in all, to intercept him while engaged in destroying the railroad. This he did at Trevilian, and a fight ensued which lasted all day and convinced Hampton that he was overmatched. He accordingly adopted the same stratagem which Lee and Jackson had employed at Chancellorsville and with equally as good success. He left a thin line in front of Sheridan, with orders in the morning, when the enemy advanced, to fight and fall back, allowing a piece of artillery occasionally to fall into the hands of the enemy. This was to continue until they should hear two cannon shots in quick succession in the enemy's rear, when they were to turn and fight. Hampton, with his main force, made a wide detour, riding all night, and in the morning he found himself in Sheridan's rear. As he expected, the Federal cavalry made their attack at daylight and were driving the Confederates in fine style, when suddenly the boom of cannon in their rear told them too plainly that their wagon trains, artillery, and all their army equipment had fallen into the hands of the Confederates. Finding themselves attacked in front and rear at the same time and all their baggage captured, every man broke to seek safety in flight. The Confederates followed them day and night until completely overcome with fatigue, capturing a great part of the force. The remnant made their escape to the rear of Grant's line.

We hastened on, following the line of the railroad until we came to some old ramshackle trains on a piece of patched-up track. These took us some distance to where we had to foot it again to Charlottesville, where we entrained again for Lynchburg, which we reached before Sunday. We marched through the town and were greeted joyfully by the people as we passed through the place. Just beyond the suburbs we saw Hunter's long line of breastworks. It was now too late in the day to make the attack; and as Rodes had not as yet arrived with his division and the artillery, General Early decided to wait until the next day to begin active operations. During the night Rodes came up, and by morning we had a line of works in front of Hunter and some artillery mounted. That day was spent in skirmishing and some artillery firing along the whole line. Every preparation was made to assault the enemy's works at daylight the next morning, but to our surprise, the enemy had fled during the night and had several hours' start of us in their flight for the mountains of West Virginia. A small force of cavalry was sent ahead to press their rear, while we hastened to follow them.

This was the beginning of some of our hardest marching during the war, the enemy making every effort to escape and General Early urging us to the utmost to overtake them. Small bodies of Federal prisoners were coming to the rear continually, and many abandoned army wagons and other impedimenta were passed on the road. The march was continued until late at night every day, and the armies bivouacked in sight of each other's camp fires until Hunter finally escaped into the mountain passes of West Virginia. We now turned back. The tired army went into camp and rested. Old Jube regretted very much that Hunter had outrun him and made his escape. He wanted him for the atrocities committed on the helpless people of the Valley of Virginia. He now turned his face in another direction to make a demonstration against Washington. D. C., no doubt under orders from General Lee to relieve the pressure of Grant against Richmond and to give employment to a great part of the fighting force of the Lincoln government. How well this was done will be the subject of a future article.

EARLY'S MARCH TO WASHINGTON IN 1864[10]

In our rapid movement from Richmond to Lynchburg we had left all our wagon trains and other army equipment, except the horses belonging to the generals and their staffs, far behind. These had now come up, rations were issued to us, and after a day of rest we were ready to begin our long march to Washington D. C. The fresh mountain air of this fine country had a favorable effect on the spirits of our men after having been confined to ditches behind breastworks in rain and mud with gun in hand while facing Grant's army. But there was much fighting and hard marching in store for us.

We took the main pike road leading north to the Potomac, which we forded and went by way of Frederick City, Md., and after a stay at that place (Washington) of one day recrossed the Potomac and leisurely pursued our way into the Valley again. But all this was not without much fighting, in all of which the enemy was defeated until in September, when we fought the great drawn battle at Winchester, after which fortune seemed to have been against us, and our little army was finally withdrawn from the Valley and once more incorporated with Lee's army to share with it in the closing disastrous events of the war.

---

[10] Ibid., May 1920, 28:176-177. Paragraphs deleted from this article to eliminate duplication. For another account of Early's march to Washington see 22:438.

The first place of importance on our route was Lexington, where the Virginia Military Academy was located. Before we entered the town we marched into the city cemetery with our arms reversed and heads uncovered, for here was the grave of our famous old commander, Gen. Stonewall Jackson. As we filed around his grave I felt that I was stepping on holy ground, the last resting place of a Christian hero. Tears came into the eyes of many as they remembered the splendid leadership of this wonderful man. Truly the hand of Divine Providence was with him. His name will be an inspiration to the South and the world as long as history is written. His name carries with it everything that is true and noble. He presented to the world the greatest military genius at the same time the most devout Christian faith. All modern military critics consider him the greatest general of ancient or modern times.

Our next stop was at Staunton, where we had clothing issued to us, for we were in rags. Here we rested a day and on the next resumed our march for the Potomac. Our small cavalry force drove off all the enemy found ahead us, and we had no trouble with them until we had crossed the river into Maryland. We reached Martinsburg on July 3 late in the evening and spoiled the great Fourth of July celebration which was to come off the next day. After tearing up the railroad for some distance, we went to Shepherdstown and waded the river, destroyed a number of canal boats, and that evening surrounded the fort on Maryland Heights over looking Harper's Ferry. This was a formidable position held by a considerable force. We skirmished with them a part of two days and made them believe it was our intention to take the place by assault, and under cover of one of darkest of nights we marched silently away. In this fight some of our men were injured by the enemy's shells. When day dawned we marched by our men who had preceded lying wrapped up in their blankets, sweetly sleeping in fields. Poor fellows! Some of them were taking their last sleep in this world. Passing them, we bivouacked, and after an hour's rest and eating a breakfast of our rough rations resumed our march toward Frederick City, Md., little thinking we were that day to fight beyond that town one of most sanguinary battles of our experience.

As we were crossing a low mountain range several miles west of that place we heard the boom of cannon in front, for our cavalry, in advance of the infantry, were in touch with the Federal army under command of

Gen. Lew Wallace, and the battle of Monocacy Creek had already begun. As the white smoke of our artillery beyond the town rose to view we hastened on, joking with each other, thinking lightly of it, only supposing it to be a force of militia which we would brush aside without any loss on our part; but in this we were sadly deceived.[11]

Walking over this battle field in 1914 I saw the excellent judgment Wallace displayed in the selection of this place to meet our army. The road from Frederick City to Washington, D. C. crosses the Monocacy two or three miles southeast of that place. A short distance east of the bridge a road leads off in a northwestern direction to Baltimore. Wallace formed his army with these roads to his back, so that he could retreat on either of them if necessary. His right was protected by the Monocacy, and we could not attack him from that direction nor get our artillery over to assist us in the fight. Gordon took our brigade by a wide detour to the south, where we managed to ford the river and come to the help of the cavalry, which had already been used up in the initial clash with the Federal cavalry. Our brigade was formed behind a low wooded mountain range out of sight of the enemy, who were formed, as I have said, with their back to the Washington Pike. Orders were given to

---

[11] For another account of the Battle of Monocacy see 36:55-57. Bradwell made the following comments on Monocacy in 40:238.

> This battle was fought principally by Gordon's Georgia Brigade, nobly assisted by the Virginians and Louisianians, who came up in time to drive Gen. Lew Wallace's army from its well-chosen position. The units of this command were the 13th, 26th, 31st, 38th, 60th, and 61st Regiments and the 12th Battalion, but the 38th was not with us in this fight, having been left behind to guard prisoners. The headstones placed by the U. D. C. in that cemetery will show for all time the casualties in the number of killed sustained by these regiments.
>
> I want the survivors of this battle, if there are any, to go with me to the place which has been made a park by the U. S. Government to attend the celebration which is planned to take place there on July 9, 1932. Those who are promoting this celebration wish to have present some old veterans who took part in the battle. Surely there are some of the old brigade besides myself still alive.
>
> Write to me at Brantley, Ala., or to Judge Glenn H. Worthington, Frederick, Md.

advance quietly over the ridge, where it was thought we would strike their left flank in the open field. We were then to charge them with the usual yell. We advanced in fine style over the mountain, but when we came to the open field we found their lines adjusting to meet us, and our yell was answered by a well-aimed volley which seriously wounded Gen. Clement A. Evans and Captain Gordon, his aide, and killed or wounded every regimental commander in the brigade, besides many of our company officers. The private soldiers were all veterans and knew what to do. They rushed at the enemy in the field and drove them to a sunken road, which they held against our left so well that our men became discouraged at their heavy loss, and finally succeeded in driving them out of their position only with the timely assistance of the gallant little remnant of the Louisiana ("Tigers") Brigade. These, after wading the river, struck the Federals on their flank and routed them. On the right the enemy was well posted in the Thomas residence and in the grove around the house, and as the 12th Battalion came up in the open field to attack them they sustained considerable loss. Finally our artillerymen got one of their guns across the river and placed it in position in the yard back of the Worthington residence. With this they opened on the enemy in the Thomas house with such deadly effect that the 12th routed the enemy from that place. In the meantime in the center we had routed them from the road leading from the Thomas place to the bridge and driven them to the protection of the Washington Pike. Behind the banks of this they maintained a stiff resistance, but were finally driven out after their right and left had fled. The enemy took the road to Baltimore, pursued by our cavalry to that place, and the next day we resumed our march to Washington.

Before the fight closed in the center there were only four men still offering resistance to the enemy behind the banks of the road. When the last squad of these ran away, my three companions and I stood in amazement and looked around. The fighting had come to a close so suddenly that we could not at first take in the situation. In every direction scattered over the field could be seen guns, army blankets, and other equipment cast off by the enemy, and on a hillside to the left a number of wounded Federals. A fire burning the wheat straw was making its way slowly toward these. Seeing their danger and hearing their cries for help, we picked up tent flies and fought the flames, which we finally subdued. The wounded men expressed their gratitude to us and begged us to fill their canteens for them. This we did and left them there for the litter bearers, who, we knew, would be along after awhile.

My curiosity led me back to the pike to see the result of our firing. As I went I picked up new blankets, linen tent flies, and such things as our men needed, and piled them up in the road. I then sat down on the bank and awaited the assembling of our men. Each one as he came showed where he was hit. I had nine bullet holes through my blanket to show. The enemy left their dead where they fell, how many I do not now remember. We had won a complete victory, but at a great sacrifice to us. The casualties of the Confederates in this engagement fell almost entirely on Gordon's Brigade and amounted to not less than five hundred men killed and wounded, while that of the enemy was much less. All of these were veterans of many battle fields, some of whom bore the scars of many wounds. Except the Louisianians, this battle was fought by Gordon's Brigade, which the numerous graves of our command in the cemetery at Frederick City will show.

We left our wounded at Frederick City to fall into the hands of the enemy, and the next day early we resumed our march to Washington, which we reached unopposed. We were all anxious to capture the city, and especially to get "Old Abe" in our hands. We wanted him for the atrocities he allowed his armies to commit wherever they went in the South. He was aware of these, but never did he do or say a thing to abate these outrages against civilization – outrages equal to those of the Germans in France. Much has been said of his kindness and sympathy, but as far as I could see from our standpoint his heart must have been as hard as flint. His assassination gave his friends cause to place his name among their deities, and many of his former enemies regretted his demise and thought it a calamity to the South; but Abe Lincoln had neither the will nor the ability to do anything for the people of the South. He always showed himself the willing tool of the extreme element in his political party, and these he did not dare offend. He was taken off at the moment of his highest achievement, and his friends were then determined to have their own way with their fallen foes, and they would not allow any obstacle to curb their resentment in the passage and execution of their Reconstruction measures. These were the result of their hatred and were more grievous to the South than the war itself.

As we marched by the Blair house [on 13 July near Silver Springs] it was wrapped in flames. No one knows who fired it. Some say it was set on fire by the enemy's shells, but this could not be, for their aim was too high. Others say it was done by General Early's orders, but he denied after the war that he had it done. I suspect it was done by some of our men who were exasperated by the numerous wanton crimes of the Federal soldiers in the South.

We stopped at Leesburg for a short rest and resumed our march to the Valley. As we were crossing the Blue Ridge the enemy's cavalry made a bold dash on our long train of wagons in the rear and captured some of them, but our men soon drove them away. And now we were once more in old Virginia among our loyal friends to begin anew a campaign against great odds in which we gave employment to five times our own number and killed or captured more of the enemy than our forces numbered.

THE BATTLE OF
MIDDLETOWN, VA.[12]

Never having seen any account of the battle of Middletown, Va., July 1, 1864, and feeling that the history of General Early's operations in the Valley would be incomplete without it, I have undertaken to write it up for the readers of the VETERAN now, quite sixty-six years after it occurred. Every scrap of our history ought to be preserved for future generations.

I suppose there is no town, village, or hamlet in the entire length of that beautiful valley that did not witness one or more engagements during the course of the war in the sixties.

---

[12] Ibid., September 1930, 38:345-346. Paragraphs deleted from this article to eliminate duplication. Editor.

How many fights were staged at this place at different times during that painful period of our history no one can tell, for there was much fighting there from first to last. I witnessed two or more myself as a participant, but this one that I am trying to write about was rather unique, as it was fought by my regiment alone, on the part of the Confederates, against a large force of Yankee cavalry as our opponents. We deserved little credit, but rather some censure for what we did, though we saved our long trains from any interference on the retreat — the very thing which we were sent to do.

We always looked on this affair as rather a reflection on our proud record as fighters. But the enemy failed to do what they set out to accomplish, and were defeated with loss by a comparatively small force. They caused a few casualties in our ranks, it is true, but failed to reach our trains or inflict any other loss on Early's forces. What loss they sustained, I do not know, but evidently it must have been considerable, since they charged our boys time and again across a wide and open field in an effort to break through our line concealed in the woods, where every man was hid behind a tree or other object to protect himself from the balls of the enemy.

They ran [during the skirmish] because they had good reason, and we ran when there was no great cause for us to do so. They accomplished nothing, and retired evidently satisfied that they had enough for that day.

After General Early had returned to the Valley from his raid on Washington, the authorities there sent large forces to surround him from several sides and capture him and his army, as punishment for his presumptuous audacity.

All these Early defeated and drove back across the Potomac. His army was scattered about in the lower part of the Valley when he found that the enemy were making other preparations, hoping to cut him off from his communications with his base while he was engaged with those in front.

A large force of cavalry was sent to cross the Blue Ridge Mountains through the gap at Front Royal and get into his rear, while those in front would again assume the offensive. But all this failed. As soon as Early understood their plans, he began a retreat which lasted until he reached Rude's Hill,(*) near Strasburg. His line of march was along the main valley pike. From the gap in the mountains at Front Royal there is a road that intersects the pike at Middletown. On this road the cavalry were advancing to attack our long line of trains and capture our wagons and artillery.

General Early had our regiment, 31st Georgia, detached and sent up this road to hold the enemy until his army could pass this point on his route. This was a bold movement on the part of the enemy, and certainly no small force would have undertaken it with any hope of success. I suppose we had gone a mile or more when our Colonel stopped and deployed his men in a piece of woods with a wide-open field in front to the east. We had at that time not more than one hundred and fifty men in our ranks, having been decimated in all the previous campaigns, and when deployed in skirmish formation, we extended perhaps five hundred yards. The right of the regiment where I stood was in the open field in a depression, and took no part in the fighting. That was done by the companies in the center and on the left. When we reached this place, we did not have to wait long for the arrival of the enemy. They soon came in sight across the field about four hundred yards away, and, immediately forming their squadrons, came in a headlong charge on our boys, hoping to break through this thin line and dash on and capture our trains. But when they came near they were received with such warm cordiality that they deemed it best to retire and let others try their hand. This they did time and again, and the fighting was fast and furious, but always with the same result to the enemy.

After this had gone on quite awhile, looking to the left I saw to my astonishment, our old Colonel going through that piece of woods to the rear in full flight. He seemed to be utterly demoralized and getting away from the fighting ten feet at every jump. He was evidently panic stricken and was acting in the most undignified manner for a field officer, who ought to be a brave man and a model for all his men.[13]

Some of his men in the center must have seen him and decided it was time for them to do likewise. Then all on the left, seeing their comrades leaving, broke for the rear in great disorder. Thinking from their unusual conduct that some disaster must have happened to our fellows, some of us on the right started off in a trot to overtake them.

---

[13] Bradwell refers to Colonel John H. Lowe.

After I had gone a short distance, I heard Lieutenant McN—, our company commander, call to me, and he asked what I was running for. As I could see no reason for it, only that it was the popular thing to do just at that time, I stopped and waited for him to come up. As he approached me slowly, I could see that he was mad as a wet hen. After we had passed through the woods, we saw a number of Confederate officers sitting on their horses behind a fence some distance ahead of us. I suppose when our Colonel saw them it had a quieting effect on his nerves, and he slowed up so that when we reached him he was cool enough to form the regiment and to march off with it to the brigade. The enemy made no further demonstrations from that direction that day, and I heard nothing more about our bad conduct until the following winter.[14]

Our regiment had at this time only one Captain left, Captain M—. All the others were either killed, disabled, or in prison; and he might have been in the same fix also, but he had not been with us much—had been at home or sick a great part of the time; yet he was a gritty little fellow and felt the disgrace of this affair very keenly. He attributed it all to the bad conduct of our Colonel. He worried over this incident very much, and to wipe out the disgrace which he considered resting on the regiment, he took it upon himself to prefer charges against the Colonel—a very dangerous thing for a captain to do, for court-martials were not always just in their decisions.[15]

Now, in talking about this fight with my comrades some time afterwards, I remarked that our Colonel was not the only one who ran away and acted badly that day; that we all had done so and were to

---

[14] Bradwell refers to Lt. Daniel McNair. Henderson, *Roster*, 3:643. "Lt. Daniel McNair. 4th corporal November 11, 1861. Appointed 1st Sergeant May 13, 1862. Elected Jr. 2d Lieutenant October 1, 1862. Captured at Fredericksburg, Va., December 13, 1862. Exchanged December 17, 1862. Elected 1st Lieutenant February 1863. Surrendered, Appomattox, Va., April 9, 1865."

[15] "Capt. M—" refers to Captain Nicholas W. Miller of Company H, 31st Georgia Regiment. Henderson, *Roster*, 3:636. "2d Lieutenant November 13, 1861. Elected 1st Lieutenant December 1, 1861. Captured at Sharpsburg, Md. September 17, 1862. Released November 11, 1862. Elected Captain June 1, 1863. Wounded at Hatcher's Run, Va. February 6, 1865. Captured in Richmond Va. hospital April 3, 1865. Died, result from amputation of left leg, in Fair Ground Hospital June 5, 1865. Remarks: "Embalmed and sent home.""

blame. Some how this went to the Colonel. The following winter, we were sent back to Lee's army and allowed to build huts for the winter at Hatcher's Run below Petersburg, though we did not enjoy them very long.

One evening I was surprised to receive a message from the Colonel to come to his headquarters at eight o'clock, as he wanted to see me on business. What business could the Colonel have with me, only a private soldier in the rank?

Promptly at the hour I "reported" and was ushered into his big tent, where I found the Colonel, Dr. B— and Dr. F—, and perhaps others, seated before a warm fire.[16]

The Colonel politely requested all to retire, as he wished to talk with me alone. As soon as they had gone and were out of hearing, he drew from the breast pocket of his coat a long official envelope, and I could see from his manner that he was very angry.

Tears were in his eyes as he said: "Charges have been brought against me for cowardice, and who do you suppose brought them? Captain M—." He called Captain M—'s name with great contempt, as if he were the last man to bring such a charge against anybody.

He then told me that perhaps he would want me before the court as a witness and would let me know.

I was very glad that he did not call for me to testify, for I could not say any thing in his favor; but as it might have been expected, he was acquitted and brave little Captain M— had acquired the Colonel's bitter resentment.

When the findings of this court came to the Colonel, we had just formed our ranks to march off some where, and Captain M— was standing at the head of his Company ready to march with it. The Colonel mounted his horse at his tent and rode up to Captain M—, and, trembling with rage, drew from his pocket the charges, then, shaking his sword in a very threatening manner over Captain M—'s head, said: "I will remember you, Sir, for this."

Poor, brave Captain M—. He was always with us after this and never lost a day until his fatal wounding and death, which took place not long after.

---

[16] "Dr. B" is Dr. Judson Butts. Editor.

Thirty years after this little incident, I met one of my old comrades in Alabama whom I had not seen since, asked him how it was that he had disappeared from our ranks. He asked me if I remembered the fight our regiment had with the Yankees at Middletown. At first I couldn't recall the incident. He told me a comrade was shot in this engagement and he assisted him out to an ambulance in the rear, and, while helping the wounded man to get in, he himself was shot. He was sent to the hospital, was furloughed home, and when recovered enough to return to the army, found himself cut off from his command by Sherman's army. After thinking about it, it all came back to my mind. I wonder how many of my young comrades of that glorious regiment are still alive—I should be pleased to hear from any of them.

(*)But Old Jube didn't go much further until he stopped to give his enemies time to come up and fight if they wanted to do that.

He waited at Rude's Hill for them, but when they came in sight they did not seem anxious for an engagement. After he had failed to bring on hostilities, he decided to assume the offensive and, during the next week, General Mulligan, their commander, was killed, and all of the forces sent to Captain Early and his army were on the north side of the Potomac except those who lost their lives in the fighting, or were prisoners.

It was the merest good luck for them that any of them escaped. A full account of all this I wrote for the readers of the VETERAN several years ago. In the subsequent fighting under Early in this campaign and afterwards, even to the end, this regiment did its full duty and the little incident at Middletown had no bad effect on the minds of our men.

They were ever ready to suffer and die, if necessary, for the cause they had defended so long.

———————

ON TO WASHINGTON[17]

On the 10th of July, 1914, just fifty years after the battle of Monocacy, in company with Judge Glenn H. Worthington, who was reared on the ground, I walked over the location to refresh my memory; after which he took me to the city cemetery, where the good people of the community had buried the bodies of my comrades who were killed on that occasion in a long straight row near the grave of Francis Scott Key, author of "The Star-Spangled Banner," to rest until the judgment day. At the head of each grave stands a small white marble slab with the name and regiment on each; but on these I noticed some mistakes. Our pioneer corps had hastily buried our dead the next morning where they had fallen, but they later received a more decent burial as I have said, at the hands of our good friends of the place.

This battle ended suddenly an hour or more before sundown and after I had walked over a part of the ground where my brigade had fought, and had gathered up all the plunder I thought my comrades would want and piled it up in the middle of the Georgetown Pike, I sat down on the bank of the road to rest and to await their return. I then called their attention to the pile of goods and told them to help themselves; but none cared to take any of it except one little fellow, and the next morning, when we set out for Washington, he looked like a foot peddler with his pack on his back.

We stacked arms and bivouacked there on the north side of the pike, and the next morning at dawn we were in ranks and on the march.

The next day, the 11th of July, when we were still several miles from the city, the enemy in the works around the town opened on us with their big guns. As these shells passed high over our heads, our boys in the ranks laughed at the marksmanship of the "melish" behind the guns. We knew then that our enemies were a set of fellows untrained and badly frightened. When these big shells came over and exploded far in the rear, I suggested to my comrades that the enemy was shelling our wagon trains; but none of them did us or the teams any harm. They made the greatest noise of any guns I heard during the whole war.

---

[17] *Confederate Veteran*, March 1928, 38:95-96. Paragraphs deleted from this article to eliminate duplication. Editor.

These shells, in passing through the air, reminded me of the noise made by a railroad train.

We were all in high spirits and felt that we were about to enter the city with little or no opposition, where we would drag "Old Abe" out, hiding somewhere there, and carry him in triumph off with us as a trophy to show our comrades on the other side of the Potomac.

That evening, I and others of Gordon's Brigade, were put ahead of the infantry as a vanguard to arrest any of our men too eager to be first to enter the city, and, therefore, we were among the first to come in sight of the place.

Out in front of Fort Stephens we halted and formed our line. Skirmishers were thrown out, and the usual preliminaries of battle began. The enemy, behind their earthworks, busy sending far over our beads their big missiles, as large as a nail keg, but doing no damage, when General Gordon ordered up a battery of twenty-pound Parrott field pieces, pretty good guns themselves. These brave gunners unlimbered in front of the brigade out in the open field in full view of the Yanks about four hundred yards away, and replied, knocking up the red dirt around the muzzles of the big fellows in the fort, while the enemy continued to aim at the moon and stars. The report of these, our biggest guns, sounded like firecrackers or popguns in comparison.

The sun was still shining in the bright blue western sky, and we lay there expecting every moment the command to arise and advance. But this order, to our regret, never came, and, after lying there that night and part of the next day, we marched away toward the fords of the Potomac, which we waded without any loss or inconvenience.

General Early's wagon trains, prisoners, and stock captured in the enemy's territory, stretched out a long way, and he managed well to cross a wide and deep stream and return to Virginia without loss. After we got across, we marched leisurely away toward Leesburg, while a battery located on a hill overlooking the river drove back the Yankee cavalry, which had followed us from Washington.

When we reached a large blue spring near that place, we bivouacked and, after we were fully rested, resumed our march to Snicker's Gap, where we crossed over the Blue Ridge into the Shenandoah Valley to camp and rest. But that did not come to us. The forces assembled at Washington to capture Early were sent after him with very little success, as I have already related in previous articles.

On this last day's march, we stopped on the roadside to take our usual ten minutes' rest at a barn surrounded by a high plank fence made of one-by-twelve oak boards. Not far off was the residence of the owner of the barn, all old gentleman perhaps sixty-five years old. As soon as he saw us, he came out to where we were, smiling, and said:

> Right here, boys, not long ago, I saw one of the smartest tricks of the whole war. One evening late Mosby and his men, about thirty, came in a gallop, opened the big gate, rode in, unsaddled their horses, closed the gate, and began to prepare to spend the night. They didn't put out any pickets to guard against a surprise, and in a few minutes after their arrival a whole battalion of Yankees that had been riding hard after them that evening came up and surrounded the place, Mosby and his men.
>
> When I saw what had happened, I clapped my hands together and said: 'They've got old Mosby this time sure.' But not a bit of it. Without taking time to bridle and saddle their horses, they mounted them with only halters on their heads and, with pistols and swords in their hands, they threw open the big gate and rode boldly out among their enemies, and every one escaped.

It was wonderful what this man Mosby accomplished here inside the Yankee lines. His captures kept the Confederate army supplied with much that they needed, and he gave employment to a large body of the enemy that would have been otherwise free to operate against Early in the Valley or Lee at Richmond. He and his men were desperate, knowing as they did that if they fell into the hands of the enemy it meant death.

I should be pleased to hear from any Confederate soldier who was with us in this campaign. I do not know of a single man now living who had a part in these stirring events. On this long march many of our men were in rags. Our company, now reduced to a mere squad, was under command of Corp. John W. Thursby, whose pantaloons were worn off up to his knees; but a truer or better soldier never lived.

WHEN GENERAL MULLIGAN
WAS KILLED[18]

On the 24th of July, 1864, near Kernstown, a suburb of Winchester, Va., where more battles were fought during the war of the sixties than anywhere else in the South, occurred the death of James A. Mulligan, commanding Federal forces. He was a brave old Irishman, and, like many of his countrymen who were fighting on our side, lost his life for a cause he considered right. In one of these numerous engagements in the Valley between the Confederates under Early and the Yankees under Sheridan, we lost brave old Colonel Monahan, of the 5th Louisiana Regiment, at the time in command of his brigade. Too corpulent to keep up in a headlong charge, he always rode his splendid bay horse to carry him over ditches and rough ground. He was leading his men when a ball passed through his body and ended his career as a soldier of the Confederacy.

When Cleveland was elected President, he rewarded Mulligan's widow, who was living in Chicago at the time, by appointing her postmaster at that city in place of Mrs. Logan, widow of General Logan, who was very popular with his political party at the time.

After our demonstration against Washington, D. C., we retraced our route and waded the Potomac at White's Ferry into Virginia, and rested awhile at Leesburg. The next day we reentered the Valley at Snicker's Gap and made our camps nearby in the open country. By some oversight, our officers neglected to leave any pickets in the Gap to guard against a sudden approach of the enemy, who were following after us to capture, if possible, our wagon trains.

Late in the afternoon of July 18, a large force of their cavalry, finding this place unoccupied, placed their artillery there and opened on the camp of Gordon's Brigade. Our men seized their arms and were ready to meet their attack; but another large force, at the same time having

---

[18] Ibid., January 1927, 35:14-15.

crossed the mountains farther to the north, advanced on us from that direction. These two divisions united, and we had quite a fight with them, which lasted till a late hour of the night. While we occupied their attention in front, General Rodes struck them unexpectedly on the flank and routed them, killing and capturing many of them. The next day we followed after them many miles to the north in a running fight, in which there were few casualties on our side.

But this was only a part of the enemy's plan. I suppose the authorities at Washington were exasperated by the boldness of General Early in his attack on the national capital, and they determined to send a large force to the Valley to capture him and his whole army. This, the main army, was advancing from Shepherdstown in Early's rear along the Valley Pike.

As soon as he was made aware of this, Early began a retreat to the vicinity of Strasburg, where he rested his army two or three days and awaited developments.

In the meantime reenforcements for the Confederates arrived; and since the enemy had stopped their advance near Kernstown for some reason and did not show any disposition to fight, Early assumed the offensive and decided to capture General Mulligan and his army.

I don't know how many men he had, but from the length of his line of battle, which extended at least three miles, he must have had several divisions.

The enemy's line when we drew up in front of them extended from southwest to northeast about that distance. It was evident to the minds of the Confederates, as soon as the skirmishing began, that aggressive leadership was lacking in the ranks of the enemy, and that victory would be easy.

But that was not what Early wanted. It was his purpose to capture the whole force sent against him and show the authorities at Washington his contempt for their effort to take him and his army. His plan was to make a heavy demonstration along the whole line except on the enemy's extreme left, where General Breckinridge was to face on them in a rapid charge, so as to get into their rear, when the whole line would move forward and rout the enemy, thus cut off from any way of escape toward the Potomac and safety.

Everything was carried out according to the plan. Breckinridge moved forward, and a bitter engagement began. The enemy was driven forward, and we who were facing Mulligan and his men on their extreme right could hear, far to the north, the angry rattle of musketry and the boom of artillery, and we knew that our men were far in the rear of those we were facing. We were lying flat on our faces in a piece of woodland to avoid the balls of the enemy, while our skirmishers, concealed in a ravine below us, were having a lively time with those of our friend Mulligan over the way around a large handsome brick residence and apple orchard about the premises. This house must have been his headquarters, for here he was mortally wounded perhaps by the sharpshooters of Gordon's Brigade and taken into it, where he died that night. He must have endeared himself to the occupants of the house by his kindness to them, for we heard that his death was very much regretted by them and all who knew him.

But the noise of battle in their rear was a warning to the enemy in our front which they were not slow to heed, and they proved to us that they had as good legs as we had and knew how to use them when in a tight place. Seeing their lines beginning to waver, the whole Confederate force moved forward in a rush, but the fighting, though sharp, was over in a few minutes, for the enemy, after the wounding of their general, had lost heart and thought of nothing but making their way to the fords of the Potomac and safety in their fortified position on Maryland Heights. They managed to escape from Breckinridge in their rapid flight. We pursued them through Winchester to Stephenson's Depot, and then camped after dark. The cavalry pressed after them, now fleeing in great confusion, and found the road strewn with abandoned wagons, ambulances, dead horses, and every manner of army equipment.

As we rushed past the residence where Mulligan was lying wounded, we could hear him groaning, and we were told about the circumstance. Though an enemy, we could not refrain from sympathizing with him in his suffering, for he had the reputation of being a magnanimous foe.

General Mulligan had served early in the war out in Missouri against General Price, and, if I am not mistaken, was captured by the Confederates.

Among the soldiers of this army who saved themselves from capture with the greatest difficulty was Maj. William McKinley, who afterwards was elected President of the United States. It so impressed him that he never forgot his experience in this affair.

General Breckinridge's failure to push in a little farther so as to block the Valley Pike alone saved them.

What old Jube would have done with so large a bunch of prisoners at a time when all Southern prisons were overflowing with captives is a question.

WITH EARLY IN THE VALLEY[19]

To describe in detail all the battles and skirmishes with the enemy from the time we returned to the valley from the march to Washington—about two months—until the great battle of Winchester, September 19, 1864, would require too much space; but in all this fighting we invariably routed the enemy. Early's activities were a great source of uneasiness to Lincoln, who was always nervous and apprehensive for his own safety at Washington. It was decided to send a picked force from Grant's army large enough, with those already there, to overwhelm Early's little army and destroy or capture it. These were armed with breech-loading rifles, and every man was a seasoned soldier and well equipped. Sheridan was selected to command the army, which numbered nearly four times as many as the Confederates. Ten thousand of these were well-mounted veteran cavalry. He collected the various commands which had been operating against Early into one compact army and took position behind a range of mountains to the east of Winchester and adopted the Fabian policy of delay. He was now between Washington and the Confederates, and no doubt the authorities there felt easier. These tactics continued so long that General Early, who knew that heavy reenforcements had come, felt a contempt

---

[19] Ibid., November 1914, 22:504-506. For another account of this battle see 28:218-220.

for Sheridan and his big army. But I would call attention to the fact that the range of mountains not only shielded the Federal army from view, but their signal stations on top of it had a fine view of all the valley and every movement of Early's army and all of his maneuvers.

This was the status when Early, for some unaccountable reason, decided to take Gordon's Division, which was about half of his small army, and a few cavalry and go away from Winchester, where his presence was so necessary, to Martinsburg, about twenty-one miles to the north. He left General Rodes with the rest of the army, about six thousand men, to hold Sheridan in check. This movement was signaled to Sheridan from the top of the mountain range, and he saw that his opportunity had at last come. He now set his army in motion and crossed the mountains and the Opequon River at its base and attacked Rodes in a spiritless engagement.

This was on the 18th of September. General Early proceeded on his wild goose chase and late that evening arrived at his destination after his cavalry had driven the Federal cavalry out of the town. Just as his infantry arrived, tired from their long march, a courier came in great haste from General Rodes with the news that fighting was in progress, that his force was not able to hold the enemy in check, and that our communication with the rear was about to be cut. Early marched his men back that night over the same road by which he had come and bivouacked at Bunker Hill, about halfway on his return to Winchester. Long before day the army was in motion, and about nine or ten o'clock in the morning we could see far to the south small knots of white smoke in the blue sky made by bursting shells and hear the sound of artillery. Before we reached the vicinity of the fighting, we left the main pike to the right and traveled somewhat parallel with it, but bearing a little farther to the east. Flankers were thrown out on our left to prevent our falling into an ambuscade. When we had reached a point about east of Winchester our brigade took up a position in the edge of a forest in a deep but narrow ravine, with high ground in front. Here our line was formed, and skirmishers advanced to open the engagement with the enemy.

As these brave fellows started to move forward some one said to them: "Go and drive those Yankees away; we don't want to be bothered with them." In another moment, to our surprise, they came running back to us down the steep hill in great confusion, and our men shouted: "What's the matter? What' the matter?" The reply was: "You'll soon see." Colonel Lowe, of the 31st Georgia Regiment, who was seated on his horse at the head of his command and could see farther from his more elevated position, called out to the entire brigade: "Forward! Forward!" Sheridan's whole line of infantry, supported by another in the rear and extending far to our right and left, was coming down the hill on us, without supports on our flanks.

Here it is proper to say that at this time the brave and accomplished Rodes was bringing up his old division to our help when, unfortunately for us and the South, he was killed by a shell, and the army lost one of its greatest generals.

We were hidden from them, and they were not expecting to meet us so suddenly. At the command of Colonel Lowe the brigade moved up the hill as one man and found themselves face to face with the enemy's line advancing with their arms at "right shoulder shift." Without waiting a moment, a sheet of fire flashed out from one end of the brigade to the other, and the blue line broke in disorder, with the Confederates in pursuit and making the panic worse by yelling, as usual. It was the Wilderness over again, as we thought, where twenty-five hundred of the enemy threw down their guns and surrendered, and everything was going in our favor when the regiment on the right suddenly became panic-stricken and gave way in confusion. Then the one on the left was seen to waver and fall back also. The regiments in the center continued to advance and drive the enemy for some time; but seeing that they were about to be enveloped on the right and left, they were compelled to fall back to their original position in the ravine. Here they found the Alabama brigade of Rodes's Division forming on the same ground and General Gordon galloping to and fro in the rear of them, shouting to his own men as they were coming back, mixed up in great disorder, saying: "What in the world is the matter, men? Fall in here and fight with General Rodes's men." Seeing the confusion, the enemy took courage and advanced, but were met by the Alabamians on the same ground and were driven through the woods and a field to the protection of a forest beyond.

These brave fellows made a splendid charge and could have driven the Federals from their last stand, but there was no one to lead them, and every one did as he pleased. They met the enemy face to face, and the lines came together. The writer of this article saw the color bearer of one regiment take the standard out of the hands of a Federal soldier and drag it along on the ground, while he held aloft our colors and led the charge. Having heard General Gordon say, "Fall in here with General Rodes's men," he did so and fought with them until late in the afternoon, when they were finally driven from the shelter of the woods. He then rejoined his own command. A few of them held the right all that dreadful evening under fire from the left, front, and right, and with the ammunition found on the bodies of the dead held back the heavy lines of the Federals.

It is but just to say that the Federal officers exhibited the greatest gallantry in rallying their men and bringing them up to renew their assaults on the thin gray line, as they were broken and scattered by the deadly fire of the Confederates. But for their efforts and those of General Gordon, who rallied his old brigade and formed it far to the left and north of the position held by Rodes's men, Early's army would have been annihilated. The only reason this did not happen was that the Federal army was not properly handled. The whole thing on both sides was a series of bungling. When the engagement was at its height the Federal cavalry massed an overwhelming force and rushed on to our thin picket line of cavalry, deployed to hold the left, and swept them from the field. They then rode into Winchester, where our wounded men had taken refuge, and among our surgeons, who were busy in their ministrations to those who needed attention. Our wounded comrades who could do so came back to us on the firing line and told us that there was no safety in the rear, as the enemy's cavalry was everywhere.

Night and the lack of ammunition on the part of the Confederates put an end to this battle, our first defeat, in which our small force of about 12,000 men, according to Early's report, lost 3,611 in killed, wounded, and missing; while Sheridan's force of 43,000 lost over 6,000 in wounded alone. If our men had been properly handled, we would have been more than a match for Sheridan's big army.

That night the enemy followed us with cavalry, but General Gordon, who was always active and resourceful, somehow secured a little ammunition and placed what was left of the Louisiana brigade in a favorable position on both sides of the pike to receive our pursuers. As they came up in full gallop in the darkness, the road was blocked with dead men and horses. This put an end to the fighting, and we made our way that night and the next day without molestation to Fisher's Hill, a short distance to the south of Strasburg, where we rested for two or three days before the enemy made his appearance.

THE BATTLE OF FISHER'S HILL[20]

In the beginning of this article I wish to correct an error made in my observations on the battle of Winchester, Va., September 19, 1864, on page 218 of the VETERAN for June, in which I gave the Louisiana Brigade credit for putting a stop to Sheridan's pursuit of the Confederate army that night. I should have said that it was done by the 38th Georgia Regiment, under Colonel Davant. This I have learned since the communication was published, and I take pleasure in giving that noble band the honorable praise due them for their heroic conduct on this occasion. No regiment in our army deserved more than these brave fellows for their conduct in this affair as well as in many other equally important engagements.

As we marched slowly along the pike that night toward Strasburg, our stragglers came up, and by morning all the regiments of Early's army were fully reorganized. We bivouacked at Newtown, about ten miles from the scene of the battle, and the next day marched to Hupp's Hill, south of Cedar Creek and north of Strasburg, where Early began to fortify; but as this position could be flanked easily on the right and left, he withdrew to Fisher's Hill, south of that town, where we found excellent breastworks already constructed extending from the Valley pike at the foot of Massanutten Mountain on the east to Little North Mountain on the west. Here he deployed his small force, now not more than eight or ten thousand men, in a thin line entirely across the valley, I suppose to stop the farther advance of Sheridan and prevent the devastation of that beautiful and fruitful region, so loyal to the Southern

---

[20] Ibid., September 1920, 27:338-340. For another account, see 25:109.

cause and necessary to the support of its armies. Stonewall Jackson was too shrewd a military man to make this fatal mistake when hard pressed by an overwhelming force in the spring of 1862, but passed on south by this place until the psychological moment arrived for him to strike. This he did at Cross Keys and Port Republic, holding one superior force off with a mere skirmish line, while he utterly routed another, defeating these two armies at the same time and within hearing of each other's guns.

But Early was not Stonewall Jackson, and perhaps as a military man he never had an equal. What our old commander would have done had he been with us, I will not venture to say; but this I know: he never would have staked his all on a fight at this place. Possessed of a keen vision, he had the happy faculty of snatching victory out of the most unpromising situations. General Early was brave, but rash; willing to take the greatest risks, but lacking the confidence of those under him. His position at this place was all that could be desired on the right, but on the left it was easily susceptible to a flank movement by the enemy, who could send a large force down on the west side of Little North Mountain, cross that low range, and make an attack on our left and rear. Gordon's Brigade held the extreme right of the line next to the pike and could have repulsed ten times their numbers if the balance of the line had maintained their position.

When Sheridan's army first came in sight, they stopped at Hupp's Hill and began to fortify the place. Our skirmishers were thrown out, and in the engagement that ensued we lost some of our men. At first the enemy showed very little inclination to fight; but this was only a ruse to give their forces on the west of the mountains time to get well on their way to our left flank and rear. When this movement was fully under way Sheridan's whole army advanced to the attack. Having every advantage of our men holding the extreme left as to numbers and position, they drove them back, although they fought bravely for a while. The next brigade on their right was now attacked in flank and front and was forced to give way also. This continued until our brigade alone was holding out. From our elevated position we could see that all the army was routed, and the enemy was making every effort to secure the pike in our rear. And now we, too, when the enemy was only a few yards in front of our works, were compelled to seek safety in flight or surrender. Some of our command preferred to take their chance of escape from this unfortunate situation by the pike leading south, while others thought best to cross this highway and make their way south through the Luray Valley beyond the Massanutten Mountain. These were entirely without organization, but in a country whose people were true to the Southern cause, while those who fled by way of the pike maintained some semblance of organization and resisted the onward rush of the enemy's cavalry. Gordon's Brigade and a few others were conspicuous in their stubborn resistance. No sooner were the little bands of brave spirits driven by the artillery and dismounted cavalry from one position of hastily constructed defenses made of rails or logs than they fell back to some other place that offered protection until they were again outflanked and driven back. Thus the enemy was hindered in their pursuit, and their progress was impeded so that the artillery wagon trains and fugitives were given time to get well on their way to the south and out of danger.

In this manner the retreat continued for about three days, until the army reached a point near Harrisonburg, where it quit the main pike and turned eastward toward Port Republic, where it took up a strong position at the foot of the Blue Ridge Mountains. The enemy continued to follow the pike and left off the pursuit. Here Early rested his army and reorganized his shattered forces. Though always brave and true, he was never a popular leader, even when victorious; but now no one had any confidence in him, and the spirit of his army was at a low ebb. For these misfortunes he blamed the army, while the soldiers blamed him. Here we rested quite a while, and many of those we considered killed or captured returned to us, and we found that our loss was not so great as we had supposed. The enemy was now unopposed and had a free hand to destroy with fire and sword to their hearts' content. Everything that could afford subsistence or shelter to mankind was utterly destroyed from Harrisonburg to Strasburg, about seventy miles. All this destruction we could see from our position, but in our helpless condition could not prevent. The whole valley before our eyes was filled with smoke of burning houses, haystacks, shocks of corn standing in the fields. etc., while the crack of carbines brought to our ears the destruction of all farm animals so necessary for man's use. Poor dumb creatures shot down in cold blood only to satisfy man's perverse nature! Who ordered this inexcusable crime? Who was responsible for it? Was it the so-called "gentle, kind hearted" Lincoln, who had "charity for all and malice toward none?" We are afraid behind a benignant face he concealed the instincts of a tiger. Was it Grant, the conqueror of the ragged remnants of Lee's exhausted army? Let history answer, while every American who loves justice and mercy hides his face in shame. Let us forever be silent when we hear others condemn the Germans for their conduct in the late war. They received instructions how to wage war from General Sheridan, who told Prince Bismarck at a great banquet in Germany given in his honor that nothing should be left to their enemies but their eyes to weep over their misfortunes. These orders came from some one higher up to Sheridan and from him to Custer, who did the work and whose Nemesis followed him to the battle of the Big Horn, where he received his recompense at the hands of the Sioux Indians. All those who blackened the pages of our history have gone to their reward, and we only hope in Christian charity that they repented before it was too late.

But all this may not interest the reader so much as an account of the writer's part in these events and what fell under his own observation. When we left the breastworks, the enemy was only a few yards in front of them. In the scuffle and confusion there a comrade, after firing at the enemy, jerked his gun back and struck me above the right eye with the sharp piece of metal on the butt end of his gun. From the wound the blood gushed out and ran down over my eye, so that I could see with difficulty. Turning around, I saw my comrades running toward the pike. When I got there, to my surprise just on the other side of the road I saw Col. E. M. Atkinson, of the 26th Georgia Regiment, holding on to the wheel of a piece of artillery that had been abandoned there when the men whose duty it was to serve it saw that there was no possible means to save it from falling into the hands of the enemy. The fight was hot and at short range, but there stood this brave though indiscreet officer trying to halt every man that passed to get this gun away by hand. In this storm of bullets not a man stopped except the writer. Being young and having been taught to obey orders, and especially by a regimental officer, I seized hold of the opposite wheel and held on to it until the enemy was only a few feet away and commanding us to surrender. I now deemed it about time to consult my own safety and left the colonel, still holding on to the wheel of the gun in his insane effort to get it away. For the next two hundred yards and until I placed a small hill between me and the enemy was only a brief period. Here I sat down to take breath. Looking back, I saw coming toward me a brave man of our regiment. He had held his ground and fought to the last minute; but once he had turned his back on the enemy, he had become completely demoralized. Like a runaway horse, he had lost control of his mind. He had thrown away his gun and accouterments, lost his coat, and was now divesting himself of his shirt. His long beard stood out in the air on each side of his face, and his eyes were wild and staring. As he passed me in his flight I called to him to stop and rest, as we were now safe. But he only glared at me and passed on.

From this little incident I have decided that the bravest men may sometimes lose their heads in great danger. Colonel Atkinson held on to the piece of artillery in his delirium to save it until he and it both fell into the hands of the enemy where he remained until the war closed. He was a brave officer and very popular with the soldiers, but a man of poor judgment.

Night now came on, and, wandering about alone on the open field, I finally fell in with two soldiers from my own State, with whom I made a solemn agreement to remain together until we should make our escape and rejoin our commands. I suggested to them that we go back to the pike and ascertain if it were possible to make our way to our friends by that route. When we reached that highway we concealed ourselves in the bushes while the Yankees passed in a few feet of us. It was too dark to tell the color of their uniforms, but we knew who they were from the foreign brogue of the Irish and German soldiers and what they were talking about as they passed us. There was nothing now for us to do but to retrace our steps, climb Massanutten Mountain, and enter the Luray Valley beyond. When we reached the lonely summit the night was far spent, and we stood still a moment to rest and decide what to do. Far down in the valley we heard the barking of a dog that indicated human habitation. Down the rocky side of the mountain we made our way and came, just as the first signs of day made their appearance, to a comfortable-looking residence on a public road. Some stragglers soldiers hailed, and a window in the attic opened. A young lady put her head out and addressed them in very uncomplimentary terms for leaving their colors and giving up the country to our enemies; but finally she told them to follow the road to the river where there was a mill. Above the mill we could find a battery concealed in the bushes on the bank of the stream. In this we could cross over to where we would be safe from any farther pursuit on the part of the enemy. That day we met several citizens who assured us of our safety and told us the enemy had come into that valley only once during the war, but that they met with a reception so warm that they never cared to come back again.

Where we camped that night there were perhaps eight hundred or one thousand stragglers, and the next day we crossed over again into the Shenandoah Valley to rejoin our commands, supposing we were now ahead of them and our enemies. As we went down the mountain we could see at a distance on the main pike a scattered remnant of our brave army still offering resistance, while the enemy's infantry, cavalry, and artillery were decimating their thin ranks.

When we reached the foot of the mountain we decided to prepare a hasty meal, for we were very hungry, and had just kindled a fire and put on a hoecake when a cavalry scout came along in a trot and told us that the enemy was just behind. We took the road leading south along the foot of the Blue Ridge in an effort to keep up with the cavalrymen. Finding it impossible to do this, some of the men decided that, rather than expose themselves to being captured and suffer the wrongs inflicted on our soldiers in prison, it would be better to climb the mountain and defy the enemy there. This they did; and although the Yankees surrounded the place with pickets, they never attempted to attack them. They subsisted by sending out foraging parties at night, who slipped through the blockade and resumed with such food as the country afforded. Thus they lived for many days high up on the mountain top, where they could see the enemy's pickets and could be seen also by them. In the course of time the enemy became tired of this unprofitable business and withdrew, and our men came down and returned to their commands. Having had experience enough in the mountains, this scribe preferred the open country and continued on to Brown's Gap, where he found the remnant of our once splendid army resting.

In the reports that were made to headquarters, it was found that we had lost in killed, wounded, and prisoners about twenty-five hundred men out of the twelve thousand who had fought Sheridan's army of five times their own number at Winchester and Strasburg. Sheridan reported after the battle at Winchester a loss in that engagement of six thousand and five hundred. His loss at Strasburg and in the fighting on Early's retreat was much less. The country was now open for Sheridan to march, practically unopposed, to Richmond with his victorious army fully as large as Lee's army and put a stop to the war. This Grant urged him to do, but he preferred to return to his old policy of delay, perhaps because he remembered his experience at Trevilian Station a few months before, when Wade Hampton, with a small force, utterly routed his army, an affair in which he and a few of his men escaped into Grant's lines with the greatest difficulty.

THE BATTLE OF CEDAR CREEK, VA.[21]

This battle, which was fought on the 19th of October, 1864, between the Confederate forces, about 12,000 in number, under Gen. Jubal Early, and about 43,000 Federals under General Sheridan, was the last battle of the Valley Campaign. Until noon this engagement was the most signal victory the Confederates ever won over the overwhelming numbers of the enemy; but by the bad management of some one it turned into our utter defeat, with the loss of all our artillery and that taken from the enemy, about seventy pieces in all. Our success in the morning was due to the foresight and good judgment of that superb leader, Gen. John B. Gordon. Who was to blame for this disaster I shall leave it to others to say.

After the hard-fought battle of Winchester between the same forces on September 19 and the rout of our men at Fisher's Hill a few days later, Early's army reorganized in the upper valley near Weir's Cave, and after resting a while a few reenforcements came from Lee's army, and Early decided once more to try conclusions with Sheridan and even up with him for his wanton destruction of the Shenandoah Valley. We set out on our march and in a few days were in the vicinity of Strasburg on the old Fisher's Hill battle field. Here we camped and rested a few

---

[21] Ibid., July 1914, 22:315-316. For another account, see 27:411.

days, while General Gordon reconnoitered and took observations of the Federals left to hold that part of the valley while Sheridan retired with the rest of his forces to Winchester. Here (at Strasburg) the Massanutten Mountain attains its greatest elevation and ends abruptly. Around its northern base one branch of the Shenandoah River winds, flowing toward the east, and, after it passes the mountain, Cedar Creek, a large stream, flows into it from the north.

While resting his men in camp General Gordon was always on the lookout to take some advantage of the enemy. He discovered that the Federals had placed a signal station on the highest point of the mountain, from which they had a fine view of the country to the north, east, and west; but on account of the wooded nature of the mountain they could not see what was going on at its base. Seeing this advantage, he took a few select men and with these he followed the course of the river until he came to the foot of the mountain, where he deployed his men in skirmish formation and advanced up the steep and rocky mountain side. The Federal guard, not suspecting an attack in this elevated and secure place, had stacked their arms at the outside of the camp and, lying around in a careless way, were not aware of the approach of the Confederates until they had passed their guns. They saw that resistance was useless and all surrendered without firing a shot. General Gordon was now able from this commanding position to take in the situation and make his arrangements to surprise and rout the enemy in their breastworks on the north side of Cedar Creek. He conceived the idea of marching the army around the foot of the mountain in single file at night over a trail near the foot of the mountain to a ford on the Shenandoah.

At 4 P.M. on the 18th all the officers of General Gordon's brigade assembled at his headquarters, and he gave them instructions to march without the least noise, as we were to pass very near the enemy's pickets, and to keep every man in place so that at dawn we could rush across the river and fall on the Federal left; the rest of the army at a given signal would cross the creek and enter their earthworks while the enemy were still asleep in their tents.

All this was carried out and proved a perfect success. The entire line of Federal works was carried and all their equipment fell into our hands. The surprise was so complete that thousands of the Federals fled, minus guns, shoes, hats, with nothing to cover their bodies but what they slept in the night before. Had Gordon's plans not been interfered with, history would have been different from what it now is.

Well do I remember how we plunged into the icy waters of the Shenandoah as day was beginning to dawn, the struggle to get to the bank on the other side, and the effort to reach the top of the high embankment, now made slick by our wet clothing; how some comrade jostled me just as I reached the top and I slid back into the cold water and had to try it all over again. We were trotted up the road and formed facing the wagon camps at the enemy's left, where they were trying to bum wagonloads of supplies. We advanced and drove their infantry across a field into a deep ravine and out of this to their works, protected by a formidable abatis of fallen timber, and out of this also to the open fields and woods beyond toward Newtown, halfway to Winchester. Crossing the breastworks at an elevated point on our right, we could see small detached bands of our men still pursuing and driving the enemy, who were keeping up a very effective fight with some artillery they were fortunately able to keep from falling into our hands. This artillery was served with great skill and kept back the few Confederates who were maintaining some sort of a line.

Looking toward the left, we were surprised to see our wagon trains and artillery coming across the bridge onto the battle field. All these that evening fell into the hands of the enemy. Whoever ordered this movement during this temporary lull in battle must have been drunk or crazy, and we all thought so at the time. Finally our scattered fragments were collected and formed some sort of a line to face the hot fire of the artillery; but the spaces between the different units were so wide that it was evident to every one that if the routed infantry of the enemy would only reform and make an effort we would be obliged to give way.

In the meantime the noise of battle and the arrival of the half-naked fugitives at Winchester caused Sheridan to awake from his slumbers and make his celebrated ride toward the scene of battle, bringing with him a fresh army. All this consumed time in which the commander of our army could have made arrangements to meet the storm gathering to crush us; but little or nothing was done, although every private soldier saw the necessity of it.

An order now came to Captain Harrell, of our regiment, to take his company and two others, in all about thirty men, and go to the extreme left of the line of infantry and assist our cavalry there. When we arrived at that place there were no cavalry to be seen. He deployed his men about thirty steps apart with orders to hold their ground against the enemy, now reformed and reenforced and forming two splendid lines in our front. We maintained our line intact until the entire army had given way, which we could see from our elevated position; and now the advance began in our front, and we were swept away and forced to seek safety in flight. The artillery succeeded in crossing the slender bridge over Cedar Creek, but was overtaken before it reached Strasburg in a sunken place in the road by the Federal cavalry, and the foremost teams were cut down. The entire train of artillery and many baggage wagons had to be abandoned and fell into the hands of the enemy.[22]

General Gordon was so mortified at this turn of affairs which he had planned and carried forward so successfully that he took it upon himself to organize a small force to fall suddenly on the enemy during the night and drive them away and recapture his artillery, but his men were too much exhausted and the night was so far spent that he was obliged to give up the idea. The next morning the army withdrew from Fisher's Hill, south of Strasburg, up the valley to New Market, and went into camp.

After the battle of Cedar Creek the army remained in the valley until December and offered battle to the enemy, but they were not disposed to fight. General Lee then at last did what he ought to have done when he detached the old Stonewall Corps from his army in June and sent us on that long march to meet Hunter at Lynchburg and on to Washington, D. C. This was removing brave old Jubal Early and putting Gen. John B. Gordon in command. General Early was as true a soldier as ever drew a sword in defense of his country, but there were reasons why he should have been left under the direction of the commander in chief.[23]

---

[22] Henderson, *Roster*, 3:624. "John A. Harrell. A. Private May 5, 1862. Appointed 5th Sergeant August 15, 1863. Elected 1st Lieutenant April 15, 1864; Captain October 25, 1864. Paroled at Stuart Hospital, Richmond, Va., April 18, 1865."

[23] This and the next three paragraphs are from the *Confederate Veteran*, November 1914, 22:504-505.

The army was marched to the railroad and sent to Petersburg, where it did much hard service and no little fighting under its new commander. He enjoyed the love and confidence of every man under him. His commanding voice, his soldierly bearing, and his engaging manner won and inspired his men and made every one of them a hero in battle. If General Lee, General Ewell, and General Early had listened to Gordon the evening of the first day's battle at Gettysburg and acted on his advice by taking possession of the heights then occupied by a beaten and demoralized mass of the enemy, history would have been quite different. When he had begged them in vain to let him drive them off that evening, it is said he turned away sadly and said: "O for Stonewall Jackson!"

Again, at the Wilderness on the second day of the battle, when he saw his opportunity and begged his superiors so earnestly to let him strike a stunning blow to Grant's army, his request was not heeded until sundown. Though too late to relieve the pressure on Longstreet on the Confederate right, he doubled up Grant's right on his center and captured Generals Seymour and Shaler and many prisoners. Night alone put a stop to his progress. If this charge had been made earlier in the day, the whole Federal army would have been routed as completely as Stonewall Jackson did Hooker at Chancellorsville a year before.

Again Gordon showed his good judgment and foresight on May 12, 1864, at Spottsylvania C. H., where General Lee's army was cut in two and about to be destroyed. With three regiments of his brigade and his sharpshooters and with some other troops he struck the vast numbers of the victorious Federals such sledge-hammer blows on their flank as to win the victory when everything seemed to be lost and saved the army from utter defeat. But his promotion came too late to save the Southern cause.

———————

SCOUTING IN THE VALLEY[24]

After Early's defeat at Winchester, September 19, 1864, at Fisher's Hill three days later, and at Cedar Creek October 19, Sheridan adopted the German policy of destroying the country and everything in it that drew the breath of life except a few old men and women and children too young to interfere with his operations. Perhaps I should say the Germans adopted his methods in their war on France and mankind, only that Sheridan and Custer were a little more cruel in one respect, in killing all Confederate scouts and those suspected of being scouts when they fell into their hands. Sometimes, however, their captors showed a little mercy in allowing them to run for their lives before shooting them down in cold blood. The writer of this article does not pretend to say that General Sheridan was the author of this policy, but he certainly put it into execution. He hopes whoever was to blame for it repented, if that were possible, before he was called to stand before the Great Judge.

After these defeats, which were brought on the Confederates partly by the overwhelming forces of the enemy and partly by the mismanagement of our commanding general, the remnant of the army, scattered along the foot of the Blue Ridge Mountains, could do nothing but look on at the smoke of their burning homes rising to heaven and pray that in some way and sometime justice might be meted out to the perpetrators of this crime. After resting here for some time General Early decided to follow the enemy down the valley and see if there was yet an opportunity to strike the enemy a sudden blow, to encourage his soldiers, and to show them that he was still in the field. When he reached the lower valley he found the enemy in large force, well protected by earthworks, unsuspecting as when we routed them at Cedar Creek; but our force was too weak to attack with any hope of success. General Early now slowly withdrew up the valley, keeping the Shenandoah River between him and the open country, the enemy's cavalry having little or no opposition beyond it.

Stopping to rest one day, the colonel of my regiment came from the rear and, passing our company, called to Sergeant W. P. Warn and told

---

[24] *Confederate Veteran*, March 1919, 27:92-93. Paragraphs deleted from this article to eliminate duplication.

him to detail two men from the company for scout duty across the river with Sergeant McLemore and a squad of men who would be along in a few minutes. Warn, always ready for any enterprise, however hazardous, if only it promised an opportunity for plunder or getting a good meal, decided to go himself and detailed me as the other man. McLemore now came up and asked him for the men, and we fell in. The banks of the river at this place were very steep on both sides, but the river was fordable. As soon as we got across McLemore suggested to Warn that he should strike out due west to a forest some distance from the river with his man, while he would go up the river some distance and move out into the country in the same general direction, intending, as I suppose, to meet again somewhere and make up a report of our observations. This was the last I saw of him and his men for months, but more about him later.[25]

We saw no sign of the Yanks anywhere and went to an elevated place in the woods where we could make observations of the open country. To our surprise we saw a farmhouse at no great distance and the smoke from the chimney ascending peacefully. This was an unusual sight in this devastated country, and no doubt the idea of a good breakfast came into "Bill's" mind. He told me to stand behind the body of a large oak and watch while he went up to the house and found out from the folks within about the Yankees. He instructed me to keep a sharp lookout and, if I saw the enemy approaching, to whistle and he would run back to me, and we would defend ourselves as best we could. He went to the yard fence and stepped over. When he appeared at the big, open front door the family, consisting of the old man, his wife, and three grown daughters, took him for a Yankee scout dressed in gray clothes, as they had no idea that there were any Confederates in that part of the country; but he could elicit no information from them. He stood there in the yard gesticulating and seemed to be in earnest conversation with some one in the house whom I could not see, as the house faced to the east and I was to the south. I became restless and was about to abandon my position when he beckoned me to come. When I reached the fence the girls came running to me, saying: "O, he's a Rebel! He's a Rebel!" They were now willing to give us any

---

[25] Henderson, *Roster*, 3:582. "James McLemore. Private November 1, 1861. Surrendered, Appomattox, Va. April 9, 1865."

information they had about the enemy. They told us about the cavalry fight there the day before, and how our men drove them away, and that they had picked up two of the breechloaders, Spencer rifles, that had been left in their flight. These they had hidden in a patch of briers, and they showed them to us. My comrade, already well armed, wanted to take both of them, but this they objected to and let him have only one. We went back to the house with them, where they gave us something to eat and detained us quite a while, until I told "Bill" that we had not come over the river to eat and have a good time with the girls, but to find the enemy and report. As we started off the girls urged us to come back to dinner. This made little impression on me, but Bill remembered it, and at noon he was willing to turn back from our tramp, in which we saw nothing to report. When we reached the house the whole family was at the door to invite us in to a big dinner on the table awaiting us. Without hesitating a minute Bill walked in, stood his two guns up in the corner of the dining room, and proceeded to divest himself of his accouterments. Taking one more glance in every direction for the enemy before following him, I saw on the hills at a distance on the other side of the river the tattered battle flags of our brigade moving off. I knew these were observed by the enemy's cavalry and that they would advance immediately. Standing outside, I told Bill, who was now seated at the table and helping himself, that we had better go, while the whole family was almost ready to drag me inside to eat with them. I asked him what he meant by his conduct. He said: "I'm going to eat my part of the dinner these folks have prepared for us. You come in here, you fool, and do likewise." Finally, when I saw I could not get him out, I said: "Good-bye, old fellow. I never expect to see you any more."

I started in a brisk walk for the woods through which we had come in the morning, but had gone only a short distance when, hearing the rustle of a woman's skirts and footfalls behind me, I looked back and saw one of the girls with a plateful of dinner, who ran up to me and said: "You shall have some of it." I opened my haversack, saying, "Put it in here quick," and off I started. Before I reached the edge of the wood Bill overtook me in a run, saying: "You were in a mighty hurry." A minute later one of our cavalry scouts, pressed by the enemy, came riding up at full gallop and said: "Hurry up, boys, they are just behind.

If you can keep up with me until we get to the river, I will help you across." We thus overtook our command before night.

Months after this McLemore and his men came to us, and I had a desire to know something of his experience. He told me that they took a public road some distance up the river leading out in the valley, but saw nothing of the enemy until late in the afternoon, when he decided to return by the same route. Looking ahead in the dusk, he saw a large body of cavalry going in the same direction. As they did not notice him, he followed on; but, seeing others coming up behind, he and his men broke for the cover of a forest and escaped capture. They remained in hiding long after the army had left the valley and lived upon whatever the good people gave them, hiding in the day and foraging at night.

Sometime after the war, in conversation with my old schoolmate and war comrade, I asked him if he remembered this little incident in our war experience and the beautiful young lady who led us to where the rifles were hidden. He answered in the affirmative and promised to write to her—Miss Sue Miller, then living at Cross Keys, Va., on the site of one of Jackson's battles. A few days after this he showed me a letter in beautiful handwriting from the lady. She told him, among other things, that it was well his comrade on that occasion did not come in, as we were hardly out of sight in the woods when the house was surrounded by Yankee cavalry, who dismounted and ate the fine things prepared for us. Poor Bill! He has long since answered the last call in consequence of a wound received at the first day's battle of the Wilderness. Peace to his ashes! I hope the beautiful and accomplished Miss Sue Miller still survives and that her eyes may fall on these lines.

THE VALLEY CAMPAIGN AFTER THE BATTLE OF CEDAR CREEK[26]

In my article on the battle of Cedar Creek I forgot to mention the important fact that we captured in our first dash on the enemy's works that morning twenty-five hundred prisoners of war. When our army was routed late that evening, those prisoners attempted to make a dash for liberty, but the guards fired into them and made them turn back. They were hustled on up the pike on their way to Staunton. Again General Sheridan failed to see his opportunity to finish the war by going straight on to Richmond. If he had pressed his advantage and pursued us vigorously, he could have captured all of Early's army; but he preferred to return to his camps in the vicinity of Winchester and lapse again into his former state of inactivity, while we retired unmolested to New Market and made our camp. This was a hard march, for we had been having a strenuous time for two nights and a day before we started, and we were not allowed much rest.[27]

General Early seemed to be in a very bad humor with his men and gave orders that any one found out of ranks with his gun should be shot. Late in the afternoon, when we had already marched about twenty-five miles and I was almost ready to die from extreme exhaustion, a comrade said to me: "I must drop out of ranks. Won't you take my gun and carry it for me a few minutes? I'll be back soon." I took it, as I did not want to see him suffer so severely for such a slight offense, and trudged along in ranks as well as I could under this new burden for several miles; but my friend, if he deserved the name, did not show up any more that day. When we reached camp the sun was just setting as we stopped in a body of woods. The order was given to stack arms and then "Rest." When this was given I fell backward where I stood and remained motionless as I had fallen until the sun was up and smiling over the landscape the next day.

After I had awakened from my Rip Van Winkle sleep, I was very much refreshed, and in a short while Eugene Granberry, the colonel's

---

[26] *Confederate Veteran*, October 1920, 28:374-376.
[27] Article referred to is 27:411.

orderly, came along and said to me: "Don't you want to go over the river with me to get something to eat? I can ride the colonel's horse, and you can ride Dr. Butt's. They told me to go and see if we could get some bread, milk, and apples." It suited me exactly, and we were soon mounted and on our way. We struck out west and were shortly at the ford of the Shenandoah. Crossing this stream, we came to a house in an out-of-the-way place which Sheridan's cavalry had missed, the house of John Kipps. He and his good wife were true Southern sympathizers, and they filled our haversacks with bread and apples and our canteens with milk. When we returned to camp, the colonel and doctor were so well pleased with our trip that they decided to send me and two more men as a guard to protect Kipps's property from any depredation on the part of our men. This we did as long as the army remained at New Market. The weather had become very cold, but we guarded his fields day and night. We had become accustomed to the rough fare incident to Confederate soldiers and sleeping in the open on the frozen ground, and we expected nothing else; but these good people insisted on our coming in at midnight and sleeping in the house. When we returned at that hour, stiff and numb with cold, we spread our blankets on the floor of the sitting room and slept soundly. They gave us plenty to eat while there; but orders finally came to us to report to our command.

This was about the middle of November. General Early had decided to have another interview with the enemy. Our men were very much refreshed by their rest at New Market, and their spirits were somewhat improved also. Sheridan had sent his cavalry as far south as Mount Jackson, but when we met them they retired without much of a fight, and we returned to our camp. On the 10th of November we started down the Valley. On the 14th we were at Cedar Creek. We found our enemy in a well-fortified position at New Town; but General Early, having sent part of his army to General Lee, did not feel strong enough to make an attack, but marched back to our old camp at New Market, where we rested with little to do until we were finally ordered, about the 10th of December, to march to the railroad at Waynesboro and entrain for Lee's army. Brave old Jube Early's habits had so disqualified him for command that General Lee had reluctantly ordered him to turn over his army to Gen. John B. Gordon, who was the idol of the soldiers of our brigade and the whole corps. What a pity it had not been done long before our old soldiers, who had won such renown under

Stonewall Jackson, had ever suffered defeat! But this change of commanders, even after so many disasters, inspired our men with new courage, and Gordon was able at that dark hour to gain victories over the enemy.

Some of my personal experiences on this last march down the Valley may be of interest. The colonel sent me out twice on this trip to scout, and I was fortunate in getting back to him, while some of our party did not return for many weeks. Scouting at this time was a dangerous business, for Sheridan's and Custer's Cavalry were in the habit of killing every one of our men they caught in that business. The second time he sent me alone to ascertain if the town ahead of us was occupied by the enemy. The brigade halted at the bridge just south of the village, and he ordered me to go across, investigate fully, and return to him. He cautioned me as I started off to be careful and not be killed.

Before I reached the little town I quit the main turnpike which passed through the place, for I knew that if there were any Yankees in the town they would be there, and I would have a poor chance of escape. I therefore went around to the east side and approached the main highway from that direction, but I saw no one passing. The old blacksmith in his little shop told me that there were no Yankees in the town; that they had all just a few minutes before evacuated the place. Not feeling sure that he was telling me the truth, and not wishing to go back to Colonel Lowe without satisfying myself that this was true, I went to the main street, intending to go to the other side of the village before returning. Passing up the center of the street, clothed in my old dirty rags, with my gun on my shoulder and my other equipment on my person, looking ahead for the enemy, suddenly as I was in front of the most imposing residence in the city a beautiful young lady, about sixteen years old, opened the front door and dashed out to me and, throwing her arms around me, implanted a kiss on my dust-covered cheek. As she did so she wheeled around as suddenly as she had come and flew back to the porch, saying at the same time, "I've done it, I've done it; I told you I would," speaking to a lady who had now come to the door. The whole thing was so unusual and unexpected that I almost forgot my mission, and I was in doubt whether it meant the act of a friend or a foe. They both now began to beg me to come in, take off my accouterments, and have something to eat, saying I looked so tired and hungry. I told them that I had been sent by the colonel to find if there were any Yankees in the town and to report to him at the bridge, where the brigade was awaiting my return; but that did not satisfy them, and they still insisted on my coming in, as the Yankees had just disappeared from view as I came up and that it was useless for me to go farther or to return with the information.

This interview consumed a little time, and I knew the colonel would become impatient and come on before I could get back; so I listened to their solicitations and went up on the porch, taking a chair, with my loaded gun handy. They were extremely anxious to do something for me—invited me to come into the dining room, but I knew that would never do; then they begged me to let them fill my canteen with water. They asked me many questions and were very anxious to see General Gordon. I told them he would be along in a few minutes. About this time I heard the sound of our regimental band, and, casting my eye toward the bridge, I saw our general riding at the head of the column, surrounded by his aids and couriers. Behind these was our band, followed by Colonel Lowe and our regimental officers on horseback. The general looked at me and passed on, but I expected the colonel to reprove me severely. Behind him was the regiment coming up in fours. As soon as the men saw me sitting there on that porch with the ladies they began, every one of them, in the most uncomplimentary manner to yell at me, some saying, "You are a pretty scout, settin' up here talkin' to them gals," and others, "Come down out o' that." All this was so embarrassing to me that I grabbed up my gun and started down the steps to escape from it all and disappear in the ranks of my companions, when the ladies said: "O you must shake hands with us before you go and tell us good-bye." At this the yelling began anew and worse than ever: "Go back and shake hands with them gals." They insisted on my stopping there again if I should ever pass, but I never had the pleasure of seeing them again. The young lady explained her conduct by telling me that when the Yankees were in possession of the place she had made a vow to her sister that she would kiss the first Southern soldier she saw, and she remembered her vow when she saw me in the street. They were true Southerners and told me their names, but the whooping and yelling of our men made me forget it, or I should have made some effort to get acquainted with them afterwards.

On returning from this expedition the weather had become very cold as we were approaching, after a hard day's march, our old camp, near New Market, about midnight. My haversack was empty as well as my stomach, and I thought of the good things to eat at the house of my friend Mr. Kipps. I suggested to a comrade that we slip out of ranks unobserved by the officer in command, cross the river, and get a good supper and have our haversacks and canteen filled. He liked the suggestion, for he was of a very bold, adventurous disposition, not afraid of anything. I was sure I could rely on him. No one seemed to see us as we dropped out or to care, and we were soon on the bank of the river, which was, I suppose, about one hundred feet wide at this place and about three and a half or four feet deep. The water was liquid ice and the air very cold. We soon divested ourselves of our pantaloons and plunged in. When we struck bottom, my comrade danced around a moment and declared that the water was too cold; that he could not stand it long enough to wade across. I begged him to go on with me, but he would listen to no argument and got out and returned to camp. When I reached the other bank of the stream, my limbs were numb; but I put on my pants and walked briskly until I reached my destination. Friend Kipps and his wife gave me a good supper and asked me many questions until a late hour of the night. They wished me to remain there till morning; but I knew that if I should be captured over there I would be considered a deserter. "O," they said, "there is no danger of that. If the Yankees were to come, we would hide you where they would never find you." But I did not care to take the risk by myself and told them I must go. Mrs. Kipps filled my haversack and canteen, and I bade them adieu. The night was quite dark, and the rough mountain road was frozen. Before I reached the river I heard ahead of me a noise that chilled the blood in my veins, and my mind ran back to those dreadful ghost stories which our black nurse used to relate to me and my little brothers and sisters at home. I must confess that I was scared. But I remembered that I had been scared before and nothing came of it, so I trudged along. On each side of the road was a high fence, and I was disposed to climb over and go around the "ghost," but then I thought how cowardly that would be, even if my comrades were not there to guy me about it afterwards; so I put on a bold face and determined to dance up to the music, whatever it might prove to be. Louder and louder the noise grew as I advanced step by step toward it until I came up to the dreadful snorting creature with its head raised high over me. My hair was now standing on ends. Looking up, I discovered between me and the blue sky the two long ears of one of our old army mules. Then I saw others grazing peacefully near by. Poor creatures, they were glandered stock driven over there to die or be killed. I hastened on to the river where there was a mill and a crossing just below made by putting slabs from one rock to another. The water rushing over these slabs was frozen to a thick sheet of ice. I made my way all right until I was more than halfway across and was congratulating myself on my success in getting over when my feet shot out from under me, and I slid into the icy stream, with my gun and other equipment to carry me under. But I soon struck bottom, righted myself, regained the slab, and made my way out. In less than a minute my clothes were frozen stiff, but I got back to camp all right and was not punished for my little venture.

On being relieved of his command General Early was ordered to march the army to Waynesboro, on the railroad, where we entrained for Petersburg. I suppose he was in a very spiteful humor at this time from the way he treated us. We broke camp about eleven o'clock on the morning of December 11 and marched twenty-six miles without a stop to rest and made camp just at dark. Our men were completely broken down from this uncalled-for test of their strength.

This was the close of Early's Valley campaign, begun when we left Lee's army at Cold Harbor in June, in which our little army, not more than twelve thousand men at any time, had fought many battles and numerous skirmishes, inflicting on the enemy, according to official reports, a loss of twenty-two thousand men, and had given employment to sixty thousand of their select troops who would have been employed against Richmond. We had even threatened the capture of Washington, D. C. We had invaded the enemy's territory several times and subsisted to a great extent on supplies taken from them and kept Lincoln and his cabinet in a state of uneasiness for their own safety. In all of this campaign our loss was only about five thousand men in killed, wounded, and prisoners. But we were now about to enter upon a new field of operations and under a commander quite different in every respect from our old general—a general whom we all loved and admired, the gallant Gen. John B. Gordon, our old brigade commander, than whom we had no greater unless we except the matchless Stonewall.

CHAPTER SIX

1865

GORDON'S BRIGADE AFTER THE VALLEY CAMPAIGN[1]

We entrained at Waynesboro, a small village on the railroad east of Staunton, on December 12 and arrived at Petersburg two days later. We were sent immediately to Hatcher's Run, where we built good winter quarters as if we were to spend the rest of the war there without molestation by the enemy; but in these we were not to remain long, for General Grant, with his overwhelming numbers, was ever extending his left wing farther and farther to the west, compelling General Lee to meet these advances by depleting his already very thin line by taking men from it to meet these aggressions. Grant had now brought down from the Valley Sheridan and his army of sixty thousand select men and, like a great serpent, could wind around his enemy and crush him to death in his powerful coil. General Lee had now but one railroad on which to bring up supplies from the south to support his army defending Richmond and Petersburg, and if this should be cut there was but one of two things to do—evacuate or surrender. To escape capture would have been well-nigh impossible.

Month after month our rations grew less and less until the end. Toward the last we were almost starved and had only enough corn bread and meat issued to us to sustain life. The spirit of fortitude exhibited by our brave soldiers, now reduced to a mere handful, under these trying conditions was only an evidence of the unconquerable character of the Anglo-Saxon race. They never under our noble Gordon failed to respond handsomely to every order to attack and never failed to drive the enemy before them. Many of these poor fellows knew that their homes in Georgia were in ashes and their helpless families were destitute.

But I must go back. When we left the Valley, a few cavalry scouts still remained there to observe and to keep in touch with Mosby, who was operating in the rear of the great army Lincoln ever kept south of

---

[1] *Confederate Veteran*, November 1920, 28:418-420.

the Potomac and near Washington to guard his sacred person from the horrid Rebels. You may search ancient and modern history in vain to find a leader [Mosby] who ever accomplished so much with so small a force at his command. Hardly a week passed from the time we left the Valley until General Lee surrendered that he did not send into our lines prisoners and wagon trains loaded with army supplies captured from the enemy. Not satisfied with this, he even sent as a prisoner to Richmond the general himself who commanded these forces. Many of our sick and wounded soldiers left by our army in that part of the country when we withdrew from it preferred when they recovered to join Mosby rather than make an attempt to get through the lines to their own commands. Some of those who united with his command preferred to wage war near their own homes, where they could see their families, who were always ready to give them information of the movements of the enemy and conceal them in an emergency; while others fell in with him from a love of adventure. From his place of retreat our scouts led these prisoners and booty up the Valley and into our lines. His force was augmented continually by these means until he had with him perhaps two or three hundred men from first to last. He had been left there at first by Gen. J.E.B. Stuart with a small squad of cavalry to observe the enemy's movements and send information through the lines, as he and his men were familiar with the country.

We enjoyed our winter quarters until February, when General Grant's movements compelled General Lee to do something to check him. This resulted in our fight at Hatcher's Run, in which we lost some men. What loss we inflicted on the enemy I cannot say, but it was certainly a very inconvenient place to fight. We advanced into a low, swampy forest, where the ground was covered with shallow pools of water, or bogs, interspersed with briers so that progress was hard to make by us or the enemy. We drove them through the swamp into their works on higher ground, when we became so much disorganized that we fell back to our original position. In this fighting the brigade was commanded by Colonel Baker, of the 13th Georgia. The accomplished and popular Major Grace, of the 26th Georgia, was killed here. Grant continued to extend his left, and we had to fight again a few days after this at Deep Run. Our brigade charged their works and were repulsed, but we rallied and drove them out. This was a stubborn fight in which we lost many of our veteran troops, and our regiments, already thinned by constant fighting, were reduced to the size of companies and companies to squads.[2]

General Lee now decided to relieve our brigade and division by sending us to hold the line in front of Petersburg, and the troops there took our place at Hatcher's Run. But this was like getting out of the frying pan into the fire; for while we had a different kind of fighting on our hands, it was incessant. It never ceased day or night until we evacuated the ditches on the 2d of April. We were in these works about six weeks, where we were never safe one minute of the time from the missiles that continually sizzled and buzzed in the air around and about us, striking in the ground and tearing out great craters large enough to bury an ox, while their riflemen were ever on the alert with their long-range guns to pick off any of our men who exposed themselves to view. Our only safe place was in our bombproofs, where we had to sit in a cramped position or lie down. Our regiment was posted directly in front of Fort Steadman and less than one hundred yards from it. At this place and far to the right and left of it while we were fighting in the Valley and in Maryland the previous summer General Grant had sacrificed multitudes of his foreign hordes in his attempts to take Petersburg by direct assault. General Lee had straightened out his line and built excellent breastworks, strengthened by a fort every quarter of a mile or more. Parallel with these Grant did the same thing, and in the rear of them and out of range of our best artillery he erected great observation towers, from which he had a fine view of the country far to our rear. Back of all this he constructed a railroad to carry supplies to his army. In front of his works he had a line of rifle pits about a hundred feet apart occupied day and night by his pickets. We had a line of pits also, but our pickets remained in them only from nightfall to dawn. Between our rifle pits and the breastworks was an abatis made of pine logs with arms through them so that they were very difficult to get through. They kept five or six pickets in their pits, while ours were occupied by one man only in each. These two lines of hostile pickets were about fifty yards apart and kept up a

---

[2] Krick, *Lee's Colonels*, 164. "Maj. Grace was born in Tattnall Co., Ga. He was a timber measurer at Reidsville in 1860, age twenty-two. He started in the 26th Georgia as a Sgt., and made his way up through the ranks to Major in 1863. He was killed in action at Hatcher's Run, February 6, 1865."

constant fusillade, the principal object being to keep the men from going to sleep.

For a few days after we were put in these works our Yankee neighbors were very social, and between the shooting we sometimes had some conversation and an occasional visit from them, but that was a dangerous business and not allowed often. Our instructions were to fire toward the enemy about every fifteen minutes, lest we should go to sleep on our post. The monotony of the long, cold nights out in the pits was very trying, and we devised many schemes to break it. One of these was firing rockets made of Minie balls into the enemy pickets. These were made by scooping out the leaden ball so that it was only a shell. In the cavity we packed powder that had been dampened with saliva. A charge of dry power was placed in the gun, and the ball containing the damp powder was inserted in the gun with the sharp end down. By giving the gun the right elevation the ball, with its long tail of fire following it, would fall into the Yankee pits and create great confusion among them for a while. Friend and foe alike enjoyed the joke, and after a while the enemy caught on to the trick. A brave but nervous picket on my right who was an expert at this thing was frightened out of the pit when one of these rockets fell in on him. But I am ahead of my story.

When we came to these breastworks the ground in the rear of them was full of all kinds of bombproofs made in every fashion. I and two comrades selected one deep down in the ground for our quarters. About the second night we were there the orderly sergeant of the company, an old schoolmate, came in and sat down by me and said that they (the regimental officers) had made a demand on the company to furnish another man for the battalion of pickets; and as it was a very dangerous service in which we had lost a great many men, he hesitated about detailing any one and asked me to volunteer. This I did, feeling that it was more honorable to do so than to be put on that duty by those in command. The next morning I met a comrade who was already serving in that capacity and told him I intended to go out with him that evening. He said: "All right; meet me at the head block at dusk with your gun loaded and a fresh cap on, and I will show you your pit."

Now, I had never had a good view of the situation, had only taken a peep occasionally, and at some risk, through the small hole mortised in this block from which a very imperfect idea could be formed. Promptly at dusk I met him at the place designated, and we stepped up on the platform behind the works. He looked at me and asked me about the condition of my gun and then said: "Are you ready?" I told him I was. We threw our guns up, and at one bound we mounted the parapet in a shower of balls from the enemy pickets, which always greeted us as we went on in the evening or came off at dawn. Standing there one moment, he pointed to the right and said, "That's your picket," and, darting to the left, disappeared.

Now, I did not know about that chevaux-de-frise being there or how to get through it in this storm of bullets. Just as I thought I was through one of the arms jerked me back by catching under my canteen strap as if to say, "Don't be in too great a hurry," while the enemy were making the situation very embarrassing for me. When released I plunged without delay into my pit and went knee-deep into the stinking, cold mud. In this miserable hole I sat and shivered until midnight, when I was relieved by a comrade who brought with him a plank which reached from one side of the pit to the other and afforded us a good seat thereafter. We were divided into two reliefs and alternated every night. The first relief the previous night became the second the succeeding night. We were while on duty under Lieut. "Billy" Gwyn, who had been promoted for his bravery and good sense in saving our brigade from capture on one occasion in the Wilderness campaign when it had by some means maneuvered so as to find itself at night in the rear of Grant's army. When he found out the predicament which we were in, he led us out of the trap by a secret route known apparently to himself alone. This is the same man who as sheriff of his county in Georgia was killed by the noted outlaw Tom Delk, who was hanged for the crime.[3]

For the first week or ten days after we took over the defense of this part of General Lee's line the enemy pickets conducted themselves very gentlemanly. They were very anxious to have some intercourse with us and often invited us to come over and exchange commodities with

---

[3] Spelled Gwynn elsewhere in Bradwell's letters. Henderson, Roster, 3:620: "William O. Gwyn. Enlisted as a private in Co. A, 13th Regiment, Ga. Infantry, July 8, 1861. Appointed Sergeant. Transferred to Co. F, 31st Georgia Regiment, October 25, 1864. Wounded in both knees at Fort Steadman, Va. March 25, 1865. Admitted to Washington Street Hospital at Petersburg, Va. March 25, 1865, and discharged May 11, 1865. Killed at Concord, Ga., in 1897.

them; but that was a very dangerous business and depended entirely upon the humor of the officer in command of the pickets whether a visitor from our side ever came back. One night shortly after I was put on this duty the enemy in front of me asked me to come over and have a talk, giving their word and honor as Irishmen that they would let me return. But I could not accept, as I knew that if I did I should be violating my instructions and if detained would be considered a deserter. Between the picket lines was a low place in which there were a few scrubby willows. A slight depression extended up from this to my pit. One dark night as I sat there peering out into the darkness, with my gun ready for use, I thought I heard a faint voice saying, "Don't shoot, don't shoot; I'm coming in," and then the footfalls of a man approaching I heard distinctly. He continued to repeat as he came, "Don't shoot; I'm coming in," and a big Yank, with his gun in hand and fully equipped, rolled over in on me, at the same time telling me to pass the word to the next man on the left not to shoot, as others were coming in. I called out to my little comrade, Perkins, and told him I had a deserter and not to shoot, as others were coming in. In a very short time seven men, well armed and equipped, fell over into Perkins' pit. He hallooed to me in a very excited tone: "There are seven of them. What shall I do with them?" I told him to send them to the rear. This class of men was not to be feared. They were what the Yankees called "bounty jumpers," men who enlisted only to get the thousand-dollar bounty which Lincoln was giving at the time. They deserted the first opportunity and were allowed to pass through the lines, where they changed their names and no doubt reenlisted. Our thin line at this time extended thirty-five miles, and sometimes hundreds came in during a night.[4]

As I have already intimated, our first experience in these rifle pits was only a picnic compared with what we had to endure later on. The enemy, by some means, had become aware that Gracie's Alabama Brigade, which had built and held these works from the first, had been replaced by Gordon's Georgia Brigade. They suspicioned from this circumstance that General Lee intended to make a great effort to surprise and capture Fort Steadman. Lieutenant Gwyn came around at

---

[4] A review of the 31st Georgia muster rolls reveals this Perkins likely to be James W. Perkins, a fellow private of Bradwell's and a soldier who also was at the Appomattox surrender.

night to see if any of us were asleep and usually patted us on the back and asked if we were awake. He was afraid some of us would be found in that condition by the officer of the day (night) and have to suffer the consequences. To keep us awake he revised his order to shoot every fifteen minutes and told us he had plenty of ammunition and to shoot as often as we pleased.

We now made the night lively along the full length of the brigade. This new conduct on our part confirmed them in their belief that we contemplated an attack, and bedlam suddenly broke loose. Their whole picket line arose as one man in a great panic and rushed back into the fort. We could hear the uproar over there as the men hastened from their quarters to their guns. And now the heavens and the surrounding scene were lit up by their artillery. Screeching mortar shells, with a tail of fire following them a yard long, were ascending toward the blue dome of heaven, while shells from the mouths of their rifle cannon were sweeping over our heads and bursting in the rear. The mighty noise of the big guns put a quietus to our activities, and we sat in awe, trembling in our pits. But those splendid meteors began to descend upon us with their ever-increasing, menacing scream as they drew nearer. All around us they dropped and exploded with a terrific noise, scattering dirt and gravel over us. To make the situation even worse their infantry were firing from the parapet as if the result of the war depended on their efforts. The fort was a veritable volcano in eruption, and every minute I expected one of those big shells to drop in on me and tear me into atoms. Language is inadequate to express my feelings as I sat there alone, unable to communicate with my comrades on the right and left and considering what I ought to do. My voice was too weak to be heard in the thunder of the big guns, and no one could be seen. I asked myself: "Are they all dead and I alone am left here? Shall I leave my post and seek safety somewhere else?" These and many other suggestions were in my mind.

How long I remained in this state of uncertainty I cannot say; but when I could stand it no longer, I jumped up, determined to find some one to die with me or to advise me. I started in a trot to the right down the zigzag ditch which connected the pits to find the next man, but he was gone. Hastening on and guided only by the uncertain flashes of the exploding shells, I struck my leg against a gun lying across the ditch. I fell forward in the bottom of the ditch so badly hurt that at first I could do nothing but rub my bruised shin. Poor fellow, brave man as he was, in despair of his life he had thrown down his gun here and was sitting there in the ditch with his back to the wall, awaiting his fate and crying like a child. As soon as my pain had somewhat subsided I said: "What shall we do?" His reply was that we all would be killed there that night. I suggested to him that we follow the zigzag into the breastworks and see if our comrades were yet alive. This we did, and to our surprise we found them all standing or sitting about under arms awaiting orders. One man was badly hurt by a shell just as we came among them.

ON PICKET DUTY IN FRONT OF FORT STEADMAN[5]

"Going over the top" and "No Man's Land" were phrases that came into use in the World War, but we of the sixties made the same maneuvers and had the same common territory under different names. As long as we were under Stonewall, we knew very little about breastworks. He didn't believe in them; we fought in the open. The Yankees under McClellan and Grant had them, but Stonewall always maneuvered so that their earthworks were not good; he outflanked them so that they were always facing in the wrong direction when we found them.

After Grant met with the slaughter of his army on the 2d and 3d day of June, 1864, at Cold Harbor, he crossed the James River to capture Petersburg. Lee followed him, and much hard fighting took place. After losing many thousands of his army, Grant became convinced that he

---

[5] *Confederate Veteran*, August 1930, 37:302-307. Paragraphs deleted from this article to eliminate duplication. Editor. Also see 23:20-23, 25:408-409, and 28:457-459.

must employ other tactics to succeed. Each army dug in—that is, threw up breastworks in parallel lines.

When we moved into these works in February, 1865, we did not have to move a spade full of dirt to make any improvement in them. Those who had made and held them from the first had left nothing undone to add to their safety. They were about five feet high and thick enough to withstand the fire of artillery in Fort Steadman, only about one hundred yards away. In front of these was a very formidable chevaux-de-frise, and beyond this, about thirty or forty feet, a line of rifle pits for pickets at night.

The pickets were not required to perform any duty in the daytime; they could lie up in their quarters and sleep, or spend their time in any way they pleased. Now, on account of these shells and sharpshooters, who were always alert and knocking over our comrades, I had always been prudent, but I longed to walk down the line held by the regiment to see how the other fellows were situated. Accordingly, one Sunday morning, I came out and sauntered along behind the works to the left, always with an eye on the heavens for shells, until I came to the last bomb proof on our left. This place now afforded a place of so-called safety to Company A. This splendid company, under Captain Forrester, who was killed at Second Manassas, was now reduced to three men— Sergeant McLemore, Dr. Scaife, and a sixteen-year-old boy who had recently come to us as a recruit. As I came up, I saw the three squatting down in that low dark place, eating a few ounces of cornbread and boiled beef issued to us for a day's rations.

At this moment, I was attracted by the peculiar noise made by a shell that seemed to be descending directly on my head. I had but part of a second to decide what to do—whether to stand still and receive my fate, or to move to the right or left; but the shell did not give me time to decide the question and came down, not on me, but on the bomb proof, exploding at the same time, scattering the dirt and heavy timbers with which it was covered in every direction, but doing me no harm. The whole thing was so sudden and unexpected that for a few moments I was dazed. Some one, in the confusion, set up a cry for help, and the men in the near-by bomb proofs came running out to see what had happened. They began immediately to lift the heavy timbers off the men. The sixteen-year-old boy was under the heaviest timbers and would have died if he had not received immediate help. Dr. Scaife was so badly stunned, although he survived the war and came home, he was never mentally sound. I was satisfied with my observations and returned to my quarters.[6]

Our rations for each day were a piece of cornbread, about one-fourth of a pound, and about two ounces of meat of some kind. After this fight, they were reduced so that we could hardly exist on them. I was hungry all the time. Thinking that life was very uncertain, I longed once more to appease this desire for food before I should be killed, and accordingly, when I drew my day's ration, I took it down into my bomb proof and wrapped it up in my blanket to keep till the next day, when I would have a double supply; but when I went down the next day to find it, a thievish comrade, or rat, had already appropriated it. I was now worse off than ever. All these bomb proofs were infested with big rats. They annoyed us no little at night when we tried to sleep by running over us.

Though weak from the lack of food, we otherwise enjoyed excellent health. From the time the enemy in our front found out that Gordon's Georgia Brigade had taken the place of other troops that had been facing them, they had a peculiar dread of us. They seemed to think we were no better than a set of wild hyenas that would pounce down on them at any time and eat them up, raw, feathers and all; and this little incident at Fort Steadman had a tendency to confirm their previous opinion. Perhaps some of them had had some experience with Gordon's Brigade at Gettysburg, or at the Wilderness, or other places. To the very last they made no demonstration along the line held by us. To our right, held by other troops, General Lee had stripped his works of defenders until there was not a skirmish line in them, where there were any men at all. Here the enemy attacked and killed or captured all the brave defenders after a most gallant defense against overwhelming numbers, but still they refrained from any aggression on us.

That evening, April 2d, as night spread her mantle over the world and the full moon arose in the heavens, the regiment marched out, leaving me and two other pickets there to watch. This was done, I suppose, by each regiment of the brigade. Our orders were not to shoot, but only to watch. We were told that an officer would relieve us at

---

6 Bradwell appears to be mistaken about the Doctor's name. Dr. William Scaife was at this time serving in the Confederate western army.

twelve o'clock that night. As I stood there alone behind the works and saw my old comrades in arms and the old battle flag that I had seen so often in the smoke of battle file away, I was sad and said to myself: "Perhaps I will never see them again." In front of me, and only a hundred yards or more, were thousands of enemies who had nothing to do but come over and take me; but they remained silent and did not make any movement until the hour appointed for our relief had arrived and I had become restless. No relief was in sight and not likely to come, so I decided to see Haynes, on the left, and advise with him what course to pursue. When I approached him, I found him silently watching in the direction of the enemy. He had not seen any officer and could give me no advice. I suggested that we go to the right and see Williams, but we found no officer there. Though the youngest of the three, I suggested that we leave our post and follow the army, which we did. And it was very fortunate for us and our comrades, whom we overtook sometime the next day. When we passed out of the zigzag covered way, we had to go up through a field where the enemy could see us in the bright moonlight. It was too far for them to use their rifles, but they opened up on us with their rifle cannon. Their missiles passed by us without doing us any harm, but we quickened our pace to a trot. We were so weak from our long fast that we soon slackened our steps and let them shoot as much as they pleased.

I visited this place in 1907 and found that all the breastworks had been leveled, the shell holes made by mortars had disappeared, and young corn was growing peacefully where war had done its worst. The "crater" where so many men had died was still there, and perhaps will remain until the end of time as a reminder to future generations of the dreadful struggle that took place there. Pine trees were growing in it large enough to make good-sized saw logs.

Evidently a kind Providence was with me in all this and even to the present, for I am now in my eighty-eighth year, having been born March 15, 1843.

FORT STEADMAN AND
SUBSEQUENT EVENTS[7]

In the October number of the Veteran, page 460, the article on "Fort Steadman's Fall" contains so many inaccuracies that I deem it the duty of some one who took part in that engagement to correct some of these misstatements. No doubt Captain Carson gave the author a true account of this affair; but the writer, whoever he was, got things "mixed." He says that the events he is about to describe occurred about half a mile to the left of the Crater. Now, I visited this place a few years ago and walked over the ground and noted carefully everything, as events which were enacted there in 1865 made a vivid impression on my mind, and I was anxious to see the place where I fought and suffered so much when we knew that everything was lost to our cause save honor.

Our brigade, then commanded by Clement A. Evans, extended from the Crater to the left toward the Appomattox River across the railroad, and at the nearest point it was less than one hundred yards from this great fort [Ft. Steadman].

The night before this affair I was on the first watch and was exempt from duty the next day; but while trying to sleep in my underground bombproof I could hear the regiment getting ready for the assault, which was made by the entire brigade and not by the sharpshooters alone, as this writer would make it appear. What part these brave fellows took in this desperate enterprise I cannot say, but I am sure they acted with their usual dash and courage. Here I wish to correct another misstatement by saying that they were not "armed with the celebrated Whitworth rifle of the latest pattern." They were armed with Enfield rifles. Every short Enfield which came into possession of any of our men was taken away and given to these men; but there were not enough, and some of them had the common long Enfield. Both kinds had a long range and were very effective. The short guns were given them, as they were lighter and handier and because they were considered the picked men of the brigade, and nothing was too difficult for them to do.

---

[7] *Confederate Veteran*, January 1915, 23:20-23. Paragraphs deleted from this article to eliminate duplication. Editor.; also see 29:56-58 and 28:457-459.

There were but two of the imported Whitworth guns given to our brigade. One of these was given to Irvin Spivey, a noted rifleman of the 26th. His duty was to watch his opportunity and pick off Federal officers, but I cannot say how much of this he did. These men were selected from every company in the entire brigade in the winter of 1863 by General Gordon, and Captain Keller, a handsome and daring young officer of the 61st Regiment, was put in command of them. When he fell into the hands of the Federals at Martinsburg, Va., on the 18th of September 1864, Captain Kaigler, of the 13th, took command. Later Captain Carson held the command.[8]

The entire brigade rushed to the assault just before day; but as I was not in the rifle pits when the charge was made, I am obliged to rely upon what others told me and what I saw after I entered into the melee. Feeling that it perhaps was my duty to lend a helping hand, I came out of my underground bombproof and mounted the works and stopped a moment, gun in hand, to locate if possible in the haze of the morning and the smoke of battle the colors of my regiment. Almost before I could think a ball took my hat off and, I thought, my right ear with it. It was indeed a close call, and I decided that it would be better to be killed fighting bravely with my own men than as a spectator in the rear. With this in mind, I rushed forward to join our men, who had just captured the fort; but before I got to the Federal rifle pits I saw General Gordon talking to a well-dressed Yankee officer, and as I was passing a few feet away he reached out his hand and beckoned me to come to him. He then said to me: "This is General McLochlin, of Kentucky. I want you to take him to the iron railroad bridge, where he will be out of danger, and keep him there until after the battle is over. I want to

---

[8] Henderson, *Roster*, 6:164. "Benjamin F. Keller. Jr. 2d Lieutenant April 21, 1862. Wounded at Fredericksburg, Va., December 13, 1862. Elected Captain in 1863. Captured at Winchester, Va., September 19, 1864. Released at Fort Delaware, Del. June 17, 1865." Keller was actually in the 60th Georgia. Editor. "William Kaigler. Sergeant July 8, 1861. Elected Jr. 2d Lieutenant May 9, 1862; 2d Lieutenant December 2, 1862; 1st Lieutenant April 4, 1864; Captain October 3, 1864. Commanded Division Sharpshooters. Surrendered, Appomattox, Virginia April 9, 1865. (Born December 29, 1833. Died April 1910. Buried in Dawson, Ga.)

talk to him. Be sure not to let any one else go with you. You are enough to guard him, and treat him with respect."[9]

I had gone but a few steps when two of our men fell in with me and, in spite of my protest, went all the way with us until I delivered my prisoner to the proper authorities in Petersburg and got my receipt for him. The place General Gordon designated was an elevation to the south of the railroad bridge, a short distance from where the fighting was in progress. When we reached this place we found it anything but "a place of safety," and I said: "General, this is a dangerous place, and I think I had better take you somewhere else. I am afraid you will be killed here." He replied: "It does not matter with me whether I am killed or not. I have fallen into the hands of the Rebels, and I don't care what happens to me." This remark rather nettled me, and I violated orders by replying that he had fallen into the hands of civilized people, who would do as well by him as circumstances would permit. He said: "But wait a moment; I want to see the progress of the battle."

From this point we could see the vast numbers of the Federals gathering from every direction to drive off our weak detachments, which were in possession of Fort Steadman and were assaulting another fort to the right of it, while a scattered few were formed on the hill beyond Steadman to meet the vast host now assembling to attack them and recover the works. After viewing the battle a moment, he turned his back and, as we walked away, said: "O, it's only a matter of time when they will be driven back." As we entered the city we saw a number of soldiers coming from our left on another street with a dandy young Yankee officer, and when he was quite a distance from us he shouted: "Hello, General, have they got you too?" The General said: "Let me stop here a minute. I see they have got one of my staff. I want to talk with him."

We stopped on the corner, and when the officer came up he said: "General, how did they get you?" He replied: "This morning before day I heard a great melee in the—Pennsylvania Regiment, and I got up with my sword and pistol in hand and rushed out there to see what was up, and I soon found myself among the Rebels."

---

[9] Brig. Gen. Napoleon B. McLaughlin was captured by Lt. Gwyn of the 31st Ga. Robert G. Stephens, Jr., *Intrepid Warrior*, (Dayton: Morningside, 1992) 535. Also see 37:302-307.

The whole time the general, who seemed to be quite a gentleman and no doubt a brave man, appeared to be extremely mortified and angry at his misfortune. As our boys mounted those formidable works, which were made almost impregnable, and jumped down into the fort among the bayonets, in the darkness and confusion of the fighting the general met Lieutenant Gwyn, of our sharpshooters, who ordered him to surrender. This the general at first refused to do and asked him if he was an officer. To this Gwyn replied: "It does not matter, sir, whether I am or not, surrender or I will blow out your brains." And surrender he did.

If our brigade had been properly supported, they could have held these forts; but General Lee was now too weak to render assistance, and our men fell back with some loss to their original position, which they held until the night of April 2, 1865, when they evacuated the works. All these were captured or abandoned except a small part held by the Louisiana brigade of Gordon's Division on the right of the Crater sometime during the day.

I suppose we had the distinction of being the last of Lee's army to give up the lines which had been held so stubbornly and for the capture of which the enemy had put forth their best effort and sacrificed so many thousands of lives. As we passed the houses in the city the women peeped out and said to us sadly: "Good-bye, Rebels; we never expect to see you again." A little farther on we found lying across the sidewalk one of our soldiers who had been to the fire, where he had imbibed too freely of the old "apple jack" stored there. Poor fellow! I suppose he found himself a prisoner when he sobered up, if he did not swim the Appomattox that night. In the glare of the burning city I saw an old citizen coming toward us in a great hurry, pushing before him on the railroad track a hand car loaded with provisions from the burning commissaries. A barrel of flour rolled off, and its head fell out, spilling a quantity of its contents. I rushed up and filled my haversack and secured a piece of meat and then filled my canteen with sorghum syrup from a barrel near by. It was very fortunate for me and my comrades that I did this, as we were now about to enter upon a period of starvation which tested our endurance to the utmost. If we had had an idea at the time how hungry our boys were and how little we were going to live on for the next two weeks, we would have run the risk of being left on that side of the Appomattox and gone to the fire and loaded up with rations for them.

We now struck out for the bridge, and when we reached it we saw a man on the other side with a light in his hand, and he hallooed out: "Come on, boys; I am going to blow it up now. Hurry up." As we passed him we told him we had left others behind in the city and begged him to wait a little until they could come. When we reached the top of the hill on the other side, we heard a tremendous explosion, and, looking back, we saw the timbers of the bridge rising high in the blue sky, now beautifully illuminated by the full moon.

We sought a quiet place and slept a short while, then resumed our journey, and sometime that day rejoined our command. They were all glad to know that I had reached them safely, and especially glad to see my well-filled haversack, as they had not had anything to eat since they started on the march. Although hungry, our spirits began to revive when we felt that we were once more in the open country and clear of the ditches and the mortar shells which had been raining on us day and night for so long from Fort Steadman. For many weeks our rations had been only half a pound of corn bread and two ounces of meat a day, and consequently we were very weak to begin this retreat, in which the enemy made the greater effort to harass our progress and worry us in every way possible. After two days without rations, the situation became acute and began to tell on the strength and spirits of our men. Some manifested it by throwing away their guns, and others cast off their old ragged shoes; while others, whose homes were not far off from our line of march, deserted. No one could blame them now, since every one knew that all hope for the Confederacy had long since fled, and it was only a matter of a very few days when the whole army would have to surrender or die of starvation.

Bad as the condition of the men was, it was even worse with the poor horses and mules, which had always served us so faithfully. These poor creatures were so weak for want of food that the drivers in many cases dumped the contents of their wagons, and many abandoned vehicles were left standing by the roadside. The artillery horses were too weak to pull the ammunition wagons, and a great part of it was piled up in a field and exploded. I thought at the time that this was a great pity and that it would have been better if it had been expended in driving back the lines of the enemy, who were now pressing us so hard. Matters grew worse and worse from day to day; but a few of us held on to our guns and ammunition, determined to cut our way out, free ourselves from the enemy, and continue the fight to the bitter end unless we could secure some fruits of the long contest and the sacrifice of so many of our brave men who had died in defense of the South. Animated by this thought, we resisted the ever-present pangs of hunger, fatigue, and the efforts of the enemy to destroy us, with a faint hope that something would turn up to our advantage, as had often been the case before when fortune seemed to be against us.

Finally we came late in the night into a piece of woods near the little village of Appomattox C.H. and bivouacked. There was quite a number of stragglers from other commands with us; but we could only pity them, and we treated them kindly as they sat around our fires in their forlorn condition. Here cooking utensils were issued to us and some provisions that came from somewhere, and we were just preparing it when fighting of a severe character started in the little village near by. We were called to arms and marched to that point. Before we reached the scene of the engagement it was over with, and when we got into the little town we saw a number of pieces of artillery, which our men or the Federals had left there, standing silently without any one near. We remained here only a short while and marched back to our bivouac, where we had a few hours of sleep. Before day we were in line again on our way to the village, where we were to meet our old enemies for the last time in battle. The whole landscape was enveloped in a fog so thick that it was difficult to see but a short distance ahead of us. To the right of the road leading south from the courthouse was a battery of artillery firing down the road at the enemy. To the right of the artillery was General Rodes's old division, or what little there was left of it, formed in line of battle. When we saw the dim outline of these men lying there in the mist of the early morning, their glorious achievements on the many battle fields in which they had supported us on the right filled our minds, and we resolved to give the enemy once more a taste of what we had done for them so often before.

Our line was now formed on the left of the road, and Rodes's men were ordered forward. Glancing in that direction, I saw a handsome young artilleryman, standing bravely at the breech of his gun, fall dead, and the thought instinctively passed through my mind: What a pity! How many battles and dangers he has passed through, only to lose his life now at the end of it all!

Rodes's men moved forward in fine style, as usual, and when they had disappeared in the fog and smoke, driving everything ahead of them, we were ordered forward. Our old brigade moved with its old-time vigor and very soon developed the enemy's line, which broke as soon as it was opened upon and fell back, leaving in our hands a piece of artillery which our men turned on the fleeing foe. We were now in hot pursuit when word was passed along the line to cease firing. When some one suggested that General Lee had surrendered, many of our brave men, who had faced all kinds of danger and endured every hardship incident to war, wept like children. We were ordered to retrace our steps, and in doing so we could see the forces of the enemy assembling to make an attack on our left and rear. From the left we saw a Federal officer riding at full gallop into our lines, waving before him a red bandanna handkerchief. When he came near enough to be heard, he inquired who was in command, and some one said: "General Gordon." He then went on, waving his handkerchief, until he met the General and had some conversation with him in connection with the surrender. When he galloped by us and in easy range, a brave soldier of the 31st Georgia Regiment, whose face was wet with tears, threw his gun up and said: "I'll get that scoundrel." But some one who was more thoughtful knocked his gun up and said: "Don't, John; it may be that the surrender has already taken place, and it may cause trouble." Thursby replied: "That's not a white flag, and I am not bound to respect it." But his comrades would not allow him to shoot, and Custer, the bloody tyrant (shall I use the word?), who had shed so much innocent blood and devastated the Valley of Virginia with the torch, rode on, not knowing how near he came to the expiation of his heartless cruelty, only to meet a fate later on which he richly deserved if the command, "Thou shalt not kill," means anything. We only hope that he repented and was forgiven before that event. He was one of those who chose to make war as cruel as possible and seemed to delight in riding rough-shod over a helpless and defenseless foe.[10]

---

[10] Henderson, *Roster*, 648. "John W. Thursby. Private November 11, 1861. Appointed 3d Corporal February 17, 1863; 2d Sergeant May 1863. Surrendered, Appomattox, April 9, 1865."

We never saw General Lee nor that apple tree of which so much has been said, for we were far in advance and had been thrown forward to cut through the Federals in a last effort to escape the net which Grant had been trying to place around us. We marched away some distance to the west of the road mentioned above and stacked our arms and went into camp. Sometime that day or the next two pounds of fresh beef were issued to us, and this was all we had to live on for the five days we were detained here. The first night of the surrender some one suggested that we take our arms (for we had not delivered them up), make a bold dash through the lines, escape to the mountains, and continue the war to the bitter end or until we obtained more satisfactory terms. The news of our intentions were conveyed by some one to General Gordon, and he came to us, mounted a wagon, and from it he made us a speech in which he dissuaded us from the undertaking, advising us to return peaceably to our homes and employ the same energy in restoring the prosperity of our country that we had displayed in its defense. A new battle flag that had never been baptized in the sulfurous smoke of battle was fastened to the staff, and all decided that it was better to take the counsel of our general, whom we loved so much, than to go into an enterprise so hazardous.

Our paroles were given us by our own officers, and we expected to be disbanded immediately; but we were detained here for five days, as I have already said, until we were nearly dead from starvation. Finally we were ordered to take our arms and were marched to the road referred to, and there on the east side and about a hundred feet from it was a long line of Yankee soldiers facing toward us. We were formed in front of them and stood quietly for some time. We were now so weak from our long fast that we could hardly stand up in ranks and were clothed in rags, so that our appearance made a poor contrast with that of our well-fed and well-clothed enemies. The silence was finally broken by some one in their ranks, and the whole line then began to curse and use the most opprobrious language. This continued for some time, when an officer, riding to and fro in the rear of their line, spoke to them and said: "These Confederate soldiers are brave men. If you were half as brave as they are, you would have conquered them long ago. If I hear another cowardly scoundrel curse these men again, I will break my sword over his head." We all now gave a shout for the major, and silence prevailed.

Colonel Lowe, Dr. J.A. Butts, our regimental surgeon, and Captain Walker, of Eufaula, Ala., who had ever since the organization of our regiment at Savannah been our commissary and quartermaster and later on had been General Lee's main dependence for securing supplies for his army, spoke to us when we had stacked our arms and said: "If you have anything on your person that belongs to the Confederacy, put it on the stack." When this was done, Captain Walker said: "Now, men, if you will follow us to-day, we will take you to a mill twenty-six miles from here, where you can get meal to-night; and if you will follow us again to-morrow, we will take you where you can get meal and meat." We were told to break ranks, and our officers rode slowly away; but we were so nearly dead that we could go only a short distance before we were exhausted and had to rest. Somehow we seemed to gain strength as we progressed, and a few kept ahead in sight of the officers, and at dusk we came in sight of the mill, which was in operation when we reached it. When the enemy was sorely pressing us on the retreat, I found a new frying pan which some one had thrown away, and, thinking perhaps I might have need of it in the future, I took it along. I also had a new tin cup. As soon as I could get through the crowd to where the meal was coming out I placed the cup under the spout, and when it was full I stepped just outside and got water, kindled a fire, and soon had a hoecake, the sweetest morsel I had ever tasted, I thought. The next day we were much stronger and made the journey much more easily to the next mill on our route to the nearest railroad point.

After this day our officers rode on, and we made it by easy stages to Danville, Va. From this place we made our way partly on foot and partly over the railroads to our homes in Georgia and other States. The writer reached Albany, Ga., with others of his command, and found that the stage to Quincy, Fla., was about to depart on its last trip under its contract with the Confederate government. He secured passage on it and arrived safely at Bainbridge, Ga., his old boyhood home, from which he had gone to the war in 1861. He felt grateful to Divine Providence for preserving him through so many hardships and dangers while most of his comrades and schoolmates who had gone away with him were either maimed or sleeping beneath the sod.

MAKING OUR WAY HOME FROM APPOMATTOX[11]

By the terms of the surrender we were not to be molested in returning to our homes with our paroles; but Gen. Joseph E. Johnston's army in North Carolina had not as yet surrendered, and there were many hostile forces between us and our homes. For our protection our company decided to maintain our organization as a means of mutual benefit. We had no idea what difficulties were to be met with on our way. We were unarmed, and if attacked by Sherman's soldiers or deserters we had no means of defense.

Fortunately, we had no trouble with any of our old enemies, none of whom we met until we reached Macon, Ga. which place we found full of Wilson's Cavalry, who had arrived there a few days before. They had heard of Lee's surrender and did not interfere with us. After we had supplied our haversacks with a sufficient quantity of meal at the mill mentioned in my previous article, we marched leisurely toward Danville, Va., where we found an abundance of commissary stores sent there by the authorities at Richmond. But if we had not been fed by the enemy, the army would have perished before we got to these supplies. We found the town full of soldiers who had outtraveled us; and as there was no train for Greensboro, N. C., that day, we decided to take a much-needed rest, cook up food for several days, and otherwise prepare for our long journey home. One of our men borrowed a big wash pot, in which we placed a quantity of dry speckled peas, choice food with us at that time, and a shoulder of very salty bacon. A great fire was kindled around it, and we sat about on the platform of the railroad watching it. We watched and waited while the meat rose to the surface and sank again in the boiling water. Our mouths were watering for a taste of that bacon and the peas. Occasionally some one would run down and examine to see if the contents were done and add fuel to the fire, but they were always found to be as hard almost as when we put them in the pot. It did not seem that our dinner would ever get done

---

[11] *Confederate Veteran*, March 1921, 29:102-103. Paragraphs deleted from this article to eliminate duplication. Editor.

enough to eat. Finally a comrade suggested that we watch the pot and save his part of the contents while he went down to the arsenal, some distance away, and got some powder and lead to take home.

He was gone quite a while, and we still sat there watching the performance of our pot, when all at once we were startled by a tremendous explosion that shook the entire town, and pieces of shell began to drop about us and everywhere in the city. Soon we saw men running with stretchers toward the scene, bringing mangled boys and soldiers away. Our comrade finally returned and reported that he had just got out of the building and far enough away not to be killed when the explosion took place. It seemed that the soldiers doing police duty in the town, when they found that General Lee had surrendered, refused to obey the orders of the mayor and keep the little boys, negroes, and soldiers out of the building filled with guns and all kinds of explosives. Crowds rushed to this place, where the floors and cellar were covered an inch or more deep in powder. A boy snapped a gun to see if it was loaded and blew up the place jam full of boys, negroes, and soldiers. Our comrade told us that two women going down the street on the other side at the time of the explosion caught fire. In their pain and fright they dashed forward to the river and plunged in, only to lose their lives by drowning.

Nothing remained of the building the next day. The cellar alone marked the spot where it had stood. The mayor had the remnants of human beings collected and put in a large box and thus buried. How many of our brave soldiers perished in this unfortunate catastrophe no one will ever know.

After waiting here some time, we got transportation on freight cars to Greensboro, where we again had to wait over some time. Here we first came in touch with Gen. Joseph E. Johnston's men. What attracted our attention most was the various gambling games in progress everywhere. Our men had long since eliminated this vicious habit, and we were surprised to know that it still survived in the Army of the West.

While waiting at the depot Generals Beauregard and Joseph E. Johnston rode up. I thought I never saw handsomer men in my life except General Lee. They looked like kings as they sat on their fine horses giving orders to their soldiers. The nobility of their characters was as admirable as their persons.

The railroad tracks were in a shocking condition where they could be used, and the freight cars were equally bad; but when we had the opportunity our men crowded into them and on top of them as long as there was space to crowd in. Once more we started and managed, by walking part of the way, to get to High Point. This is now a beautiful and flourishing manufacturing city; it was then a little old dilapidated village. Here we had to lie over again. The next morning some comrades and I were preparing our breakfast at a little fire when a very gentlemanly soldier from Texas approached us and said: "Boys, have you heard of old Abe's demise?" "No," we replied. He then told us that John Wilkes Booth had killed President Lincoln. We could but feel at the time that it was only an expiation for the atrocities he had allowed his soldiers to commit and the treatment accorded our defenseless prisoners in his hands, doing so much to create bitter sectional feeling by the methods he employed, when he could have accomplished the same ends by a more humane policy. Many think that if he had lived there would never have been the persecution of the South in Reconstruction days, but no argument could be more false. Lincoln would have been just as wholly in the hands of the most radical element of his political party and could have done little in opposition to their wishes.

Once more we mounted those old ramshackle cars that had done duty during the whole war without repair. We were packed in them and on top like sardines. When we reached Blackstock Station, in South Carolina, in the darkness, our engine ran into a freight car standing on the track, and the top of the one on which I was riding broke in, dumping us down on our companions sleeping below. Strange to say, nobody was seriously hurt. We now decided to abandon the railroad and make our way on foot across the country to Aiken, S. C. Reaching that place, we went to the broad piazza of the hotel to rest. The proprietor came out and said: "Gentlemen, I am sorry I cannot entertain you better, but you are welcome to occupy my front porch."

From Aiken we went to Augusta, Ga., where we found one of our comrades, who had by some means outtraveled us. When the Confederate stores of every kind were opened, he secured for each one of us a new suit of clothes from head to foot and much other plunder. I took my new clothes and a piece of soap to the river at the back of the building where we were stopping, and, divesting myself of the old ragged duds I had worn so long, I cast them with all the living things they contained into the Savannah River to float on and out to the Atlantic Ocean.

On our way to Atlanta our engine ran off the track at Stone Mountain; but the train crew got it back in place, and we were soon in that city of ruins. I saw but one house that had not been burned, and it stood at the end of White Hall Street and overlooked the place. I was told that it was Sherman's headquarters while he occupied the city. As we passed along the ruined streets desperate-looking men peeped at us from cellars with the eyes of hawks. They looked like desperadoes who had followed the wake of Sherman's army to rob, steal, or murder as opportunity offered. But if they had injured one of our men, it would have cost the offender his life.

From Atlanta to Macon we rode in comfortable passenger cars and were not overcrowded, as many of our soldiers had branched off in every direction to their homes. At each station some of our comrades got off, and we bade them adieu. Macon, as I have already said, was full of Wilson's raiders, but we were not molested by them. After another delay here we entrained for Albany, then the terminus of the railroad, fifty-six miles to Bainbridge, Ga., our home town. We were informed that the stage would make its last trip under the company's mail contract with the Confederate government that evening to Bainbridge and Quincy, Fla., and that the fare was $120 in Confederate money to Bainbridge. I sold an extra pair of shoes I got at Augusta for that sum and secured a ticket. The coach was crowded, but our driver had a splendid team of horses, which was changed every ten or twelve miles. There were two ladies with us bound for Tallahassee, Fla., and to these we gave the best seats inside the coach, while we occupied the top and the seat with the driver. At daybreak the stage stopped in front of John Sharon's hotel at Bainbridge, and I stepped out amidst a crowd assembled to greet friends and to hear the news. I did not see any one I knew except Dr. Moritz Hahn, an old Jewish citizen, who informed me where to find my people in the town. This was May 4, 1865, and so many changes had taken place in my absence that I did not know the people. But I should mention that new conditions were met with after we left Macon. From that place to Albany every warehouse at the different stations along the road was piled to its capacity with Confederate corn and army supplies. It seemed that there was enough stored there to supply all the armies we had in the field, while we were starving in Virginia.

My father lived on his plantation, one and a half miles out of town. He was one of the county officials and very prominent in supporting the cause by feeding and caring for the families of the soldiers who were away fighting for their country. My oldest brother, now returned from the army, was very apprehensive lest the Yankees, when they occupied the town, would hang him for the active part he had taken. But he did not seem to care or feel any uneasiness; and when it was reported that Captain Roberson, of the 13th Maine Regiment, with a hundred men and two lieutenants, was coming from Albany to take over the government in the name of the United States, he called Sam, the carriage driver, and told him to hitch up and go to meet the soldiers and bring Captain Roberson and his officers to our house and invite him to make it his headquarters. This Sam did; and when Roberson came, my father met him on the porch and extended his hand, at the same time saying that he had sent for him to have his protection; that he had done all he could for the cause of the South, but now that we were defeated it was in his hands to bestow such treatment as he saw fit. Roberson seemed to be very sullen the whole time he was there, but his soldiers did not commit any depredations. They were relieved by a battalion of Kentucky cavalry. These men seemed to have been forced into the service to fight in a cause they did not like and so vented their anger on the poor negroes, treating them with the greatest cruelty. They came without any wagons or feed for their horses, about six hundred in number, and compelled our old foreman, Sambo, to give up the keys and helped themselves to six hundred bushels of corn and other forage. Sambo and Sam were pressed into service to haul the stuff to their camps, and when they moved to Tallahassee they took the two negroes and our teams with them. This was after all the Confederate armies had surrendered, and father was never paid one cent by the United States government. A battalion of infantry from Indiana, under Captain Mason, took the place of the Kentuckians, and during their stay our citizens began to realize the evils of reconstruction, the darkest page in all the history of our country. Our government was placed in the hands of carpetbaggers, negroes, and our own Southern traitors, many of whom had been prominent in the secession movement, but took no part in the fighting that resulted. They joined the Union League to get office and have a part in the robbery and plunder of their fellow citizens. Their management of the State government was so outrageous that we organized the Ku-Klux Klan and redeemed the country. Since that time the South has remained solid.[12]

---

[12] At the age of ninety, Isaac Gordon Bradwell wrote a letter to Col. Peter Brannon of Montgomery, Ala., concerning postwar activity (see appendix §3 for the text of this letter.

UNDER THE SOUTHERN CROSS

Editor's note: Bradwell sums up the history of the 31st Georgia Volunteer Infantry by tracing the sequence of the battle flags that flew over the regiment. His story concludes with a testimony to his regiment's bravery and sacrifice.

UNDER THE SOUTHERN CROSS[1]

The first flag of the Confederacy was called the "Stars and Bars." Its similarity to the United States flag, in the confusion and smoke of battle, made it difficult to be distinguished from the colors of the enemy, and for this reason the famous battle flag was designed, the beautiful emblem under which our men marched to victory and to death. This flag was conspicuous in the thickest fighting, and every straggler could see plainly where his unit was engaged. Some of these flags had a border of golden fringe, which added very much to their appearance. Its staff was surmounted with a formidable looking blade of shining metal, or a round knob of the same material. Many of the Virginia regiments had their State flag, which had a blue ground, with the coat of arms of the State in the center and the memorable words "Sic Semper Tyrannis" inscribed thereon. The Virginians loved that flag, for under it their fathers had won our independence at Yorktown.

When the regiment to which I belonged, the 31st Georgia Infantry, entered the service of the Confederacy at Savannah, in November, 1861, it was presented with a flag, the "Stars and Bars." This, or one like it, was hoisted on a tall flagstaff over our camp, and often as I looked on it proudly floating in the breeze, the thought passed through my mind that the existence of our government depended solely upon our ability to keep the flag afloat.

This flag was replaced by the battle flag, the "Southern Cross," under which we marched and fought until the end. One large company of the regiment from Pulaski County, Ga., under Capt. Warren D. Wood, at first had its own flag, presented before it left home, a beautiful green silk Georgia State flag, with the coat of arms of the State on one side. The color bearer was a Russian, or Polish, Jew, who had belonged to the Russian army, and wore his tall black bearskin cap, which gave

---

[1] *Confederate Veteran*, May 1925, 33:182-183.

him a commanding appearance and made him look much taller than he really was. But as the regiment did not need this extra standard, it was displayed only on dress parade. Perhaps some survivor of that command remembers this and knows what became of it.

We had been in camp of instruction at Savannah some months when the new battle flag was presented to the regiment. This flag was destined to be in much fighting, to be torn into shreds by shot and shell, and to witness the death of many noble souls who held it aloft in battle. The next year (1862), in August, when Stonewall was making his celebrated flank movement to get into General Pope's rear, at the crossing of the Rappahannock, a shell from a Yankee battery on the north side of the river passed through our flag and left nothing but the fringe clinging to the staff. But under it, mutilated as it was, the regiment marched and fought at Manassas, Chantilly, Harper's Ferry, and Sharpsburg.

On returning to Virginia a new flag of the same kind was fastened to the old staff, and, like its predecessor, was destined to have a checkered career, for it was not long until it floated in the smoke of battle at Fredericksburg, where it rested for a short time in a muddy ditch. In this engagement, our general being away, suffering from a wound received at Manassas, the brigade was badly led, or rather was not led at all, as every regiment and individual in it seemed to act independently. When we had driven the enemy out of the woods to the line of the railroad where we were to stop (if there were any such orders we never heard them), and we were in full view of that splendid Federal battery and its white horses, standing out there around the guns, our men could not restrain their desire to capture it, but rushed forward, led by our noble Adjutant General Lawton. We were not supported on the right or left by any command, and, after desperate fighting, in which many men on both sides were killed, including Captain Lawton, and fifty-four of the horses belonging to the battery, the guns were captured. But at this critical moment the enemy's reserves advanced in a long line that easily enveloped our right and left flanks. To escape being captured or killed our men abandoned the guns taken at so great a sacrifice of life and started back across the field with many prisoners, to reach if possible, the protection of the woods some hundreds of yards to the rear. The artillerymen, seeing their opportunity, ran back to their guns, and with grape and canister fired rapidly upon the fleeing Confederates and their prisoners, killing and wounding many of both.

In this disastrous affair, the young soldier carrying the colors, despairing of reaching a place of safety alive, threw the flag in a ditch full of mud and water, from which it was recovered after the battle was over.

Had the brigade been supported, the entire left wing of Burnsides's army would have been driven into the Rappahannock River, or captured, for we were in sight of that stream, only two or three hundred yards away. Their only means of escape was a pontoon bridge. The dust and mud of defeat were washed off the flag, and our colors were once more ready to wave defiantly in the smoke of battle at Fredericksburg, Chancellorsville, in May 1863, and again at Winchester in June, and at Wrightsville, Pa., and Gettysburg, where we completely broke the enemy's resistance on the first clay of the battle, capturing and killing thousands of the enemy and driving the remaining troops through the town to the heights beyond.

Returning to Virginia, our colors featured in all the minor engagements in the fall of that year (1863) and were ready to meet the overwhelming forces under Grant in the spring of 1864. They floated over the command at the first day's battle of the Wilderness, where they witnessed twenty-five hundred of the enemy throw up their hands and surrender to the irresistible advance of the regiment and brigade, and the killing of many others. And the next day advanced and crushed Grant's right wing, capturing Generals Seymour and Shaler, and many of their commands.

Under the shade of night the colors were shifted to Spotsylvania, where they were unfurled in the sulphurous air of battle on the 8th, 9th, 10th, 12th, and 13th of May, where thousands died around them.

To turn aside, as it were, for a brief season from this scene of death, they were shifted to North Anna and at Cold Harbor where they had first received their baptism of blood and thunder in 1862, only to witness again the valor of friend and foe in the shortest and most destructive battle in all the history of our country on the 3rd of June, 1864.

But now a new act in the drama of war was about to take place, in which our old colors must perform their part. The scene is shifted to Lynchburg, where they were to meet the enemy under the timid but tyrannical Hunter, and, after routing him, to be borne in triumph across the Potomac to meet and defeat Lew Wallace at Monocacy, where so many of their brave defenders laid down their lives; and to go on to the gates of Washington and float defiantly in full view of the dome of the national Capitol. After a brief visit of two days there, they were borne quietly at night across the swift blue waters of the Potomac to the friendly shores of Old Virginia, where they were to witness victory after victory over enemies who seemed afraid to measure arms with a weak but hitherto invincible foe. But overconfident in his own men, and despising the extreme caution of the enemy, our old commander, Jube Early, divided his forces in the presence of overwhelming numbers and resources. From the mountain tops the enemy saw, after hesitating so long, their opportunity to destroy Rodes and his brave but weak division. Fifty thousand blue warriors came down on this little band of gray veterans, heroes of a hundred victories, but the very sight of their battle flags seemed to cause the blue lines to hesitate in the work of extermination. Then, when almost too late to save the army, our old commander received word from Rodes and, realizing his mistake, ordered his tired forces to hasten by a forced night march to assist Rodes and his brave men. At daylight the boom of cannon ahead of us and the smoke of battle hastened our steps to the scene, and our battle flags hardly had time to unfurl, when the long blue lines overlapping us far to the right and left, with others supporting them, were down on us. Disregarding numbers, we dashed forward, driving back those in front of us, but those on the right and left swung around behind us unopposed. The right and left gave way, but the center still fought. Then the center gave ground and all was confusion. The brave Rodes was killed, but his men came up to our help and we were shifted to meet the enemy farther to the left, where we held the line all day until the sun went down and our flag was borne away, not defeated, but overwhelmed, to be planted on Fisher's Hill, only to be outflanked and driven off three days afterwards without a chance to fight. Once more we were reorganized, and, on the 19th of October, less than a month, under the guidance of our noble Gordon, we fell on the enemy's front and flank at Cedar Creek in sight of our former disaster, and our battle flags witnessed our complete victory. All their camp, artillery, and equipment were in our hands. They saved one piece of artillery to keep up a show of resistance until help came from Winchester. But now direction of affairs was turned over to "Old Jube," who did not seem to be at himself, and no effort was made to meet the gathering storm coming from Winchester under Sheridan. We were outnumbered, driven from the battle field, and our splendid victory turned into defeat.

But we clung to our colors, reorganized, and, under Gordon and Lee, met the enemy at Hatcher's Run, Deep Bottom, and Fort Steadman. Finally, the enemy at Five Forks surrounded and defeated our noble old commander, and there was nothing left for us to do but abandon the works at Petersburg, which we had held so long, and follow our comrades on the painful retreat, fighting and starving all the while. At length we reached Appomattox. A mouthful of food was issued, and we were preparing to fall down on our blankets to sleep, but the rattling noise of battle at the courthouse called us to arms again. We hastened to the scene, but found no combatants there, only the artillery standing in the silent night, and returned to our bivouac only to be aroused shortly in the heavy fog of the morning to unfurl our battle flags in their last engagement. We took our place in the line, while the cannon on our right boomed and we saw the standards of Rodes's Division disappear in the smoke of battle and mist of the early morning in their last charge in an effort to cut our way through the enemy's lines. And then we were ordered forward to assist in the same effort for General Lee and his army. We soon struck the enemy, who gave way as far as we extended to the right and left, and abandoned their artillery to us. With these guns we opened on their fleeing ranks. But at this moment we were ordered to cease firing. We asked: "What does it mean? Has General Lee surrendered the army?" Perhaps so; but can it be that, after so much sacrifice and suffering, we must surrender these battle flags which have triumphed so many times over the foe? Yes, it is too true. And our men weep.

We were ordered back toward the village and stacked our arms to await orders. The following night some one suggested that we could not submit to such humiliation and proposed that all who wished to do so could steal out of camp through the enemy lines and, reaching the mountains, continue the war to the bitter end. The old battle flag we loved so well was torn from the staff and a small piece given to each of us as a relic and evidence that we had served under it in the regiment. But our beloved commander, General Gordon, got wind of what was transpiring in camp and hastened into our midst, lest we should do something violent to cause him and us trouble. Mounting an empty wagon, he made us a speech in which he praised our former bravery and loyalty to orders and begged us to refrain from violating the terms of surrender, but to return to our homes and restore our ruined country and be obedient to the laws as we had been as soldiers to his orders.

A new battle flag was found somewhere in the wagons and was fastened to the old staff, and this was surrendered. The old one never was. I brought a piece of it home with me, as every other man of the regiment did.

What became of all the other flags of the different regiments and brigades of Lee's army? They have a glorious history that can never be told.

> "Furl that banner! true 'tis gory,
> Yet 'tis wreathed around with glory,
> And 'twill live in song and story,
> Though its folds are in the dust."

APPENDIX

The appendix includes three letters that were too lengthy to include in the text. The first is an excerpt from a letter written by Daniel Bradwell, Pvt. Gordon Bradwell's father, and it identifies the elder Bradwell as an eloquent writer and man of intellect. The letter provides insight on the philosophy Daniel Bradwell provided to his family and gives the reader a perspective on Pvt. Bradwell's heritage. Daniel wrote the letter to his son, Sumter, in 1876.

An excerpt of Daniel Bradwell's 1876 letter follows:

"You would like to know what are my consolidations, if any, during the period of old age? If one has lived righteously, he has nothing to regret. We were placed on earth under the probationary form of moral government: that our lives might long grow in capacity for truth and virtue, every day bringing us nearer the great type of perfection manifested once in Humanity as a model for man. If one breaks one of the great laws of nature by eating and drinking too much he suffers the penalty attack to the law--which is sickness. So also it is with disobedience to all the great laws of nature—such penalty must be suffered. These penalties destroy life: but when Heaven is the goal for which we are striving, how dare we shorten the time allotted to us for perfection, and sacrifice the inestimable treasure future years may per chance have in store for us. The work of preparation is not appropriated to youth or middle age, but to whole life times. We cannot cultivate so successfully with the impetus order of youth, or the unbending will of manhood, those Christian graces for which the contemplative mood of old age, when the sullener facilities of the soul hold sway, seems perfectly fitted. Old age is maturity, and on our journey of earth's existence there are many station houses. Like the marine on the great deep will stop to take truthful reckoning. Old age then gains its moral reckonings in reviewing past deeds—inquires as how many more days may be allotted to our stay on earth. Then a life thus spent grows more beautiful as it approaches Heaven, and the soul as it nears its release.... Often times in returning home, whether noon or night, from my labor of the day, my limbs are so much worn and tired, I can scarcely reach my domicile. My soul addresses to these tired and worn limbs the following and consoling language—your task is almost finished, and soon will be at rest. You have been engaged in honorable employment all your days, the work was pointed out for you by our Heavenly Father--in peace and virtue you have discharged you duty, and soon you will return to God, who is author of my being." Letter provided by Gordon C. Bradwell of Athens, Georgia.

§ 2. In *Confederate Veteran*, November 1925, Bradwell quotes a letter from W. H. Bland describing Bland's capture at Morton's Ford. See page 149.

"I was captured at Dr. Morton's house, near Morton's Ford, on the Rapidan River, on the night of the 4th of January, 1864, after we had shot away nearly all of our ammunition. My capture happened in this way: I was at Dr. Morton's house while you and others of our company were fighting from behind other houses. As you well know, our skirmish had given the Yankees a whipping, killing, wounding, and capturing four or five hundred, and there were not over forty of us fighting them, and, after our ammunition had been exhausted, the Yankees surrounded Dr. Morton's house just at dark. I had gone into the house and did not know that any part of our line had given way until Dr. Morton's house was entirely surrounded by the enemy. I did not see any of our boys leaving, so I was alone and was surrounded by about fifty Union soldiers, and I just had to surrender. They took me to the rear in a hurry, for they were scared and in bad confusion. When we got to the river, I found that it was bridged with round poles and lacked a few feet of being finished on the south side of the river, and we had to make a pretty good jump to get on to it. I made it very well, as I was an expert jumper, as did my guard, he being sober; but some of those little cut-short Dutchmen could not make it very well with the amount of whisky they had taken on. They could not reach the bridge, but did reach the water under the bridge, and some being too drunk to swim and others not able to swim, lost their lives in the icy waters of the river, while in the darkness and rain their friends could not render them any assistance.

"After we had crossed the river and had gone about three hundred yards, we found some camp fires. I was taken to them and kept there until the Yankees got across. After all were over, they formed in line and marched off and went about four miles and camped.

"They had a hard time in getting fires started with oak brush and chips in the rain. My guard and I sat down by an oak stump on our knapsacks, and he spread his oilcloth over us to keep off the falling rain. He was soon nodding, and I thought he was asleep. I lifted the cloth off me and raised it up to run; but he woke up, so I turned over my knapsack and sat down again quickly to keep him from suspecting my anticipated escape. He spread the cloth over me again, and I remained very quiet. He was soon nodding again, and I made a second attempt; but he woke again. By this time they had fires started, and he said, 'Well, Johnny, we will go to the light,' and I saw no chance of making my escape.

"Next day we marched about nine miles and reached their old camp. I was put in a guardhouse with about a dozen of their own prisoners. Being the only Johnny Reb (as they called me), I was treated kindly. Next morning I was sent for to go to General Hayes's headquarters. While going through their camps the Yankees would say, 'Hello, Johnny, when did you come over?' and I would reply, 'I was captured and brought over,' for I did not want them to think that I was a deserter.

"The General's headquarters were some four or five hundred yards away. When I got there, the guard said: 'General, here is our Johnny Reb.' The general wheeled around and said: 'Hello, Johnny, how do you feel to-day?' I replied: 'I feel very well General. How do you feel?' He said, 'I am well;' then 'Well, Johnny, do you wish to go back across the river?' I told him that I did. He said: 'O, no, Johnny, you don't wish to go back.' 'Well,' said I, 'all you have to do is to give me a showing to that effect and you will see that I go back.' 'Well, Johnny, how are you faring on your side of the river?' I told him I was faring very well. 'Well, Johnny, what do you get to eat on your side of the river?' I replied: 'Bacon, flour, rice, sugar, coffee, etc.' 'Well, Johnny, do you draw all that?' 'Yes, sir.' (Which we did, but it was scanty, especially the sugar and coffee.)

"By this time he was looking in my haversack. I happened to have two day's rations for four men, and he said: 'Did you draw all this meat, Johnny?' I said: 'Yes sir.' 'How many days is this ration for, Johnny?' 'Two days,' I replied. He then turned to another general and said, 'Look at the meat, general,' who replied: 'Yes, I see.' He then said: 'How is it, Johnny, that some of you men come over here and say that you are on starvation?' I said: 'Well, any man who will desert his country will tell you a lie.' And I further said as to my regiment and brigade: 'We fare very well, but as to the rest of the army, I can't account for.'

"He then said: 'How is Lee's army situated?' 'I guess you know more about that than I do,' said I. 'How much force has he got?' To this I replied: 'You know more about that than I can tell you.' He turned to another general and said: 'This is a fine man, general, if he is a Rebel. What was your loss, Johnny?' I told him I did not know. 'Did you see any dead men?' I told him I did not see any, then asked him his losses, and he said they lost between four and five hundred. I said: 'Well, we did very well then.' I have since learned that we had two killed, one wounded, and I was captured, which made a total of four.)

"He told me that they all got on a drunken spree, and he rushed his men over the river without orders, and that he was under arrest that day. He also told me that he rode on our skirmish line for some distance in the dark and was halted several times, but he said he told them that he was General Hayes and was allowed to go on. Saying to me: 'You have a General Hays, which was all that saved my life.'

"The general then said: 'Johnny, don't you want a drink of good brandy this morning?' I told him I could not refuse, as I had taken cold. He then poured out a fine drink and gave it to me, and I drank it. He then said: 'Well, Johnny, we will have to send you to prison.'

"I was taken to a place they called their 'bull pen,' about thirty miles away, where I found six or eight more Confederate prisoners. This was on the railroad running from Fredericksburg to Alexandria and Washington. We had plenty to eat, but we came near freezing. We stayed here two days and nights, and were then taken to the city of Washington and put in prison in the old Capitol building, which they used for a wayside prison.

"Our fare was very good for prisoners, though we were closely confined. We were in rooms about eighteen feet square, with a good fireplace, and plenty of coal and blankets were furnished us. Here a Confederate prisoner from Florida killed another from Virginia while in a mad fit, but he was afterwards very sorry for the deed.

"One day Mosby's Cavalry made a raid on the railroad near Alexandria, Va., and caused some confusion in the city of Washington. We stayed here about four months, with excellent fare; we had plenty to eat and good coffee to drink, and I weighed more than I ever did before or since. We were transferred from there to Fort Delaware. Here some Confederates made a lot of money while shut up in prison, with no other tools but saws made out of case knives, pocketknives, needle drills, hand saw files, and other small files, making bone and gutta-percha rings with gold and silver sets in them. A great many other things besides were made and sold by them. They traded with citizens, Yankee officers and private soldiers.

"Here we fared extremely bad, in fact we were nearly starved to death. I would often dream of being at home at my mother's table, with plenty of good things on it, and I would eat and eat, but it seemed that I could never get enough. I would awaken nearly dead from hunger. Our rations consisted of one-fourth of a one-half pound loaf of baker's bread. We got this twice a day. Our meat consisted of a very small, thin slice of salt pork, or fresh beef, which made about one good mouthful, with one Irish potato occasionally thrown in extra. I often gave up to die from hunger. I was so nearly starved that I was reduced from one hundred and forty to eighty pounds. This food caused scurvy among the prisoners and many of them died.

"One man bet his blanket that he could eat every bit of his bread at one mouthful. He did, and won the blanket. The prisoners ate every rat they could catch. They were fine and highly relished by the prisoners, and if we could have caught enough rats we would have gotten along a great deal better than we did.

"In extremely cold weather all the water we had to drink was real brackish tide water. It would not quench thirst, but made us want water much worse. We sometimes had river water brought to us in boats from up the river. We had this brackish water only when it was too cold to bring the other. The private soldiers were in one department and the officers in another. We could have no communication with them except to write a few lines on paper, tie it to a stone, and throw it over the wall to them when the guards were not watching us. They would often reply to us in the same way.

"About six thousand prisoners were there. Our guards were old soldiers who had been used to hard service and were mostly square gentlemen. They were kind to us and would often divide tobacco with us and show us other acts of kindness.

"I do not think we received all the government sent there for us or intended us to have. I believe it was abominable rascality and speculation of some of the managers of the prison, and I am sure that from what we heard the Confederate officers' fare was, if possible, worse than ours.

"I stayed in prison about ten months and had the smallpox in that time. There was a department in the prison for each Southern State, and one thousand private soldiers were in the Georgia department. They paroled us all, with ten Georgia officers, and marched us to the boat and put us on it. We started about eleven o'clock in the morning on the 7th of March, 1865, to City Point, below Richmond, Va. Six prisoners died on the boat and were buried on the banks of the James River near City Point.

"When we put our feet on Dixie's soil, how our hearts leaped with joy and our eyes filled with tears! We were marched along through the Yankee army, which was between City Point and our army at Drewry's Bluff. We were then put on a boat and taken up the river to a landing near Richmond and marched to Camp Lee, two miles from the city. Here we drew money and clothing and stayed four days, and then were given a sixty-day furlough. With this I started home to my mother, but I had a rough time getting there, for Sherman had torn up a great many of our railroads. I was weak and emaciated from confinement and starvation and could walk but a short distance at a time, but finally arrived at home on the 27th of the month. I took those at home by surprise, for they all thought I was dead, as they had not received any news from me in about fifteen months."

§ 3. At the age of ninety, Isaac Gordon Bradwell wrote a letter to Col. Peter Brannon of Montgomery, Ala., concerning postwar activity:

"In you article prepared for the Sunday issue of the Advertiser you mention the name of Capt. Sanders who deserted my Regiment (31st Ga.) in Virginia, came home to Alabama, raised a company of deserters and terrorized all of West Florida and Southeast Alabama.

I knew Capt. Sanders well as a brave and true soldier as long as he remained with us and was surprised and ashamed to know that he turned his back on his former comrades to become an enemy to them and their families at home—an outlaw of the worst character.

He didn't leave our regiment without a good reason for he was degraded and humiliated by the Colonel of the regiment when there was no cause for such treatment. He was advised by his men to do this, to return home, raise another company or join another command where he would be respected and at the time perhaps he intended to do this but when he got back his old home he realized that he was a deserter; under evil influences and still chafing with resentment he decided to take the course that brought ruin, death and disgrace to himself and misery and suffering to wide sections of our country. In this Georgia regiment there was one company (Co. C) from Alabama made up form the counties of Dale, Barbour, Henry and Coffee. This was a fine company of soldiers and there was not a braver man among them than Sanders. He was only a non-commissioned officer at first but rose in the estimate of his comrades by his meritorious conduct on every occasion. When the regiment was sent from Savannah in the spring of 1862 to Stonewall in Virginia the company lost heavily in the battle and Co. C. had no captain. The men of the company considered him the most worthy of all and elected him their captain. This so displeased the Colonel that he refused to recognize him as a captain in his regiment and reduced him to the rank of private.

"The last time I remember seeing Capt. Sanders he was standing up on the Confederate earthworks at Falling Waters, Maryland where General Lee was waiting for Mead to attack him after Gettysburg and for the arrival of ammunition from Richmond. Capt. Sanders was standing up on the breastworks with field glasses taking observations of Mead's defenses. I had no idea then that this brave Captain would become one of our bitterest enemies to attack us in the back.

"But what became of Captain Sanders? Perhaps there is nobody in Alabama except myself that can answer this question. There were hundreds, perhaps thousands, of returning Confederate soldiers who were determined to kill Sanders for this treatment of their families while they were away in the Army.

"Sanders knew this and crossed the Chattahoochee river into Decatur County, Ga., where he was engaged in building a mill. He was living with a women he called his wife in a little log shack. The few people that lived in that sparsely settled country knew little or nothing of his reputation and he went about his daily labor unmolested by anybody. Nobody there knew that he had an enemy in the world – but he had very many of them where he came from and by some means they had found out where he was and how situated.

"The citizens of Georgia never knew who those Alabamians were that crossed the river that night and poked the muzzles of their guns through the cracks in the humble home and shot Capt. Sanders to death as he sat at the table with his wife eating supper.

"The colored ferryman at the river told the authorities that quite a number of men on horseback, all well mounted and carrying double barrel shotguns, came to the ferry late on the day before Sanders was killed and he put them over. The next morning early he ferried them back to the Alabama side but he said he did not know any of them.

"p.s. Col. Brannan, I am not a native born Alabamian. I was born in Georgia, served from 1861 to 1865 in the 31st Georgia Regiment under Lee, Stonewall, and John B. Gordon. Am now 90 years old, a citizen of Brantley, Ala., a member of the Methodist church and living in the fear of God and in love and charity with all mankind. Very truly yours, I. G. Bradwell."

Isaac Gordon Bradwell *Confederate Veteran* Bibliography
(articles listed in chronological order of publication)

1. "The Fight at Winchester, Va.-Jim Graham," (15:411, 1907)
2. "Battle of the Wilderness," (16:447-448, 1908)
3. "Gordon's Ga. Brigade in the Wilderness," (16:641-642, 1908)
4. "After the Surrender at Appomattox," (17:467, 1909)
5. "First of Valley Campaign of General Early," (19:230-231, 1911)
6. "What Became of Adjutant Hill," (21:57, 1913)
7. "Early's Demonstration Against Washington in 1864," (22:438-439, 1914)
8. "The Battle of Cedar Creek, Va.," (22:315-316, 1914)
9. "With Early in the Valley," (22:504-506, 1914)
10. "Fort Steadman and Subsequent Events," (23:20-23, 1915)
11. "The 31st Georgia at Chancellorsville," (23:446-447, 1915)
12. "Soldier Life in the Confederate Army," (24:20-25, 1916)
13. "The Battle of Gaines Mill," (24, p. 23, 1916) and (33:382-383, 1925)
14. "Troops Demoralized at Fisher's Hill," (25:109-110, 1917)
15. "In Front of Fort Steadman," (25:408-409, 1917)
16. "Mine Run-A Ghost Story," (26:445-446, 1918)
17. "Scouting in the Valley," (27:92-93, 1919)
18. "The Burning of Wrightsville, Pa.," (27:300-301, 1919)
19. "Battle of Cedar Creek, Va.," (27:411-412, 1919)
20. "Battle of the Wilderness," (27:458-459, 1919)
21. "Second Day's Battle of the Wilderness, May 6, 1864," (28:20-22, 1920)
22. "Spotsylvania, Va., May 8 and 9, 1864," (28:56-57, 1920)
23. "Spotsylvania, Va., May 12, 13, 1864," (28:102-103, 1920)
24. "Cold Harbor, Lynchburg, Valley Campaigns, etc., 1864," (28:138-139, 1920)
25. "Early's March to Washington in 1864," (28:176-177, 1920)
26. "Early's Valley Campaign, 1864," (28:218-220, 1920)
27. "The Battle of Fisher's Hill," (28:338-340, 1920)
28. "The Valley Campaign After the Battle of Cedar Creek," (28:374-376, 1920)
29. "Gordon's Brigade After the Valley Campaign," (28:418-420, 1920)
30. "Holding the Lines at Petersburg," (28:457-459, 1920)
31. "Last Days of the Confederacy," (29:56-58, 1921)
32. "Making Our Way Home from Appomattox," (29:102-103, 1921)
33. "From Cold Harbor to Cedar Mountain," (29:222-225, 1921)
34. "From Cedar Mountain to Sharpsburg," (29:296-298, 1921)

35. "General Lee at Sharpsburg, 1862," (29:378-380, 1921)
36. "The Georgia Brigade at Fredericksburg," (30:18-20, 1922)
37. "How It Started," (30:65, 78, 1922)
38. "A Stampede," (30:170, 1922)
39. "Chancellorsville," (30:257-260, 1922)
40. "Capture of Winchester, Va. and Milroy's Army in June, 1863," (30:330-332, 1922)
41. "Crossing the Potomac," (30:370-372, 1922)
42. "From Gettysburg to the Potomac," (30:428-429, 437, 1922)
43. "The Grand Review," (31:16-18, 1923)
44. "A Love-Sick Volunteer," (31:62-63, 1923)
45. "The Irresponsible Race," (31:132-134, 1923)
46. "How Captain Bryan Earned a Good Dinner," (31:173, 1923)
47. "Picturesque Soldiery," (31:212-214, 1923)
48. "A Tribute to a Brave Comrade," (31:291-292, 1923)
49. "In Camp Near Savannah, Georgia," (31:338-339, 1923)
50. "Memories of 1860," (31:382, 1923)
51. "Cooking in the Army," (31:419-420, 1923)
52. "Gambling in the Army," (31:464, 475, 1923)
53. "Bravery and Cowardice in Battle," (32:131-133, 1924)
54. "Presentiments," (32:375-376, 1924)
55. "David and Goliath," 32:419-420, 1924)
56. "Under the Southern Cross," (33:182-183, 1925)
57. "First Lesson in War," (33:382-383, 397, 1925)
58. "Morton's Ford, January 4, 1864" (33:412-414, 1925)
59. "One Hour Saved the Union", (34:252-254, 1926)
60. "Carlos Maximilian Casini, Our Old Band-Master," (34:333-334, 1926)
61. "When General Mulligan Was Killed," (35:14-15, 1927)
62. "With Early in the Valley, 1864," (35:96-97, 1927)
63. "That Apple Tree, and Other Trees," (35:262-263, 1927)
64. "Old Kentuck," (35:380-381, 1927)
65. "In the Battle of Monocacy," (36:55-57, 1928)
66. "On to Washington," (36:95-96, 1928)
67. "The Battle of Monocacy, Md.," (37:382-383, 1929)
68. "Sheridan and Trevillian Station," (37:452-455, 1929)
69. "On Picket Duty in Front of Fort Steadman," (38:302-307, 1930)
70. "The Battle of Middletown, Virginia" (38:345-347, 1930)
71. "North Garden Station, Va., 1862," (39:374-377, 1931)
72. "On Monocacy Battlefield," (40:238, 1932)
73. "Colonel Hugh M. King," (40:258-260, 1932)

INDEX

Butts, Dr. Judson, 95, 95n, 104, 133, 170, 240

Campbell, Annie, xx
Camp Beaulieu, see Beaulieu, Camp
Camp Jackson Hospital, Va., see Jackson, Camp
Camp Wilson, Ga., see Wilson, Camp
Capers, Lt. Col. Henry D., 173
Carson, Capt., 233
Cassini, Carlos Maximilian, 13, 47-50, 47n
Cedar Creek, Battle of, 74-75, 197, 203-207, 212-213
Cedar Mountain, Va., Battle of, 74, 82
Chancellorsville, Battle of, 41, 110, 115, 174, 207
Cold Harbor, (Gaines's Mill, 1862), Battle of: description of battle, 26-27, 64-68, 131; Hoboken Battery, 26, 44, 65, 68-69; McGehee House, 43-44, 65, 70; Gen. Porter at, 86; Powhite Creek, 25, 69; prior to, 24-25; searching battlefield after, 70-71; soldiers throwing away playing cards before, 35; Waters, Sol, death of at, 43-45
Cold Harbor (1864), Battle of, 172-174, 217, 228
Compton, Lt. Charles M., 139-141, 139n, 159
Confederate Veterans, United (Camp Gracie), xxv
Cooking, see Soldier Life
Cooper, John, 95, 95n
Costigan, Pat, 14, 14n
Cox, Lt. Carey W., 49, 49n
Crenshaw County, Al., xxiii
Crews, Col. C. C., 36, 36n

Crowder, Capt. John T., 11, 12n, 89
Culpeper Courthouse, Va., 51, 74-75, 144, 147
Custer, Maj. Gen. (Bvt.) George A., 114, 121, 200, 214, 238
Cutts, Col. Allen S., 111

Darrow, Mr., 80
Davant, Col. Phillip E., 197
Davis, Dr., 79, 81, 127
Decatur County, Ga., xxiii, 4, 19, 45
Delevan Hospital, Va., 79
Delk, Tom, 225
Douglas, Col. Marcellus; at Sharpsburg, 42, 82, 88, 90-92; bravery of, 85, 88; as a pre-war lawyer, 95; physical discription of, 95
Drinking, see Soldier Life

Early, Lt. Gen. Jubal: artillery of, 8; bad humor of, 212, 217; burning of Blair mansion, alledged, 126-127, 181; at Chancellorsville Campaign, 111, 114; at Charlottesvile, (June, 1864), 175; command, removal from, 206, 213, 217; description of, 98; drinking problem, 97, 213; leadership of, 198, 206; at Lee's inpection of troops (Sep, 1863), 142; at Fredericksburg, 101-102; at Gettysburg, 207; at Harrisburg, Pa., 123; at Middletown, Va., (July, 1864) 181-183, 186; in Shenadoah Valley prior to Fredericksburg battle, 97; at Spotsylvania, (May 6, 1863), 156; Valley Campaign, 1864, 190-191, 193-199, 202-203, 217; Washington, march on, 176-

Lawton, Capt. Edward P., 101, 105, 250

Lee, Gen. Robert E.: 1863 fall operations of, 138, 140; appearance of, 149, 242; Gen. Early, attitude toward, 97-98; Gen. Early, removal from command, 206, 213; at Cedar Mountain, 74; description on horseback; 142; leave, granting of, 147; at Gettysburg, 130, 132-134, 207; Gettysburg Campaign, forbidding tresspass in, 120, 126; Malvern Hill, orders at, 72; Manassas, at Second, 83-85; Maryland invasion, strategy for 1862, 86; and Mine Run, 135; prisoner observations of, 149; Petersburg, defense of, 221-223. 230; review of troops (Sep. 1863), 141-142, 144; at Sharpsburg, 87-88, 91, 93-94; Sharpsburg, strategy after, 96; at Spotsylvania, "Lee to the rear," 168; surrender, troops reaction to, 238; at The Wilderness, 156

Lee, Lt. Gen. Stephen D., 87

Lewis, Capt. George W.: prewar activities of, 19, 47; at Mine Run (Morton's Ford), 136-137; orgainization of Bainbridge, Ga. soldiers, xxi, 20, 47; sick leave at North Garden Station, Va.,79-81; at Spotslvania, 166-167; at Wrightsville, Pa., 129

Lincoln, President Abraham: assassination, reaction to, 243; Burnsides, replacement of, 103; Gen. Early's desire to capture, 180; election of, 7; Fredericksburg, public reaction

to shelling civilains at, 99; McClellan, disagreements with, 94; McClellan, failure to send reinforcements to, 24; Shenandoah Valley, blamed for destruction in, 199-200; South, attitude toward, 180; Southern pre-war sentiments for, 4; Washington, uneasiness over safety of, 23, 193, 217

Longstreet, Lt. Gen. James, 84-85, 96, 103, 144

Lowe, Col. John H.: at Appomattox, 240; election to major, 11, 12n; granting of sick leave to Pvt. Bradwell, 170; at Middletown skirmish, 183-186, 183n; Capt. Miller, incident with, 183-186; in the Shenandoah Valley, 214-215; at Winchester (1864), 195

Lucas, Charles, 78-79

Madison County, Va., 98

Maine, 13th Regiment, 245

Malvern Hill, Battle of, 69, 71-72

Manassas, Battle of Second, 74, 83-85, 143

Mansfield, Gen. Joseph, 91

Massanutten Mountain, Va., 197, 199, 201, 204

McClellan, Maj. Gen. George: at Gaines's Mill, 24; at Malvern Hill, 71-74; organizational ability of, 86; at Shapsburg, 90-91, relationsip with Lincoln, 94; relieved of command, 94, 96

McGehee House, see Cold Harbor (1862)

McKinley, William, 192

McLaughlin, (McLochlin) Brig. Gen. (Bvt.) Napoleon, 233, 234n, 235

McLaws, Maj. Gen. Lafayette, 87
McLemore, James, 209, 209n
McNair, Lt. Daniel J., 167, 184, 184n
Meade, Maj. Gen. George, 131-135, 138, 140-141, 147
Middletown, Battle of, 181-186
Middletown, Va., 87
Miller, Capt. Nicholas W., 40, 184-185, 184n
Miller, Sue, 211
Milroy, Gen. Robert, 114-119
Mine Run, Va., 135-137, 147
Mitchell's Geography, 3
Monahan, Col. William, 190
Monocacy, Battle of, 177-180, 187
Moore, Green Berry, 62, 63n
Morgan, Sig, xxv
Morton's Ford, Va., 135-137, 147-149
Mosby, Col. John, 189
Mulligan, Brig. Gen. (Bvt.) James A., 190-192

Nelson Courthouse, Va., 77
North Carolina troops: 1st Regiment, 118; Hoke's Brigade, 74
North Garden Station, Va., 77-80
Norwood, Col., 12

Perkins, James W., 226, 226n
Petersburg, Va., defenses of, 221, 224-228, 229-231, 234-235
Pettigrew, Brig. Gen. James J., 133
Phillips, Col. Pleasant J., 10, 10n, 13-14
Pikes, see Joe Brown pikes
Pope, Maj. Gen. John, 73-74, 82-83, 85
Porter, Maj. Gen. Fitz John, 85-86

Powhite Creek, Va., see Cold Harbor (1862)
Presidential election, 1860, 4, 6-7
Pride, Capt. Rodolphus, 84, 84n, 152

Quincey, Fla., 35, 240

Ricks, Sgt. John M., 54, 54n, 140-141
Rodes, Maj. Gen. Robert E.: band in Division of, 49; at Gettysburg, 125; at Lynchburg, 175; review of troops by Gen. Lee (1863), 142; at Winchester (1863), 116, 118; at Winchester (July 1864), 191, 194-196
Russel, Willis M., 6

Savannah, Ga., 10, 20, 22, 41, 48, 143
Scaife, Dr. William L., 229, 230n
Scott, B. C., 77
Scouting, 208, 214
Secession, attitude toward in Decatur Co., Ga., 4, 5
Sedgwich, Maj. Gen. John, 110
Seegar, Alan, 104
Seven Days' Battle, The, 64, 71
Seymour, Maj. Gen. (Bvt.) Truman, 141, 159, 207
Shaler, Maj. Gen. (Bvt.) Alexander, 141, 159, 207
Sharpburg, Battle of, 42, 86-95, 104
Sharpsburg, Md., 120
Sheridan, P.H., Maj. Gen.: at Cedar Creek, 205; during Gen. Early's 1864 Valley Campaign, 121, 193-194, 196, 202-203, 212-214; at Fisher's Hill, 198; tactics, compared to Germans in WWI, 200, 208; at Trevilian Station, 174